JESUS AND THE MYSTERY OF THE TAMID SACRIFICE

Michal E. Hunt

Jesus and the Mystery of the Tamid Sacrifice

ISBN 978-0-578-79836-3

Unless otherwise noted, Scripture verses are from the
Revised Standard Version Catholic Edition
of the New Testament Copyright 1965
of the Old Testament © 1966 by
Thomas Nelson Publishers for Ignatius Press

Nihil Obstat: Fr. David Rasner, M.A., S.T.B., Censor Librorum
Imprimatur: Bishop Timothy Doherty, Diocese of Lafayette-in-Indiana,
September 19, 2011
Revised edition 2020

Cover art by Steve Vanderbosch

Dedicated to my beloved husband Jerry,
my partner in life and the spread of the Gospel, and to all
those who are called to teach the Gospel of salvation in
the spirit of Eldad and Medad from within the camp
(Numbers 11:24-29; Mark 9:38-41).

The coming of God's Son to earth is an event of such immensity that God willed to prepare for it over the centuries. He makes everything converge on Christ: all the rituals and sacrifices, figures and symbols of the "First Covenant." He announces him through the mouths of the prophets who succeeded one another in Israel. Moreover, he awakens in the hearts of the pagans a dim expectation of this coming.

Catechism of the Catholic Church, 522

TABLE OF CONTENTS

LIST OF ABBREVIATIONS

Bible Editions

All quotations are from the Revised Standard Version Catholic Edition unless otherwise noted:

New American Bible (NAB)
New Jerusalem Bible (NJB)
The Interlinear Bible: Hebrew-English (IBHE, vol. I – III)
The Interlinear Bible: Greek-English (IBGE, vol. IV)
Catechism of the Catholic Church (CCC)

New Testament Books

Matthew (Mt)
Mark (Mk)
Luke (Lk)
John (Jn)
Acts of Apostles (Acts)
Romans (Rom)
1 Corinthians (1 Cor)
2 Corinthians (2 Cor)
Galatians (Gal)
Ephesians (Eph)
Philippians (Phil)
Colossians (Col)
1 Thessalonians (1 Thes)
2 Thessalonians (2 Thes)
1 Timothy (1 Tim)
2 Timothy (2 Tim)
Titus (Tit)
Philemon (Phm)
Hebrews (Heb)
James (Jm)
1 Peter (1 Pt)
2 Peter (2 Pt)
1 John (1 Jn)
2 John (2 Jn)
3 John (3 Jn)
Jude (Jude)
Revelation (Rev)

Old Testament Books

Genesis (Gen)
Exodus (Ex)
Leviticus (Lev)
Numbers (Num)
Deuteronomy (Dt)
Joshua (Jos)
Judges (Judg)
Ruth (Rt)
1 Samuel (1 Sam)
2 Samuel (2 Sam)
1 Kings (1 Kng)
2 Kings (2 Kng)
1 Chronicles (1 Chr)
2 Chronicles (2 Chr)
Ezra (Ezra)
Nehemiah (Neh)
Tobit (Tob)
Judith (Jud)
Esther (Est)
1 Maccabees (1 Mac)
2 Maccabees (2 Mac)
Job (Job)
Psalms (Ps)
Proverbs (Pro)
Ecclesiastes (Ecc)
Song of Songs (SS)
Wisdom (Wis)
Sirach (Sir)
Isaiah (Is)
Jeremiah (Jer)
Lamentations (Lam)
Baruch (Bar)
Ezekiel (Ez)
Daniel (Dan)
Hosea (Hos)
Joel (Jl)
Amos (Am)
Obadiah (Ob)
Jonah (Jon)
Micah (Mic)
Nahum (Na)
Habakkuk (Hab)
Zephaniah (Zp)
Haggai (Hg)
Zechariah (Zec)
Malachi (Mal)

PREFACE

In God's gift of divine Law and the Liturgy of worship to Israel at Mount Sinai, He ordained a single sacrifice as the center of the sacrificial system—the Tamid sacrifice. The Hebrew word *tamid* means "standing" as in perpetual or continual. According to the Law of the Sinai Covenant, the ritual of the perpetual burnt-offering of the *'olat ha-Tamid* was a communal sacrifice for the atonement and sanctification of the covenant people. This daily sacrifice became the focus of religious life for the Israelites in covenant union with the God of their forefathers. It consisted of two liturgical services, one in the morning and the second in the afternoon (evening for the Jews), in which the sacrifice and offering of a single, unblemished male lamb with wheat flour mixed with oil, an unleavened bread wafer, and red wine. The entire day revolved around the offering of the Tamid lambs. No other sacrifices were to take precedence over the Tamid sacrifice, and it was to continue for as long as the Sinai Covenant endured.

The covenant people initiated the Tamid liturgy at Mount Sinai after the dedication of the Sanctuary, and it continued until the destruction of the Temple by the Babylonians in 587/586 BC. During the seventy years of the Babylonian exile, the people remembered the Tamid sacrifice and worship service in their morning and afternoon prayers, and they immediately reinstated the Tamid liturgy after their return from exile. The daily ritual of the Tamid sacrifice ended forever forty years after Jesus' resurrection when the Roman army destroyed the Jerusalem Temple in AD 70.

Within the events of the crucifixion of Jesus of Nazareth, the Tamid sacrifice played a role that has been largely ignored by Christian and Jewish scholars. The Passion of the Christ reveals the mystery of the single sacrifice of two Tamid lambs in He who is both fully man and God. Jesus, in His self-offering on the altar of the Cross, became the single sacrifice of the true Tamid Lamb that all past Tamid lambs prefigured, fulfilling and abolishing the necessity for all Old Covenant animal blood sacrifices.

The purpose of this book is to present Jesus of Nazareth as the true Tamid lamb. Just as the unblemished Tamid lamb was the "standing" sacrifice offered continually on the altar of sacrifice in the Jerusalem Temple, Jesus is the unblemished Lamb "standing" before the throne of God in the heavenly Temple. He offers a sacrifice that is continually made present on the Eucharistic altar and banquet table in the sacrifice of the Mass: *And between the throne and the four living creatures and among the elder, I saw a Lamb standing as though it had been slain* ~ Revelation 5:6.

ACKNOWLEDGEMENTS

I could not have completed this journey without the encouragement and faithful assistance of a group of friends who have been my companions in the study of Sacred Scripture. When I first announced the book project to my students, a "faithful remnant" willingly stepped forward and offered their help. We began the book project in September 2007. We continued to meet every Wednesday, carving a path from Genesis to Revelation in our pursuit of an in-depth understanding of the unique role that the daily blood sacrifice of the Tamid lambs played in God's plan for humanity's salvation.

I wish to thank Diane M. Chandler, Jason Hull, Mary D. McCorkle, Michael J. McLeish, Patricia Murphy, Theresa Verde, Vangie Vescovi, Deborah Vespo, Rosie Zatkulak, Tina Zimmerman, and my husband, Jerry Hunt. We constantly sought the guidance of God the Holy Spirit as I wrote, as we studied, and as they dissected and discussed the material I presented to them. We explored the mystery of the Tamid, beginning with the declared necessity of blood sacrifice as a means of atonement and restoration as presented in Sacred

Scripture, together with information gathered from the writings of the first century AD Jewish historian Flavius Josephus and the second century AD Jewish *Mishnah*.

I also want to thank Lauren Amundson, Mary Jo Richards, Elizabeth Bridgewater, Lucille Surette, and my husband Jerry Hunt who helped me edit the manuscript. My journey with these companions gave each of us an even deeper appreciation of God's faithful covenant love for His children and for His divine intervention in the history of humanity by providing a definitive plan for man's salvation through the blood sacrifice of His Son on the altar of the Cross.

Finally, I want to thank Fr. David Rasner for his careful reading of my manuscript. His thoughtful comments and suggestions helped me improve the final version of the book, the goal of which is to present my premise that Jesus Christ is the true Tamid Lamb that the sacrifice of every Old Covenant Tamid lamb prefigured.

INTRODUCTION

In the first century BC, political unrest erupted into armed rebellion in the eastern regions of the Roman Empire. The whole system of credit and finance, the very prosperity of the Empire, was bound to the tribute revenues collected from the various provinces and client kingdoms under Roman domination. The Roman Senate responded to the threat that challenged Rome's supremacy by deploying General Gnaeus Pompeius Magnus (Pompey the Great) and four legions of seasoned soldiers across the Mediterranean Sea. Pompey's mission was to crush the rebellion, eliminate the rebel leader, King Mithridates of Pontus, re-establish order in Asia Minor, and most importantly to restore the valuable revenues of the eastern provinces and client kingdoms that were necessary for the continuing prosperity of the Roman Empire.[1]

Pompey's aggressive pursuit of the enemy resulted in a successful campaign. He swiftly engaged the rebel forces that left the army of Mithridates with no option but annihilation or surrender. Pompey then proceeded to re-establish Roman authority over the rebellious territories, quickly securing the continued flow of tribute from the provinces and client kingdoms into the coffers of Rome and thereby safeguarding the financial credit as well as the glory of the Empire.

Flushed with their recent victory but still hungry for conquest, Pompey and his legions swept southward and took control of the old Greek Seleucid kingdom. The Seleucid kingdom of Syria, torn apart by various claimants to the throne, resisted with more of a whimper than a howl and fell like an overripe plum into greedy Roman hands. Satisfied with their Syrian victory, the Romans set up their winter camp. The next prize came seeking them.[2]

While Pompey encamped with his victorious Roman legions at Damascus, two rival princes, Hyrcanus II and Aristobulus II of Judah, sent emissaries to him pleading for his political support. These brothers, descendants of the heroic Maccabees and the last heirs of the Hasmonean dynasty of the nation of Judah, were locked in a deadly struggle of succession. To break the deadlock and avoid a civil war, each brother submitted his claim to the throne of Judah to the Roman general. When Pompey decided in favor of Hyrcanus II under the guidance and protection of Rome, Prince Aristobulus defiantly claimed the throne for himself. With the assistance of his loyal supporters, Aristobulus took possession of Judah's capital, the holy city of Jerusalem.

This conflict was the provocation Pompey needed to employ the powerful arms of his legions to reach out and squeeze Judah and Jerusalem into submission.[3]

The Roman siege of Jerusalem began in the early spring of 63 BC. Jerusalem is a naturally fortified city built 2,300 to 2,500 feet above sea level on a crest of the central range of the Judean Mountains. The ancient walled city was built on two mountain ridges with the steeply sloped Kidron valley to the east and the equally steep Wadi-er-Rababy (the Biblical Ge-Hinnom) on the west. These steep slopes gave the city an excellent defensive position that was only vulnerable to attack from the north. Despite the natural barriers and other fortifications and resources, intrigue allowed the Romans to take possession of the lower sections of the city and to capture the rebellious Prince Aristobulus. The loss of their leader, however, did not dampen the resolve of Aristobulus' forces. His capture only strengthened their determination to resist their enemies. They refused to surrender and barricaded themselves inside the walls of the holy Jerusalem Temple on the heights of Mount Moriah. Fortified within this sacred precinct, the Jews defiantly resisted the Romans for three months.[4]

Before the arrival of Pompey's army, the Jews dug a defensive ditch on the Temple's north side. It was a formidable sixty feet deep and two hundred and fifty feet broad. General Pompey built his military camp across from the defensive trench. He ordered his soldiers to fill it in and to raise a bank from which his state-of-the-art siege engines could do the most damage. After three months of preparation, Pompey brought in his mechanical siege engines and battering-rams from the coastal city of Tyre.[5]

During the siege, General Pompey observed that, because of their piety and strict obedience to their religious laws, the Jews did not fight or even defend themselves on their most holy day, the Jewish Sabbath. Therefore, he directed the full force of his assault against the Temple Mount on each successive Sabbath.[6] Placing the siege engines on the bank the engineers prepared for them, the Roman soldiers began to mercilessly pummel the entire area of the Temple Mount with huge boulders that cascaded into the Temple complex. Despite the downpour that caused death and destruction all around them, the priests of Yahweh continued to perform their ministerial duties prescribed in the Law of God's covenant with Israel for the liturgical worship service of the sacred Tamid sacrifice.

The center of daily liturgical worship in the Temple of Israel's God was a whole-burnt, communal offering on the altar fire. It was called the Tamid (pronounced tah-meed), meaning the "standing" as in continual or perpetual [sacrifice]. God commanded the sacrifice to be offered daily so long as the Sinai Covenant endured. The whole-burnt sacrifice of the Tamid was one single sacrifice in the offering of two unblemished male lambs: one lamb offered in a morning liturgical worship service at the third hour and a second lamb offered in sacrifice in an afternoon liturgical worship service at the ninth hour.[7] The Tamid was such a vital covenant obligation that the entire twelve hours of the daytime and the daily ritual of Temple worship revolved around this holy sacrifice offered for the atonement and sanctification of the covenant people and the hoped-for salvation of the entire human family.[8]

On the Sabbath of the 23rd of the Jewish month of Sivan in 63 BC, the Temple ramparts fell, and the defenders and their families sought sanctuary within the Temple precincts where the Romans slaughtered them. Since it was the Sabbath, most of the Jews refused to defend themselves, and many of the desperate people leaped from the Temple walls to their deaths. No one surrendered, and twelve thousand died.[9]

The Jewish priest/historian, Flavius Josephus (c. AD 37-100), reporting on these events a little over a century later, wrote that the piety of the Jews was so great, and the Tamid sacrifice was so sacred that, despite the danger, the priests stubbornly continued the liturgical service during the assault on the Temple. Without hesitation, they continued to perform the ritual of the Tamid sacrifice as prescribed by the Law of the Sinai Covenant, even though their brother priests were dying all around them. Josephus wrote: *and anyone may hence learn how very great piety we exercise towards God, and the observance of his laws, since the priests were not at all hindered from their sacred ministrations by their fear during this siege, but did still twice each day, in the morning and at about the ninth hour, offer their sacrifices on the altar; nor did they omit those sacrifices, if any melancholy accident happened, by the stones that were thrown among them; for although the city was taken on the third month, on the day of the fast, upon the hundred and seventy-ninth Olympiad, when Caius Antonius and Marcus Tullius Cicero were consuls, and the enemy fell upon them, and cut the throats of those that were in the Temple, yet could not those that offered the sacrifices be compelled to run away, neither by the fear they were in of their own lives, nor by the number that were already slain, as thinking it better to suffer whatever came upon them, at their very altars, than to omit anything that their laws required of them; and that this is not a mere brag, or an encomium to manifest a degree of our piety that was false, but is the real truth.*[10]

In the Roman attack on the Temple, the priests resisted the impulse to run away or to defend their lives in their commitment to fulfill the covenant people's most sacred ritual. The sacrificial requirement of the Tamid originated from the time of Israel's covenant formation at Mount Sinai when God first called the children of Israel to become a holy nation set apart from the other nations of the earth. However, the ritual of blood sacrifice for the atonement and sanctification of God's people as prescribed in the daily Tamid sacrifice was not a concept that originated at Mount Sinai. Blood sacrifice was the requirement for expiating sin and the restoration of fellowship with God. It was a remedy for sin that reached back into the distant past when Adam's willful act of rebellion resulted in God's divine judgment for the occupants of the earthly Sanctuary of the Garden of Eden. Adam's sin separated humanity from divine grace, making the ritual of blood sacrifice God's necessary remedy for the atonement of sins.

Blood sacrifice became the necessary means of atonement for humanity's sins and the first step in the restoration of fellowship with God, but the ritual of blood sacrifice also pointed forward in time to a promised future redemption. In the event of man's fall from grace in Eden, God's divine judgment was tempered by His mercy in the promise of humanity's future salvation. The judgment of humanity's sinfulness united to God's mercy in His promise of a future Redeemer-Messiah resulted in humanity's participation in the great drama of salvation history that reached its climax during the sacrificial rite of the afternoon Tamid in the spring of AD 30.

Endnotes: Introduction

1. Cary and Schullard, *A History of Rome*, pages 250-255.
2. Seleucus I Nicator (c. 312-280 BC), one of the generals of Alexander the Great, founded the Greek Seleucid Kingdom.
3. Josephus, *Antiquities of the Jews*, 14.3.2-4 [37-52]; Cary and Schullard, *A History of Rome*, page 254-255.
4. *Ancient Israel*, page 265-266; Josephus, *Antiquities of the Jews*, 14.4.1-2[57-9].
5. Josephus, *Antiquities of the Jews*, 14.4.1-2 [60-62]; Strabo, *Geography*, 16.763. Strabo recorded that the defensive ditch was 60 feet deep and 250 feet broad.
6. Josephus, *Antiquities of the Jews*, 14.4.2 [63]. God established the Sabbath "rest" on the seventh day of Creation in Gen 2:1-2, but the observance of the Sabbath did not become a covenant obligation until the formation of the covenant with Israel at Sinai in Ex 20:8-11 (repeated in the Pentateuch eight times in Ex 23:12; 31:12-17; 34:21; 35:1-3; Lev 19:3; 23:3; Num 15:32-36; Dt 5:12-15), at which time a covenant judgment was attached to the Sabbath requirement (Ex 31:14).
7. The third-hour Jewish time is 9 AM modern time, and the ninth hour Jewish time is 3 PM modern time. The Jewish day began and ended at sundown; their "evening" is our afternoon (*Jewish book of Why, vol. I*, pages 9-10); Josephus,

Antiquities of the Jews, 14.4.3 [65]; *The Temple: Its Ministry and Services*, Alfred Edersheim, pages 113–115.

8. Philo, *The Special Laws I*, 35 [168]: *And since, of the sacrifices to be offered, some are on behalf of the whole nation, and indeed, if one should tell the real truth, in behalf of all mankind.*
9. Josephus, *Antiquities of the Jews*, 14.4.3 [66–71].bid., 14.4.3 [65–68].

CHAPTER I SACRIFICE AND COVENANT

And he said, "Behold, I make a covenant. Before all your people I will do marvels, such as have not been wrought in all the earth or in any nation; and all the people among whom you are shall see the work of the LORD; for it is a terrible thing that I will do with you."
Exodus 34:10
(the word "LORD" is a substitute for the Divine Name YHWH/Yahweh) [1]

Gather to me my faithful ones, who made a covenant with me by sacrifice!
Psalm 50:5

THE ORIGIN OF SACRIFICE

In the first great human tragedy triggered by Satan's seduction and man's desire for knowledge apart from God, Adam and Eve were banished from the Garden of Eden after their sin of rebellion in eating the fruit from the forbidden Tree of the Knowledge of Good and Evil (Gen 3:23-24). Adam and Eve became the parents of a spiritually fallen humanity, no longer capable of communing with God in the intimacy previously enjoyed with God's manifested presence in the Garden Sanctuary. Sending them into exile, God sacrificed animals to clothe His fallen children's physical nakedness (Gen 3:21). No longer spiritually "clothed" in divine grace, humanity's physically naked condition now symbolized the loss of grace and spiritual separation from God that closed the gates of Heaven.

Deprived of divine grace, human "fathering" in communicating human nature to the next generation became an imperfect act. Man, created in the image of God, lost the grace of God's image and likeness in human fathering. Children born naturally came into the world lacking God's divine grace and inheriting the tendency to sin which the Fathers of the Church called "original sin," meaning the transmitted sin of our original parents that affected human nature. However, despite the catastrophic events of man's fall from grace, God did not abandon His sinful children. Humanity needed a Redeemer to bind the power of Satan, to resolve the deadly consequences of sin, and to restore man to the state of grace in which God created him. Pronouncing judgment on the serpent, the material form of Satan in the fall of man (Rev 12:9), and on Adam and Eve, God promised a future Redeemer born from the "seed" of "the woman." Satan would wound the promised Redeemer, but the "seed of the woman" would ultimately have victory over humanity's great Adversary, defeating Satan's power over humankind (Gen 3:15-19; 1 Jn 3:8).

In the meantime, to prevent a continual sinful state that left humanity without divine grace and separated from Him, God established the means of restoring fellowship. God provided for the atonement (reparation) of humanity's sins through blood sacrifice. Blood sacrifice was a temporary remedy for humanity's sinfulness and foreshadowed the saving work of the future Redeemer on the altar of the Cross. In God's plan for man's redemption, the lifeblood of an unblemished animal provided the means of atonement to cover the sinner's guilt: *For the life of the flesh is in the blood; and I have given it for you upon the altar to make atonement for your souls* (Lev 17:11). The inspired writer of the Letter to the Hebrews affirmed the necessity of blood sacrifice as the means of expiating sins: *Indeed, under the law, almost everything is purified with blood, and without the shedding of blood there is no forgiveness of sins* (Heb 9:22).

The sacrifice of the animal victim was, however, only the first step in the process of spiritual restoration. Blood sacrifice became the visible sign God established to teach humanity the link between the humility of the sinner who submits his life to God and the restoration of fellowship between God and the sinner (Is 66:2b). Through the ritual of animal sacrifice, the essence of the person was bound up with the life of the victim that died vicariously in his place as the life of the offeror becoming an acceptable sacrifice to God. To be a worthy offering, a confession of guilt expressing genuine contrition had to accompany the sacrifice (Lev 5:5; 16:1; Num 5:7; Ps 32:5) along with the submission of the offeror's life to the will of God (1 Sam 15:22; Ps 51:16-17; Sir 34:18-19; 35:1-7). The sacrificial blood applied to God's holy altar became the channel of grace by which atonement for sins became possible for individuals or an entire community, permitting a return to peace and fellowship with God (Ps 32:1-2, 10-11; 50 Lev 5:26).

However, until the coming of the promised Redeemer, blood sacrifice became the visual and physically enacted remedy that served as a solution for the morbidity of sin that infected all of humanity in a spiritual pandemic. It served as an imperfect and temporary remedy for the sentence of physical and spiritual death that sin imposed upon humanity (Wis 1:13; 2:23-24). Since no animal could be perfect enough to completely remove the stain of sin from the human soul (Heb 10:4, 11), the gates of Heaven remained closed to humanity, and the blood of animals shed for the atonement of human transgressions could only restore bodily purity (Num 15:27-31; Heb 9:13-14). It could not restore humanity's definitive sanctification, nor could it offer the path to eternal salvation. Nevertheless, it was the necessary remedy for sin until God's plan for man's redemption came to fulfillment in the Incarnation of God's unblemished Lamb of sacrifice, the Redeemer-Messiah, Jesus Christ.

In the time before the advent of the Redeemer-Messiah, the eternal blessings and punishments made explicit in the New Covenant of Jesus Christ were only dimly understood and applied in God's hidden providence (Heb 9:15). While Adam's sin closed the gates of Heaven, it did not open the gates of Hell. Before the atoning blood sacrifice of Jesus on the altar of the Cross, physical death consigned all humanity, the righteous and the wicked, to *Sheol*. *Sheol* was the grave/netherworld (*Hades* in Greek) that held all the souls of the dead until the coming of the Redeemer-Messiah (Lk 16:19-31). Even those souls who died in the time of the Great Flood resided in Sheol until they would hear Jesus' Gospel message of salvation when He descended into Sheol from the grave to rescue the souls of the redeemed (1 Pt 3:18-20; 4:6; CCC 536, 632-33, 1026).

BLOOD ATONEMENT DURING THE AGE OF THE PATRIARCHS

For the remnant of Adam's family that remained in covenant with Yahweh, the ritual of sacrifice and the application of the life-blood of designated ritually clean, unblemished animals to God's holy altar became the means of both redemption and covenant continuation (Gen 4:3-5; Lev 17:11; 22:20-22; Ps 50:5). In the ritual of sacrifice in the time of the Patriarchs, they built altars, sacrificed animals, and brought forward their offerings of the fruits of the earth. These actions took place whenever the patriarchal head of the family, acting as God's priestly representative, felt the need to invoke God's Divine Name (Gen 12:8), to make atonement by drawing near to God's presence in demonstrating his humility and gratitude, and to receive the benefit of God's covenant blessings (Gen 8:20; 12:8). In this early period in salvation history, sacrifice to God took place at any site deemed suitable by the firstborn sons in covenant with Yahweh (*Mishnah: Zebahim*, 14:4IA).

God's covenant relationship with the faithful remnant of humanity continued through the Flood judgment in the re-established covenant with Noah and his sons (Gen 9:8-11). The role of God's representative to those faithful to Yahweh continued through Noah's righteous first-born son, Shem, who replaced Noah as the covenant mediator (Gen 9:26-27). Then the direction of salvation history took a decisive turn when God instituted a covenant through Shem's descendant Abraham. The covenant promises God made to Abraham included land for a kingdom, a multitude of descendants, and a world-wide blessing (Gen 12:1-3; 15:18-21; 17:2-8; 22:15-18). It was a covenant that continued through Abraham's son Isaac, through Isaac's son Jacob (who God renamed "Israel"), and through Jacob-Israel's twelve sons who became the physical fathers of the twelve tribes of Israel (Gen 17:19; 26:3-4; 28:13-16). This centuries-old pattern of priestly fathers building altars for sacrifice and offering worship to the God of Creation who identified Himself to the Patriarchs as El Shaddai (Gen 17:1; 28:3; 35:11; 43:14; 48:3; 49:25) and by His covenant name expressed in Sacred Scripture by the consonants "YHWH" (Gen 4:1; 15:2, 7; 16:2, 5; 18:1, 13, 14, 17, 19 twice, 20, 22, 26, 33, etc.) was changed forever in the momentous event of the Israelite's Exodus out of Egypt and their rendezvous with the Divine at Mount Sinai. [2]

THE EXODUS LIBERATION AND THE JOURNEY TO MOUNT SINAI

Then Yahweh said to Abram, "Know this for certain, that your descendants will be exiles in a land not their own and be enslaved and oppressed for four hundred years. But I shall bring judgment on the nation that enslaves them and after this they will leave, with many possessions."
Genesis 15:13-14 (NJB)

In the ancient world, powerful nations and their vassal states relationships maintained their relationship through covenant treaties. In the adoption of the twelve tribes of the children of Israel as a vassal people, God, through His covenant mediator Moses, employed the covenant treaty as the formal means of establishing a continuing relationship with the Israelites. Covenants are not contracts. Contracts address material concerns like property rights, privileges, and the exchange of money. Covenants address intangibles like honor, loyalty, and fidelity and are the formal documents in adoptions and marital unions that create new family bonds.

God defines His relationship with humanity through the sacred bond of the covenant. This bond began with the covenant formed with Adam, continued in the covenant with Noah and Creation, to the covenant with Abraham and Israel as a corporate covenant people, and finally with the New and eternal Covenant established with the blood of Jesus Christ (see the list of Yahweh's Eight Covenants in Appendix I).

After God's covenant with Adam, Noah, and the family of Abraham, the Sinai Covenant treaty became God's next step in His plan for the salvation of humanity. However, the covenant treaty with the children of Israel did not erase the other, previously formed covenant family bonds. Yahweh's covenants are not separate and unrelated unions. Each succeeding covenant integrates into the past and builds on the future. The Noahide Covenant in which God granted permission to eat the meat of the sacrifice in a sacred meal (Gen 9:3) and the prohibition against drinking blood and eating raw flesh (Gen 9:4; Lev 3:17; 7:25-26; 17:10-12, 14; 19:26; Dt 12:16, 23-27; 15:23) continued in the Sinai Covenant with the children of Israel. So too, did the rite of circumcision that was the covenant sign with Abraham (Gen 17:9-14) and the importance of blood sacrifice in worship and liturgy. All these elements from previous covenants continued in the next level of covenant formation in the Sinai Covenant.

Before the ratification of the Sinai Covenant gave a new direction for God's divine plan for salvation history, Yahweh formed covenant bonds with individuals and their families. But in a radical departure from the previous pattern, Yahweh took the descendants of Jacob-Israel and molded them into a unified covenant nation. It was a change in the destiny of a tribal people that began with God's promised liberation for the descendants of Abraham from slavery in Egypt (Gen 15:13-16).

First, the God of the patriarchs Abraham, Isaac, and Jacob took their descendants and transformed them from a primitive migratory tribal family into a vigorous community of twelve tribes in the crucible of suffering in Egypt (Ex 1:8-14). Next, He chose Moses, a man from the tribe of Levi, as His covenant mediator to the Israelites (Ex 3:7-10, 15). Then, God began their liberation through ten successive plague judgments inflicted upon the nation of Egypt (Ex Chapters 7-12). Finally, He redeemed the children of Israel and claimed them as His own on the night of the tenth and final Egyptian plague. Yahweh saved the firstborn of Israel but executed judgment on the false gods of Egypt in the deaths of the Egyptians' first-born sons and animals (Ex 11:4-7; 12:12). Once again, as in the event of the Great Flood, God extended His gift of salvation to a faithful remnant in the midst of divine judgment.

God promised to spare the children of Israel from the tenth plague's curse of death (Ex 11:4-5, 7). In obedience to God's commands, the Israelites sacrificed unblemished lambs and goat-kids and ate a sacrificial meal in their homes (Ex 12:3-10). Yahweh protected their doorways with the blood of the sacrificial victims smeared in the sign of a cross with blood-drenched hyssop branches from the threshold to the lintel to the doorposts of their houses. Under this "sign," those inside the dwelling eating the sacrificial meal were saved from death as unprotected first-born sons and animals died throughout Egypt (Ex 12:12-13, 22-23). The events that took place the night of the tenth plague were so profound that God commanded them, from that time forward, to alter time by counting the month of their deliverance from Egyptian oppression as the first month in their liturgical calendar. He commanded them to annually relive the events of their liberation in every generation so long as the children of Israel endured as a covenant people in seven God-ordained annual feasts (Ex 12:1-2, 14; Lev 23).

YAHWEH THE GOD-KING TAKES A BRIDE

Yahweh says this: "I remember your faithful love, the affection of your bridal days, when you followed me through the desert, through a land unsown. Israel was sacred to Yahweh; the first-fruits of his harvest."
Jeremiah 2:2-3a

Biblical revelation, in fact, is above all the expression of a story of love, the story of the covenant of God with man; therefore, the story of the love and union between a man and a woman in the covenant of marriage was able to be assumed by God as a symbol of the history of salvation.
Pope Benedict XVI (address to the Congress of the Roman Diocese on "The Family and the Christian Community," June 6, 2005, St. John Lateran, Rome)

In the journey from Egypt to Mount Sinai, God led the twelve tribes of Israel from servitude to sacred nationhood. As they fled from the wrath of the Egyptians, God purified them from the stains of their old, sinful lives when they passed through the miraculously parted waters of the Red Sea (Ex 14:19-31; 1 Cor 10:1-3). And as they traveled across the hostile wasteland, Yahweh taught the children of Israel to trust and obey Him. He nourished them with manna, a substance that miraculously appeared six mornings a week (Ex 16:11-36), and He gave them life-giving water from a rock (Ex 17:1-7; Num 20:7-11). God gave the children of Israel everything they needed on their wilderness journey that was a pilgrimage to fulfill their destiny in their appointed rendezvous at His holy mountain.

God's relationship with Israel is symbolically presented in Scripture as a relationship between a Divine King and His vassal people, as a Divine Father to His human children, and most profoundly imaged as a Divine Bridegroom to His covenant Bride. In the Sinai Covenant, marriage became an icon of Yahweh's loving relationship with His covenant people. Israel came to God out of her humble station as a disenfranchised people, and in His beneficence, God raised Israel from lowly slave to the chosen Bride.

In the journey to Mount Sinai, Yahweh courted the children of Israel like a bridegroom courts a bride, providing for the people's every need (Ez 16:6-14). In the miracle of the Red Sea crossing and the other signs of God's divine protection, the other nations of the earth witnessed Israel's nuptial procession. Through those experiences, God prepared Israel for the supernatural event she was going to experience at the covenant formation and ratification at Mount Sinai when the God of the Patriarchs invited Israel to become His faithful vassal people, submitting to Yahweh as the newly formed nation's Divine King (Ps 10:16; 29:10; 47:6-7; 89:18; etc.).

When the Israelites arrived at the foot of the mountain, Moses warned them of the danger of a sinful people encountering a tremendously powerful and holy God. They were commanded to keep their distance until they received the signal to approach the mountain. During these preparations, Yahweh made a solemn vow to Israel through His covenant mediator, Moses: *Now therefore, if you will obey my voice and keep my covenant, you shall be my own possession among all peoples; for all the earth is mine, and you shall be to me a kingdom of priests and a holy nation* (Ex 19:5-6).

God commanded the people to bathe and purify themselves for three days. It was the same preparation as that of a Hebrew bride before coming to the intimacy of a covenant union with her bridegroom.[3] The Israelites obediently sanctified themselves by bathing, washing their clothes, and for a three day period they entered a state of ritual purity by refraining from sexual contact (Ex 19:10-11, 14-15).

The Exodus experience reached its climax when Yahweh revealed Himself to the Israelites on the summit of the mountain. God descended upon the mountain in fire, peals of thunder, flashes of lightning, a dense cloud, and the sound of a trumpet blast while the Israelites trembled in fear (Ex 19:16-19). Then out of the thunder came a great voice that said: *"I am the LORD your God, who brought you out of the land of Egypt, out of the house of bondage"* (Ex 20:2). In the next blast of thunder, Yahweh began to recite the heart of the Law in ten commandments intended to bind Israel to Him (Ex 20:3-17). Then, Yahweh's great symphony of the Law continued as He gave Moses the additional ordinances of moral, civil, and religious commands and prohibitions. The entire body of divine Law would govern the people and serve as both a tutor and a guide in holiness for His covenant people down through the centuries to prepare them for the coming of the Redeemer-Messiah (Ex 21:1-33).

THE GIVING OF THE LAW AND THE RATIFICATION OF THE SINAI COVENANT

Hence even the first covenant was not ratified without blood. For when every commandment of the law had been declared by Moses to all the people, he took the blood of calves and goats, with water and scarlet wool and hyssop, and sprinkled both the book itself and all the people, saying, "This is the blood of the covenant which God commanded you."
Hebrews 9:18-20

The first encounter with Yahweh at Mount Sinai left the Israelites paralyzed with fear. After the terrifying visual and acoustical experience when God descended in fire upon the mountain to announce the opening chapter of divine Law, the people begged Moses act as their covenant mediator by personally receiving God's words and transmitting those words to the people. God granted the people's request, and Moses went forward to approach Yahweh "in the dark cloud" to receive the expanded articles of the Law (Ex 20:18-23:33).

Returning from his first ascent of the mountain and in preparation for the ratification of the covenant, God instructed Moses to form a delegation or hierarchy composed of Aaron, his two eldest sons, and seventy elders to serve as the representatives of the twelve tribes of Israel. Moses told the people God's words in the additional commands that he received on the mountain. In response, the people answered by swearing: *"All the words which the LORD has spoken we will do"* (Ex 24:3). Then, as God commanded, Moses began to write down the words of the Law he received from God on the mountain in what was to become the part of the Torah of Moses called the Book of the Covenant (Ex 24:4).

In the morning, Moses prepared for the ratification ceremony by erecting God's altar of sacrifice and twelve standing stones, signifying the twelve tribes of Israel (Ex 24:4). Next, he sent certain young men to offer communion sacrifices (Ex 24:5). At the ratification ceremony, Moses took half the blood of the sacrificed animals and poured the blood into bowls. The other half of the blood he ritually sprinkled on the altar of sacrifice (Ex 24:6). Then, taking up the words of God that he wrote down earlier, Moses read from the Book of the Covenant. The people once again swore their oath of obedience, saying in response to hearing God's commandments, *"All that the LORD has spoken we will do, and we will be obedient"* (Ex 24:7b).

Moses continued the ritual of covenant ratification by taking the blood reserved in the bowls and with a hyssop branch he sprinkled the blood of the sacrifice upon the people and the book, saying, *"Behold the blood of the covenant which the LORD has made with you in accordance with all these words"* (Ex 24:8b, also see Heb 9:20). Moses, in his role as the covenant mediator between Yahweh and the Israelites, symbolically united the newly formed covenant family by sprinkling the blood of the sacrificial victims on the altar that represented God, then on the people, and lastly on the book. The book was the covenant document that bound the Israelites by their sworn oath in covenant with Yahweh.

Blood is a sign of the essence of life. It is blood that unites a family—the children being of the same blood as the father. This ritual signified the birth of the sacred assembly of the Old Covenant Church, the ones "called out" (*kahal* in Hebrew) from the nations of the earth to become Yahweh's possession (Lev 20:26). Moses, as the covenant mediator, ratified the covenant in the blood of the sacrifice. The children of Israel became a covenant nation—the obedient vassal people of a Divine King and the faithful sons and daughters of a Divine Father (Dt 1:31; 14:1-2; Jer 3:19-20).

THE SACRED MEAL: THE EATING OF THE SACRIFICE IN THE RITUAL OF COVENANT

Listen to these ordinances, be true to them and observe them, and in return Yahweh your God will be true to the covenant and love which he promised on oath to your ancestors.
Deuteronomy 7:12 (NJB)

The Exodus out of Egypt and the birth of the sacred assembly at Mount Sinai became the defining experience in the history of the children of Israel. When the children of Israel entered into a new covenant relationship with Yahweh at Mount Sinai, God transformed the fabric of life and sacrifice. The Sinai Covenant marks the first time in the history of salvation when code, cult, and creed are defined. It was the first time since Eden that one earthly Sanctuary became the focus of worship and communion between God and man (Ex 25:8; Lev 17:8-9). It was the first time God ordained a ministerial priesthood (Ex 28:1; 30:30), and the covenant with Israel became the first corporate covenant in salvation history in which a unified covenant people submitted themselves to God as their Divine King.

The word "corporate" is defined as "people united collectively to form one body" (*New Webster Dictionary*). The Sinai Covenant became the precursor to the Universal Church's corporate covenant with God that is "one body in Christ" (Rom 12:4-5). It was unlike the previous covenants with Adam, Noah, and Abraham. In the age of the Patriarchs, every father served as a priest for his family, building random altars and offering sacrifice and worship. In a newly established ordained priesthood, the descendants of Moses's brother Aaron became the chief priests who replaced the patriarchal priesthood, serving God and ministering to His people by offering prescribed sacrifices and defined ritual worship at God's holy altar (Ex 28:1; Lev 9:5-24; Dt 12:13-14).

When God called Israel to become His sacred assembly and His holy covenant kingdom, He raised the children of Israel to the status of God's adopted "first-born sons" among the nations of the earth (Ex 4:22). They became a people called to fulfill their destiny in the ritual of worship as Yahweh's priestly witnesses to the other "younger sons" of world nations. In establishing the corporate covenant with Israel in the wilderness of Sinai, legitimate sacrifice and the ritual of worship was confined to one holy Sanctuary and offered by an ordained priesthood who served as God's representatives to "a kingdom of priests, a holy nation" (Ex 19:6). Through the prescribed ritual of worship in God's Sanctuary, Yahweh defined the Israelites as a liturgical people set apart from the other peoples of the earth as His holy partner in the divine plan of salvation (Ex 19:5-6; Lev 11:44-45).

Yahweh finalized the Sinai Covenant with the Israelites by the offering of blood sacrifices, the people swearing of an oath of loyalty and obedience to God their Divine King, and the eating of the communion sacrifices in a sacred meal (Ex 24:1-11). God commanded Moses to select a delegation composed of Moses (the covenant mediator), Aaron (the people's first high priest), Aaron's two elder sons (the first chief priests) and the seventy elders of Israel (the hierarchy of the governing body of the covenant people). Next, Yahweh invited them to ascend the holy mountain, and mid-way up the slope, they sat and gazed through the translucent sapphire floor of the heavenly throne room above them. They beheld what they interpreted as the form of God as they ate and drank at a sacred communion banquet in His presence (Ex 24:9-11). It was the first time since Eden that humankind enjoyed such intimacy with his Creator.

The observance of the sacrificial meal in covenant formation, covenant continuation, and the intimacy of fellowship with God was an established liturgical practice since the time of Noah when God gave His permission to eat the meat of animals offered in sacrifice (Gen 9:3-4). It signified that those who ate or "broke bread" together and consumed a common substance had a mutual relationship. These elements of covenant formation were similar to secular covenant treaties of the ancient Near Eastern. God's covenant with Israel formed by oath swearing, promised blessings, sacred blood ritual, covenant obligations and the ritual of eating a shared meal were essential parts of Biblical covenant formation (Gen 26:28-31; 31:44, 53-54; Ex 24:5-11; Jos 9:11, 14-15; Ps 50:5).

Sacred Scripture reveals the critical link between blood sacrifice, the covenant oath, the ritual meal, and the ratification of a covenant creating a family bond. The formation of a covenant in the ritual of the blood sacrifice that formed the unity between two parties, even in secular covenants (i.e., the covenant treaty between Jacob and Laban in Genesis 31:44, 53-54) took on special significance in the sacrificial meal. It was the final step of ratification in the Sinai Covenant between Yahweh and Israel, but it also became the visible sign of the continuation of the covenant relationship down through succeeding generations. In the shared sacred meal, the covenant family became united in the blood of the sacrifice as all human families linked by blood. Represented by the hierarchy of the newly formed Church at Sinai, the delegation of Israelites came to eat and drink as the children of a unified covenant family in the presence of their Divine Father. This sacred meal in the Divine Presence was the precursor of greater blessings that were to come as God moved forward His divine plan for humanity's salvation.

God's covenants always result in the formation of a unique covenant family bond with God fulfilling the role of both suzerain or dominant king and the patriarchal head of the covenant family. In the Sinai Covenant, God joined Himself to Israel in a covenant expressed in the images of a marriage between Yahweh the Great King to Israel His Bride and as the adoption of Israel as the first-born son of Yahweh the Divine Father. The concept of a covenant formation made by blood sacrifice, oath-swearing, and eating a sacred meal is a repeated Biblical theme. In the New Covenant, we relive our covenant continuation in our oath of faith through the Sacraments (*Sacramentum* is a Latin word meaning "oath") and the sacred meal. In the offering of bread and wine that becomes the sacrificial offering of Christ's Body and Blood in the Eucharist, we celebrate the "Thanksgiving" (in Greek *Euchatistia*) sacred meal of Christ the Bread of Life as the New Covenant children of God gather around the table of His holy altar (Jn 6:35, 51; Lk 22:19-20; 1 Cor 11:23-29).

In the first embrace between Yahweh and Israel at the momentous encounter at Mount Sinai, law, love, blood sacrifice, and a sacred meal bound the covenant between God and Israel. To seal their union, Yahweh, the Divine Spouse, gave Israel the gift of the Law of the Ten Commandments and their additional precepts and prohibitions (Ex 20:1-23:33), conceived in love and faithful to the oath He swore to the Patriarchs (Dt 7:7-8, 12). Gratitude and love for her Divine Redeemer moved Israel to accept the Covenant Treaty of Sinai and to offer the rituals of a sworn oath of obedience and blood sacrifice sealed by a sacred meal to bind the union (Ex 24:3-11). Love, liturgy, sacrifice, blood, and redemption bound by the covenant are the continuing themes of God's plan of salvation history in preparation for the Advent of the Messiah.

After the sacred meal, God called Moses to come up to the summit of the mountain. There Moses viewed the heavenly Sanctuary as he received the commands for the earthly Sanctuary and the plans for covenant continuation that included God's gift of Divine Liturgy in the perpetual, sanctifying communal sacrifice of the Tamid.

CHAPTER SUMMARY POINTS: SACRIFICE AND COVENANT

1. The garden in Eden was the first Sanctuary in which man had the fellowship of communion with God. The word communion is from the Latin meaning "sharing unity." In this shared unity with God, Adam and Eve enjoyed the position of divine son/daughter-ship, created in a state of holiness as sinless and immortal beings in the image of God (Gen 1:27; CCC 355, 375-76).

2. In our first parent's fall from grace, human fathering (communicating one's human nature) became an imperfect act. All sons and daughters of Adam in the human family are born spiritually lacking the grace of original holiness with souls stained by original sin (CCC 390, 399, 402-05).

3. God promised that one day a Redeemer would come to defeat Satan, the serpent who deceived our first parents (Gen 3:15; Rev 12:9; CCC 2852), and restore humankind to the original state of grace in which they were created (CCC 410-11).

4. God established confession of sin and blood sacrifice as expressions of humanity's acknowledgment of guilt, desire for redemption, and as a foreshadowing of the future unblemished sacrifice that will save humanity from eternal death that is eternal separation from God. The temporary remedy God provided was the shedding of the blood of certain ritually pure animals for the atonement of sin. Without the shedding of blood and the demonstrated humble contrition of the sinner, there can be no remission of sin (Heb 9:22).

5. Animal sacrifice was only an imperfect, temporary remedy since no animal could be perfect enough to effectively remove the stain of sin upon the human soul (Heb 10:4). The ministerial priesthood of

the Old Covenant was powerless to bring about definitive sanctification and eternal salvation (CCC 1540).

6. Animal sacrifice and atonement through the shedding of the blood of the unblemished victim became a ritualized preparation for understanding the perfect and sufficient sacrifice offered by Jesus Christ to one day expiate humanity's sins in all generations (Rom 3:24-26; Heb 9:11-12; 1 Jn 2:2; CCC 457, 604, 606-18).

7. To preserve the "promised seed" of Genesis 3:15, God established covenant treaties with a faithful remnant of humanity (CCC 522, 762). God's covenants are not separate and unrelated; they are continual, with each covenant built upon and integrated into the next (CCC 781).

8. The repeated link between covenant formation and blood sacrifice of animals after the Fall of our original parents established that the blood of sacrifice had a purpose in God's plan for humanity (Lev 17:11; CCC 2260).

9. The selection of a particular people, consecrated in a covenant relationship to Yahweh, was necessary to fulfill the promise of future redemption. These people needed to be trained in holiness, in an understanding of

sacrifice and re-established communion, and taught to recognize the Redeemer-Messiah when it was time for His entrance upon the stage of human history (CCC 1963-64).

10. Love, liturgy, sacrifice, blood, a sacred meal, and redemption bound in Yahweh's covenant are the continuing themes of God's plan of salvation history.

11. The Sinai Covenant marks the first time in the history of salvation when code, cult, and creed are defined. It is the first time since Eden that one earthly Sanctuary became the focus of worship and communion between God and humankind. For the first time in salvation history, a ministerial priesthood and a corporate covenant people were bound by a covenant to worship Yahweh, their Divine King, in a prescribed liturgy (public work) of worship at one altar and one Sanctuary.

12. In the Sinai Covenant, the sacred meal took on special significance as the unified children of the covenant family ate in the presence of their great King and Divine Father.

Endnotes: Sacrifice and Covenant

1. The Divine Name YHWH (translated Yahweh by most modern scholars and replaced by LORD in most English

translations) is the most frequently used name for God in the Old Testament (about 6,800 times) and is found from Genesis 4:2 to Malachi 3:23/4:5. Abraham addressed God directly by His Divine Name, for example, in Gen 15:2 and 8. God identified Himself to Abraham using the Divine Name in Gen 15:7; and Sarah/Sarai used God's Divine Name in Gen 16:2. Eve is the first person in Scripture to use the Divine Name in Gen 4:1.

2. In Ex 3:15b, God commands that all generations should know Him by His Divine Name, YHWH (Yahweh). Bible scholar Robert Vasholz writes that the better translation of Ex 6:2–3 is: *I am Yahweh. To Abraham, Isaac, and Jacob, I appeared as El Shaddai; by my name, Yahweh, I indeed made myself known to them.* He argues that the particle often translated as a negative should instead be an emphatic particle (Vasholz, *Leviticus,* page 132, note 5). Vasholz's argument makes sense in the context of Sacred Scripture. God's holy covenant name, YHWH (Yahweh) connects God with both the Patriarchs and Moses. The first century BC/AD saw the introduction of false piety in which it became forbidden for Jews to invoke the Divine Name except in the daily Tamid Temple liturgy.
3. In Jewish tradition, the bridal *mikveh*, or ritual bath, signifies the spiritual rebirth of the bride as she begins her new life (*The New Jewish Wedding*, Anita Diamant, Simon & Schuster, Inc., N.Y., 1985, 2001).

CHAPTER II THE SANCTUARY AND THE INSTITUTION OF THE SACRED LITURGY OF THE TAMID SACRIFICE

The LORD said to Moses ... "And let them make me a sanctuary, that I may dwell in their midst. According to all that I show you concerning the pattern of the tabernacle, and of all its furniture, so you shall make it."
Exodus 25:1a, 8-9

THE BIRTH OF ISRAEL AS A COVENANT PEOPLE

The rendezvous between God and the children of Israel at Mount Sinai was a crossroads in salvation history. It was the three-way intersection between love, law, and liturgy. God expressed His love for Israel in His gift of the Law and in the promised blessings Israel received for living in obedience to His commands and prohibitions. In return, Israel expressed her love for God through her obedience to the Law and in the faithful practice of prescribed liturgical worship. Beyond the impact of the terms of the covenant on this tribal people, Israel's uniquely divine election and covenant formation established them as a liturgical people "called out" (*kahal*) by God and set apart to be His possession as a sign to the other nations of the world. It was a sign that prefigured the New Covenant in Christ when all the nations of the earth are "called out" from a world of sin and into the baptism of a new and universal covenant formation, lifting man's understanding of God from a focus on temporal blessings to the promise of eternal salvation. [1]

With the ratification of the covenant completed in a blood ritual and sacred meal, Yahweh commanded Moses to come up onto the mountain to receive additional instruction and the covenant documents (Ex 24:12). The glory of Yahweh rested on the mountain's summit in what appeared to be a dense cloud with a devouring fire. Moses waited for six days; then, on the seventh day, Yahweh called to Moses from inside the cloud. Moses ascended the mountain, disappeared into the dense mist, and was absent from the children of Israel for forty days (Ex 24:16-18). It is significant that Moses entered into Yahweh's presence on the seventh day after ascending the mountain. In the symbolic significance of numbers in Scripture, the number seven represents perfection, fulfillment, and completion. In the Biblical account of Creation, it was on the seventh day that Adam and Eve entered into Yahweh's rest when God ceased His work of creation and blessed the seventh day (Gen 2:2-3). The giving of the Law and the liturgical requirements for worship in Yahweh's earthly Sanctuary established Israel as a new creation among the nations of the earth, and a unified people that makes holy the seventh day as a covenant sign of communion with the One True God (Ex 31:12-17).

God's first command was for Moses to collect a free-will contribution from the Israelites to build the sacred space for God to dwell in the midst of His covenant people (Ex 25:1-2, 8; 29:45). The people were to build a structure that was a copy of the heavenly Sanctuary (Ex. 25:9, 40, 26:30). Yahweh commanded the building of the earthly Sanctuary and its Tent of Meeting (Tabernacle) in three sections within one enclosure: a courtyard and a Tabernacle divided into two sacred spaces designated the Holy Place and the Holy of Holies.

They were to furnish the Sanctuary with seven pieces of furniture copied from what Moses saw in Heaven.[2]

The purpose of the earthly Sanctuary was to unite Heaven and earth in the liturgical expression of divine worship. The Sanctuary was to be a sacred space where a holy covenant people worshiped and experienced their God who was sacramentally present not only in the visible white cloud that rose from the fire of the altar of sacrifice in the courtyard but also in His invisible presence within the innermost sacred space of the Holy of Holies. The Holy of Holies was a cube-shaped room containing Yahweh's earthly throne, a wooden box clad with gold inside and out and covered with a solid gold lid. It was called the Ark of the Testimony or the Ark of the Covenant (Ex 25:22; Num 10:33), and its lid was the "Mercy-seat" or "Seat of Atonement," in Hebrew the *Kapporeth* (Ex 25:17-21).

The Ark of the Covenant became the Israelites' prized possession and the focal point of worship for God's covenant people. The Ark would hold the covenant treaty documents that were God's precious gift to His chosen people. The documents were written by "the finger of God" on the front and back of two stone tablets (Ex 31:18; 32:15-16; 34:1) and were known as the Decalogue ("ten words") or the Ten Commandments God spoke to the Israelites at their first encounter on the holy mountain (Ex 20: 1-17; 34:28). The divine testimony of God hidden in the Ark of the Covenant became the guarantee of the fulfillment of the promises of the Covenant Treaty made between God and Israel at Mount Sinai. The presence of Yahweh was to dwell among His people enthroned on the gold lid of the Ark of the Covenant, resting between the wings of the two golden cherubim statues that overshadowed the Mercy-seat. The Ark, therefore, became the earthly throne of Yahweh the Great King, the footstool of His heavenly throne, and the place from which God communicated with His people (Ex 25:17-22; Lev 16:2; 2 Sam 6:2; 1 Chr 28:2; Ps 99:5; 132:7).

After God gave Moses the detailed commands for building the earthly Sanctuary (Ex 25:1-27:20), He gave Moses instructions for the ordination of the ministerial priesthood. Yahweh told Moses: *In the tent of meeting, outside the veil which is before the testimony, Aaron and his sons shall tend it from evening to morning before the LORD [YHWH], it shall be a statute forever to be observed throughout their generations by the people of Israel. Then bring near to you Aaron your brother, and his sons with him, from among the people of Israel to serve me as priests* (Ex 27:21-28:1). This command not only addressed the first investiture of a ministerial priesthood, but it was the formation of a covenant with Aaron and his priestly descendants within the Sinai Covenant (Num 18:7, 19; Sir 45:7/8, 15/18-19; Jer 33:21; see the chart on "Yahweh's Eight Covenants" in Appendix I).

God commanded the anointing of Aaron and his sons as the chief ministers of the Sanctuary. Aaron was to serve as Yahweh's High Priest with spiritual authority over the people. It was the function of the High Priest and the chief priests to serve as God's authorized mediators in offering sacrifices in liturgical services and performing prescribed ritual duties on behalf of the covenant people. Only Aaron's descendants were permitted to serve at the sacrificial altar as Yahweh's High Priest and chief priests (Num 3:10). Included in the instructions for the priests were the requirements for the four liturgical garments for the chief priests and the eight vestments for Aaron, the High Priest (Ex 28:1-43). Then, God gave the instructions for the ritual of the priestly investiture ceremony (Ex 29:1-35) and the consecration of the bronze Altar of Burnt Offerings (Ex 29:36-37).

Word repetition in Scripture is like underlining. It denotes emphasis and importance. It is significant in the Hebrew text of Exodus that the word "altar" is repeated four times in the instructions for its consecration: once in Exodus 29:36 and three times in verse 37. The repetition of the word "altar" in these verses is an appropriate introduction for the primary mission of the ministerial priesthood and the primary function of the sacrificial Altar of Burnt Offerings. The fifth use of the word "altar" in verse 38 begins the instructions concerning the one communal sacrifice that was to be the center of liturgical life for the covenant people, the core of the entire sacrificial system, and the reason for a ministerial priesthood: the communal sacrifice of the *olat ha-Tamid.*

THE DAILY BURNT OFFERING OF THE TAMID LAMB: A SACRIFICE OF ATONEMENT AND SANCTIFICATION

The law requires that out of the public expenses a lamb of the first year be killed every day, at the beginning and at the ending of the day.
Flavius Josephus on the Tamid,
Antiquities of the Jews, 3.10.1 [237]

Biblical scholar J. H. Kurtz writes in Offerings, Sacrifices and Worship in the Old Testament (page 349): This daily burnt-offering was called the continual, standing sacrifice, [olat ha-tamid] (Ex. xxix.42; Num. xxviii. 6, 10, 15, 23, 24), and at a later period ha-tamid alone (Dan. Viii. 11, 12, 13, xi.31). The Hebrew word tamid means "standing," as in perpetual or continual, and the word olat is from the Hebrew verb l-h (olah), meaning "to go up or to ascend." The ascending smoke rising to Heaven is the distinguishing visible feature of all altar sacrifices consumed by fire. Of all the sacrifices established in the rites of the Sinai Covenant, no other sacrifice was as important or took precedence over the Tamid; all other compulsory sacrifices were offered "in addition" to the Tamid (repeated fifteen times in the Book of Numbers, Chapters 28-29). It was a single sacrifice offered twice daily for the atonement and sanctification of the entire covenant community, and the sacrifice Yahweh commanded be established as the focus of daily liturgical worship.

The Tamid was a "whole-burnt offering (holocaust) where the animal was completely consumed on the altar fire and described in the Hebrew text simply as olat ha-Tamid: [38]Now this is what you shall offer upon the altar: two [sons of] lambs a year old, day by day continually [tamid]. [39]One lamb you shall offer in the morning, and the other lamb you shall offer in the evening [between the twilights]; [40]and with the first lamb a tenth measure of fine flour mingled with a fourth of a hin of beaten oil, and a fourth of a hin of wine for a libation. [41]And the other lamb you shall offer in the evening [between the twilights] and shall offer with it a cereal offering and its libation, as in the morning, for a pleasing odor, an offering by fire to the LORD. It shall be a continual burnt offering [olat ha-Tamid] throughout your generations at the door of the tent of meeting before the LORD, where I will meet with you, to speak there to you. There I will meet with the people [sons] of Israel, and it shall be sanctified by my glory (Ex 29:38-43; emphasis added; [...] = literal Hebrew translation, IBHE, vol. I, pages 222-23).

The Hebrew word tamid is both a noun and an adverb. There are passages in Scripture where the Hebrew word tamid appears as an adverb as in Exodus 29:38 in the instructions to offer the sacrifice of the two lambs "day by day continually" [literally tamid]. There are also other passages where the word appears as an adverb but not in association with the daily whole-burnt offering of the communal sacrifice. In those passages, the word tamid appears as a modifier to describe anything constantly repeated. For example, the adverb tamid associated with:

- The instructions for the daily replenishing of the twelve loaves of bread known as the "Bread of the Presence" that were placed on the golden table in the Holy Place, representing the twelve tribes of Israel (Ex 25:30; Lev 24:8; Num 4:7).

- The command for the continual burning of the oil lamps of the seven-branched Menorah (lamp-stand) that stood in the Holy Place of the Sanctuary (Ex 27:20, 21; Lev 24:2, 3 twice, 4, 8).
- The instructions concerning the sacrificial altar included that its fire must burn continually (Lev 6:13 or 6:6 in some translations other than the RSV).
- The instructions that the burning of the incense on the golden Altar of Incense must take place twice a day, perpetually (Ex 30:8).
- The instructions for the high priest's vestments, including his breastpiece of judgment and the golden miter plate on his forehead (Ex 28:29, 30, 38).
- And in the instructions for the priestly grain offering associated with the Tamid sacrifice (Lev 6:22/16; Num 4:16).

However, when referring to the twice-daily sacrifice of the Tamid lambs, the word *tamid* is exclusively used as a noun; no word follows for it to modify, and it is always used with the article *ha*, which corresponds to our definite article "the" (e.g. Lev 6:2-6/6:8-13; Num 28: 4, 6, 10, 15, 23, 24, 31; 29:6, 11, 16, 19, 22, 25, 28, 31, 34, 38; Dan 8:11, 12, 13; 11:31; 12:12; Ezra 3:5; Neh 10:34).

Nowhere else in Scripture is the Hebrew word *tamid* used as a noun except for this unique sacrifice.

The Tamid was the communal sacrifice that ensured the continuing covenant relationship between a holy God and His chosen people. The command for the Tamid in the Hebrew text identifies the sacrifice in the singular (Ex 29:42 and Num 28:3, 6), indicating that the two lambs were to be considered a single sacrifice.[3] The sacrifice of the Tamid lamb was to take place between the altar of sacrifice in the courtyard of the desert Sanctuary and the curtain that covered the entrance to the Tabernacle's Holy Place, the sacred space that led to the dwelling place of God within the Tabernacle's Holy of Holies. The instructions God gave Moses concerning the Tamid lambs required the sacrifice of one unblemished male lamb (less than a year old but not younger than eight days) in the morning and a second lamb in the afternoon (evening for the Israelites) for the atonement and sanctification of God's covenant people (Ex 29:38-42; Lev 23:27; Num 28:4-8).

Understanding the requirements for the twice-daily Tamid sacrifice in the proper context, it is necessary to recall that for the Hebrew people each day ended at sunset with the setting of the sun also announcing the beginning of the next day (*JPS Torah Commentary: Exodus*, page 55). According to tradition, this was an observance set by God during the Creation event. The six passages in Genesis Chapter One establish this tradition with the words "there was evening, and there was morning" (Gen. 1:5, 8, 13, 19, 23, and 31). For the Israelites, the day consisted of twelve seasonal hours, as noted by Jesus in John 11:9 when He said: *"Are there not twelve hours in the day?"* High noon marked the division between the seasonal twelve daytime hours. Evening for the Israelites began at noon when the sun started to descend toward the end of the day (*Jewish book of Why*, vol. I, pages 9-10). Their "evening" is our modern day "afternoon;" therefore, when referring to the second liturgical service of the *olat ha-Tamid*, the designation will be "afternoon."

The instructions for the daily liturgy of the Tamid are in the Fifth Division of the Jewish *Mishnah*, entitled "Holy Things" in the sub-section "Tamid." The *Mishnah* is a document that contains the detailed record of ritual and worship in the Jerusalem Temple in the first century AD. It was written and compiled by Jewish scholars in the third century AD, about 130 years after the destruction of the Jerusalem Temple in AD 70. There are two commentaries on the *Mishnah* that form the Palestinian and Babylonian Talmud. After the Hebrew Scriptures, the *Mishnah* is the first canonical document of Rabbinical Judaism and is the primary source and continuing expression of Jewish law and theology. The *Mishnah* united with the *Gemarah* (its commentary) forms the most extensive compendium of rabbinic Biblical exegesis ever compiled.

Mishnah: Tamid, 4:1 identifies the two lambs as the daily whole-burnt offering of the dawn and twilight. "Twilight" is the translation of the time marker recorded in Scripture which is literally "between the twilights" (plural). The reference cannot refer to the time just before sunset since twilight was the very end of the day. Sunset marked the end of one day and the beginning of the next, and no sacrifices took place at the end of the day because there was the requirement to cleanse the blood of the sacrificial victims and purify the sacred space before sunset in readiness for the worship services of the next day. Therefore, "between the twilights" identifies noon as the time for the preparation of the second Tamid service, between the twilight of the dawn and the twilight of sunset. The Jewish chief priest and historian Flavius Josephus (*The Antiquities of the Jews,* 14.4.3 [65]), the Jewish *Mishnah* (*Mishnah: Pesahim,* 5:1) and Rabbi Telushkin (*Jewish Literacy,* page 47), identify the offering of the second Tamid lamb as an afternoon sacrifice.

Mishnah: Pesahim, the section of the *Mishnah* that records the procedure for the Passover sacrifice, notes that the regular time for the sacrifice of the afternoon Tamid was at half past the eighth-hour Jewish time or two-thirty in the afternoon. The priests placed quartered body of the animal on the altar fire at half after the ninth hour Jewish time, or three-thirty in the afternoon (*Mishnah: Pesahim* 5:1). The Mishnah account was from c. AD 200, 130 years after the Tamid liturgical service ceased with the destruction of the Jerusalem Temple. Men who never witnessed the sacred Tamid liturgy wrote the Mishnah's record of hours of Temple service.

However, writing about ten years after the destruction of the Jerusalem Temple, the Jewish historian Flavius Josephus (AD 37-100), who served as a priest in the Jerusalem Temple Tamid services before the destruction of the Temple, identified the hour of the afternoon sacrifice as the ninth hour Jewish time or about three o'clock in the afternoon according to modern time. Josephus wrote that the priests *did still twice each day, in the morning and about the ninth hour* [3 PM], *offer their sacrifices on the altar...* (Josephus, *Antiquities of the Jews,* 14.4.3). Jewish scholar Baruch Levine notes that the Rabbis also specified the time for the afternoon Tamid as the ninth hour or about 3 PM, the time in which the afternoon Tamid is remembered in the afternoon prayer time of Rabbinic Judaism (*JPS Torah Commentary: Numbers*, page 239).

The morning Tamid was led out to the altar at dawn and offered for sacrifice at the third hour (9 AM) at which time trumpets signaled the beginning of the morning liturgical service (Edersheim, *The Temple: Its Ministry and Services*, pages 72-75). The second Tamid lamb was brought to the altar at noon and sacrificed when the afternoon worship service began at about the ninth hour (3 PM). In addition to the two male lambs offered in daily sacrifice, there were other offerings associated with the Tamid sacrifice. There was one-tenth of a measure of fine wheat flour mixed with one-fourth hin of olive oil (a little less than one gallon) offered on the altar fire and one-fourth hin of red wine splashed against the altar of sacrifice as a libation (drink offering) in both the morning and afternoon sacrificial offering of the Tamid (Ex 29:40-41). The morning sacrifice was to remain on the altar fire, burning all through the day, while the afternoon sacrifice burned throughout the night until the next morning in obedience to Yahweh's command, the altar fire burned continually and was never allowed to go out (Lev 6:8-9, 12-13 RSV; 6:1-2, 5-6 in some other translations).

Together with the sacrifice of the *olat ha-Tamid*, the High Priest was commanded to provide, out of his private resources, a gift offering of unleavened wheat flour mixed with oil and formed into a small, flat, unleavened wafer baked as a griddle cake and offered in the morning and afternoon worship services. The High Priest offered it with incense, and it was designated the high priestly *minhah*, "gift offering." Concerning this offering, *The LORD said to Moses, "This is the offering [korban] which Aaron and his sons shall offer to the LORD [YHWH] on the day when he is anointed: a tenth of an ephah of fine flour as a regular cereal offering [minhah], half of it in the morning and half in the evening. It shall be made with oil on a griddle; you shall bring it well mixed, in baked pieces like a cereal offering, and offer it for a pleasing odor to the LORD [YHWH]. The priest from among Aaron's sons, who is anointed to succeed him, shall offer it to the LORD [YHWH] as decreed forever [tamid]; the whole of it shall be burned. Every cereal offering of a priest shall be wholly burned; it shall not be eaten"* (Lev 6:19–23 RSV; Lev 6:12–16 in some other translations; emphasis added; bracketed words are the literal Hebrew words, see *IBHE*, vol. I, pages 270–71). Flavius Josephus also mentioned the designated high priestly offering associated with the Tamid sacrifice: *The high priest also, of his own charges, offered a sacrifice, and that twice every day. It was made of flour mingled with oil, and gently baked by the fire* (*Antiquities of the Jews*, 3.10.7 [257]).[4]

According to rabbinic tradition, the offering of the priestly wafer took place between the prescribed flour offering for the Tamid and the wine libation (Ex 29:40; Kurtz, *Offerings, Sacrifices, and Worship in the Old Testament*, page 353). The High Priest held the priestly wafer of unleavened bread in his two hands and lifted it above the fire of the sacrificial altar in full view of the congregation of worshipers in the same way a Catholic priest elevates the host above the altar in a Catholic Mass. He then broke the bread and placed the broken pieces of the wafer with the body of the Tamid lamb burning on the altar fire. The High Priest or his representative priest made the same priestly bread offering in the afternoon liturgical service (Lev 6:20-23 RSV/Lev 6:13-16; 9:17; Sir 45:14). The unblemished male lamb, the fine flour mixed with oil, the priestly wafer gift-offering, and the wine libation, all presented on behalf of the covenant community on God's altar of sacrifice, were consumed by the holy fire. For the covenant people, the billows of white smoke rising from the salted sacrifices were the visible sign that Yahweh graciously accepted their offerings (Lev 2:13; Ez 43:24).

The Tamid was a sacrifice that God commanded must be *a continual burnt offering [olat ha-Tamid] throughout your generations* (Ex 29:42). Later, Scripture abbreviates the term for this premier, single sacrifice in two parts to *ha-Tamid,* "the Tamid" (e.g. Num 28:6, 15; Dan 8:11).[5] The first description of the morning worship service and the whole-burnt-offering of the Tamid lamb appears in Leviticus Chapter 9, immediately after the ordination ceremony of Aaron the High Priest and his sons the chief priests (see Lev 9:17).

THE CONCEPT OF SACRIFICE IN THE BIBLE

Most Bible translations erroneously include the word "sacrifice" following the rendering of *'olat ha-tamid* as in "daily sacrifice." This practice does not adequately reflect either the Hebrew character or the unique use of the word *tamid* as the proper name of a special class of sacrifice expressed as *ha-Tamid*, "the Standing" (as in continual) holocaust or whole-burnt-offering. It isn't just "a daily" sacrifice; in the Hebrew Biblical text, it is **the** Tamid: *It is a* [literally *ha = the*] *continual burnt offering [literally = olat ha-Tamid] which was ordained at Mount Sinai for a pleasing odor, an offering* *by fire to the LORD [YHWH]* (Num 28:6; Hebrew = IBHE, vol. I, page 429).

God established the Tamid ritual sacrifice and all other associated sacrifices as the ultimate expression of the Israelite's liturgical service. However, our modern understanding of the word "sacrifice" does not adequately express the concept of the offering of "sacrifice" in the Bible. The word sacrifice has come to mean "the willing renunciation of something valuable to obtain something or to save someone." The Hebrew word most often translated as "sacrifice" or "offering" in the Bible is the word *korban* (*corban/qorban*). This Hebrew word derives from a root meaning "to draw near to" or "to establish fellowship with" (*The Brown-Driver-Briggs Hebrew and English Lexicon,* page 897) and appears forty times in the liturgical instructions in the Book of Leviticus (Vasholz, *Leviticus,* page 33).

The use of the word *korban* for the offering of sacrifice reveals that the Hebrew concept of sacrifice is much more than simply making a pleasing gift to appease a deity by giving something of material value. Any form of an offering to God, whether animal sacrifice, grain offerings, first-fruit offerings, or Sanctuary gifts was *korban.* The priestly offering of the unleavened wheat wafer in association with the Tamid is, for example, described as the *korban* of Aaron and his sons which they are commanded to offer in "drawing near" to Yahweh (Lev 6:20 RSV/6:13). In offering God the blood sacrifice of a ritually clean animal, the one making the sacrifice laid his hands upon the animal and confessed his sins for a sin sacrifice or offered a confession of praise for a communion sacrifice to the officiating priest (e.g. Lev 3:1-2, 6-8; 4:2-4, 13-17; 5:5-6; 7:11-12; 16:21; Ps 32:5). This action acknowledged God's sovereignty over the offeror and his dependence on God for all that is necessary for one's life.

More importantly, to offer *korban* to Yahweh is the highest form of adoration by allowing one to enter into the experience of an intimate encounter in "drawing near" to God by offering the sanctified heart and the self-surrendered life of the believer (1 Sam 15:22; Ps 51:16-17 RSV/51:17-18; Hos 6:6). The purpose of the *korban* of the morning Tamid was to sanctify the covenant people by allowing them (priests and laity alike) to confess their sins as a people, receive God's forgiveness, and "draw near" to Him during the day. The purpose of the *korban* of the afternoon Tamid was to keep the covenant people in fellowship with God and to preserve them from falling into sin as the second Tamid lamb burned on the altar throughout the night.

However, the Tamid served as more than the means of atonement and covenant sanctification for the people of Israel. The Tamid was also a sign of the hope for the future sanctification for all the peoples of the earth, as expressed by the first century AD Jewish philosopher and theologian, Philo of Alexandria. Addressing the singular importance of the Tamid, he wrote: *Accordingly, it is commanded that every day the priests should offer up two lambs, one at the dawn of the day, and the other in the evening; each of them being a sacrifice of thanksgiving; the one for the kindnesses which have been bestowed during the day, and the other for the mercies which have been vouchsafed in the night, which God is incessantly and uninterruptedly pouring upon the race of men* (*The Works of Philo, Special Laws*, I.35 [169]; emphasis added).

ISRAEL'S FALL FROM GRACE: THE SIN OF THE GOLDEN CALF

When the people became aware of Moses' delay in coming down from the mountain, they gathered around Aaron, and said to him, "Come, make us a god, who will be our leader; as for the man Moses who brought us out of the land of Egypt, we do not know what has happened to him."
Exodus 32:1

Moses remained with God on Mount Sinai for forty days, receiving the instructions for building the earthly Sanctuary, for the ordination of the ministerial priesthood, and the twice-daily Tamid worship service. It was the Law, the sanctifying Tamid liturgy in the Sanctuary, and the Sabbath obligation that bound the covenant people in fellowship with Yahweh. Finally, as Moses' period of instruction came to an end, Yahweh gave him the two stone tablets of the covenant treaty testimony inscribed by the finger of God (Ex 24:12;31:18).

Instead of this momentous experience ending in jubilation, Moses was stunned by Yahweh's words. The Lord said: *"Go down; for your people, whom you brought up out of the land of Egypt, have corrupted themselves; they have turned aside quickly out of the way which I commanded them; they have made for themselves a molten calf, and have worshiped it and sacrificed to it, and said, 'These are your gods, O Israel, who brought you up out of the land of Egypt!'"* (Ex 32:7-8). Before the "ink was dry," so to speak, on the documents of the covenant treaty, the Israelites violated the covenant agreement by falling into the sin of idolatry and convincing Aaron to fashion an idol of gold in the form of a calf. God physically took Israel out of Egypt, but the corrupting vestiges of Egyptian idol worship remained within Israel.

Moses returned to the Israelite camp to confront the people. In his anger, Moses broke the two stone tablets of the covenant treaty, symbolically demonstrating

Israel's broken covenant with Yahweh (Ex 32:19). The firstborn sons of Israel who were consecrated to God when He spared their lives on the night of the tenth Egyptian plague (Ex 11:4-7) should have been the first to respond to Moses' plea for help when he called out "all who are on God's side come to me" (Ex 32:26). But Israel's firstborn sons did not rally to Moses. Instead, Moses' kinsmen, the sons of the collective clans of Gershon, Kohath, and Merari who formed the tribe of Levi, came to Moses' aid and by force overcame the rebels.

In the collective sin of the covenant people and the failure of the "firstborn" sons in the rebellion of the Golden Calf, every Israelite family lost the priestly status of their eldest sons when the firstborn males of every family became disgraced and dispossessed sons unfit for liturgical service. Consecrated in the sacrificial blood of their fallen 3,000 rebel brethren, the Levites would replace Israel's firstborn sons. After the restoration of the covenant, by God's command, Moses dedicated the Levites to Yahweh's service as the lesser ministers of the Sanctuary (Ex 32:28-29; Num 3:6-9, 11-13). In a liturgical ceremony, the people laid their hands upon the Levites, giving them up to God as living sacrifices (Num 8:5-22; 18:1-7).

THE AFTERMATH OF THE REBELLION

On the next day, Moses said to the people, "You have committed a great sin. I will go up to the LORD, then; perhaps I will be able to make atonement for your sin."
Exodus 32:30

In His righteous wrath over the people's sin, Yahweh threatened to destroy the Israelites and create a new nation from Moses' descendants (Ex 32:10). Fortunately, Moses' plea for mercy deflected God's anger. The reluctant hero of the Exodus willingly offered his own life and his hopes of salvation in exchange for the forgiveness of the people's collective sin (Ex 32:31-32). He asked God to erase His name from the Book of Life in exchange for the forgiveness of those placed under his protection.[6] Yahweh did not agree to Moses' offer of sacrifice to atone for the sins of the Israelites, but He did grant Moses' petition to forgive Israel's sin. Moses' self-sacrificial love for his people prefigured the future sacrifice God would accept in the sacrifice of Jesus the Messiah for the sins of all people of the earth.

Through Moses' intervention, God was merciful in sparing Israel as a nation, but the Israelites were still accountable for their collective sin in the incident of the Golden Calf (Ex 32:34-35). Israel's sin of idolatry violated the sacramental covenant bond, and it was necessary for the people to renew their covenant with Yahweh. Moses ascended the holy mountain for another forty-day period where he received the new stone tablets of the Ten Commandments to replace the ones he broke. He also received the expanded laws, prohibitions, and rituals of sacrifice for the renewed covenant (Ex chapter 34).

Before the sin of the Golden Calf, there were compulsory animal sacrifices to sanctify the altar and to consecrate the priests to the ministerial priesthood. However, there was only one kind of altar sacrifice required in a continual, twice-daily liturgical service for the people as a whole, and that sacrifice was the *olat ha-Tamid.* After the people's covenant failure in the events surrounding the fashioning of the Golden Calf, Yahweh repeated the command for the twice-daily liturgy of the Tamid. However, in the renewed covenant, there was a radical change in the kinds of sacrifices and the other requirements and obligations of the Law.

In the reinstated covenant, after the sin of the Golden Calf, the Law became the most thorough attempt in history to use religion as a regulator of every aspect of the lives of a people. Yahweh established cultic purity rites, which included regulating hygiene in intimate marital relations, the eating of "clean" animals, and the avoidance of what was declared to be "unclean" (Lev Chapters 11-15). Purification rites necessary for those who became ritually unclean and unfit for worship were defined (Num Chapter 19). The prohibition against drinking blood and eating raw flesh, first established in the covenant with Noah (Gen 9:4), was repeated an additional eight times (Lev 3:17; 7:25-27; 17:10-12, 14; 19:26; Dt 12:16, 23-27 and 15:23). There were regulations concerning the wearing of distinctive clothing and the cutting of hair (Lev 19:27; 21:5; Num 15:37-39; Dt 22:11-12). All civil and moral laws were subjects of divine ordinance and guidance. Scholar E. Renen, in his classic work on the history of Israel, writes that the Law of Sinai became "the tightest garment into which life was ever laced" (*History of the People of Israel*, page 163).

In the liturgy of worship, God expanded the acceptable sacrifice of specific animals and the prescribed blood rituals that made sinners acceptable beyond the Tamid. In the renewed covenant, God restated the command to offer the Tamid as the premier sacrifice: *And you shall say to them, "This is the offering by fire which you shall offer to the LORD: two male lambs a year old without blemish, day by day, <u>as a continual offering</u> [olat ha-Tamid]"* (Num 28:2-3; emphasis added; [...] = literal translation *IBHE*, vol. I, pages 429). The divine command contained the admonition that the Tamid took precedence over all other types of blood sacrifice, including the Sabbath Sacrifice. All other sacrifices were offered "in addition" to the Tamid within the morning and afternoon liturgical services (repeated fifteen times in Num 28:10, 15, 23, 24, 31; 29:6, 11, 16, 19, 22, 25, 28, 31, 34, and 38). Those additional sacrifices included mandatory communal whole-burnt offerings for the weekly Sabbath, voluntary individual whole-burnt offerings, compulsory communal sin sacrifices, voluntary personal sin sacrifices, including sacrifices of reparation (guilt offerings), and the individual's voluntary communion sacrifices. There were also non-bloody offerings that expressed gratitude to God like grain and wine, the first fruits from the harvests, and Sanctuary endowments (see the chart on the different kinds of sacrifices in Appendix II).

The holy days that were Yahweh's "appointed times" were expanded from the weekly Sabbath obligation (first commanded in Ex 20:8-11 and restated in Ex 35:1-3) and the original three annual holy days of obligation called the "pilgrim feasts" (first commanded in Ex 20:8-11; 23:14-17; 31:12-17, restated in Ex 34:18-23 and again in Dt 16:16 and 2 Chr 8:13). The three pilgrim feasts of Unleavened Bread (*Hag Hamatzot*), the Feast of Weeks/Pentecost (*Hag HaShavuot)*, and the Feast of Tabernacle/Shelters/Booths (*Sukkot*) required the Israelites to relive the Exodus liberation and reaffirm their commitment to the covenant with Yahweh. Three times a year, God commanded every Israelite male over thirteen years of age to appear before His altar with their sacrifices.[7]

However, after the sin of the Golden Calf, other feasts were added to bring the number to seven annual remembrance festivals in which the Israelites relived their origins in the Exodus out of Egypt and the covenant formation at Mount Sinai (Lev 16:1-34; 23:5-44; Num 28:16-29:39). The annual God-ordained remembrance feasts still included the same three pilgrim feasts of Unleavened Bread, Weeks, and Tabernacles as well as the Passover remembrance sacrifice that marked the beginning of the liturgical year on the day before Unleavened Bread (Ex 12:2). In addition to the weekly Sabbath and annual feasts, there was also the monthly feast of the New Moon and the periodic observances of the Sabbatical Year (every seventh year) and the Feast of the Jubilee (every fiftieth year) that became part of the religious calendar (Ex 23:10-11; Lev 25:1-55; Num 28:11-15; see Israel's Liturgical and Civil Calendar in Appendix IV).

The most radical change in God's relationship with Israel was that the sin of the Golden Calf separated Israel from unlimited access to God (Ex 33:1-4). Under the renewed covenant, only Moses had unrestricted communication with God's Divine Presence as Israel's covenant mediator (Ex 33:7-11). In the renewed covenant, the High Priest could only enter beyond the barrier of the veil that separated the Holy Place from the Holy of Holies and God's Divine Presence above the Ark of the Covenant once a year on Yom Kippur, the annual Feast of Atonement (Lev 16:1-34). During this feast, celebrated within the liturgy of the Tamid (Num 29:11), Israel remembered her sin of rebellion and idol worship as well as Yahweh's gracious forgiveness.

On the Feast of Atonement/Yom Kippur, the reigning High Priest offered a bull as a sin sacrifice for himself, recalling the sin of the first High Priest, Aaron, who made the Golden Calf. On this day of communal repentance, the Ark of the Covenant served as Yahweh's earthly throne of grace and the vehicle of expiation for the entire covenant community. It functioned as an altar of sacrifice as the High Priest, after the offering of the perpetual holocaust of the Tamid lamb (Num 28:11), sprinkled the blood of the prescribed sacrificial victims on the Mercy-seat of the Ark of the Covenant in atonement for the people's sins in a rite of communal reconciliation (Lev 16:14-16, 34).

The expiration of the people's sins through the application of the blood of the victim on the Mercy-seat foreshadowed Christ's act of atonement when He offered Himself as both the sinless victim and the enthroned King on the sacrificial altar and "mercy seat" of the Cross (Rom 5:11; Col 1:13-14, 21-22; 2:13-14; Heb 9:11-14). On the Feast of Atonement, the people remembered the sin of the Golden Calf and their need for a Redeemer to bring them into perfect fellowship and peace with Israel's God. From the time of their separation from God's Divine Presence after the sin of the Golden Calf, until the time of Jesus' act of perfect atonement, the Israelites saw the veil that separated the Holy Place from God's Presence in the Holy of Holies as a symbolic barrier between God and His chosen people (Lev 16:2).

In addition to the expanded articles of the Law, the increased sacrificial rites, and the prohibition against unlimited access to the Divine Presence, the Israelites no longer witnessed continual manifestations of God's Divine Glory as they had in the past. Before the covenant failure of the Golden Calf, the people heard God's thunderous voice speaking directly to them from the Glory Cloud and witnessed aspects of His divine glory (Ex 16:10-11; 19:16-20, 20:1, 18-19; 24:9-11). After Israel's sin, the visible evidence of Yahweh's Divine Presence became limited to:

1. the Pillar of Cloud in which the Angel of Yahweh became Israel's guide to the Promised Land (Ex 32:34; 33:2-6),

2. the radiant glory of God reflected on the face of the ever-faithful Moses (Ex 34:29, 34-35), and

3. witnessing the cloud of smoke that arose twice daily from the altar of sacrifice signifying God's acceptance of the atoning and sanctifying sacrifice of the Tamid and symbolizing the promise of His Presence (Ex 29:42).

In the meantime, there was no remedy for the tragic consequences of Israel's sin. The fall of Adam and Eve left humanity in need of a Redeemer to remove the original sin Adam transmitted to his offspring, imperfectly fathering children born into the human family physically who were spiritually lacking God's grace (CCC 403, 1999-2003). Yahweh established animal sacrifice as a temporary means of atonement; however, it was only capable of restoring bodily purity. It offered an imperfect fellowship with God because the blood of animals was incapable of removing the transmitted sin introduced by our first parents. The blood sacrifice of animals in the liturgy of the Sinai Covenant was also only a temporary measure of restoration of fellowship with God and was incapable of removing Israel's collective sin in the rebellion of the

Golden Calf or any individual's deliberate personal sin (Num 15:27-31; Rom 3:20; Heb 9:9-10; 10:4; CCC 708, 1963).

The people of Israel individually needed a personal Redeemer to restore forgiveness and divine sonship lost in Eden. However, the sin of the Golden Calf also left Yahweh's corporate covenant people in need of a Redeemer to purify the curse of their collective sins and to restore their holiness as a priestly people (Lev 26:14-43; Dt 28:15-68; Gal 3:13-14; 1 Pet 2:9-10; CCC 1546). The blood of the communally sacrificed Tamid could only serve as a partial remedy for the repented communal sin of the people. The coming of the Redeemer-Messiah, planned since before the foundation of the earth (1 Pt:1:20), was needed to heal the rupture caused by the people's collective sin and to re-establish unhindered communion between God and His covenant people (Heb 10:5-7, quoting Ps 40:6-8 LXX).

Despite Israel's fall from grace, the central themes of the subsequent narratives in the Pentateuch focus on God's great compassion and faithfulness. Yahweh re-instated Israel as His covenant people. However, they were a covenant people who, because of their obstinate and "stiff-necked" condition in refusing to bend to their Divine Master's "yoke," required more discipline

(Ex 33:3). The expanded laws not only ensured Israel's well-being during the forty years of enforced wandering in the wilderness, but the observance of the Law became the Israelite's daily lesson in obedience and submission (Num 14:32-34). The covenant people had to learn to rely solely upon God to protect and provide in every way for His Bride Israel in the procession to her new home, the Promised Land of Canaan. It was in the crucible of the wilderness that God molded a new generation of Israelites through law, love, and liturgy into a holy people God called to be His possession and a vehicle of salvation to the nations of the world.

In the restored covenant, Israel's sanctification, atonement for sin and restored fellowship with God depended on the Tamid worship services and the different classes of acceptable blood sacrifice together with grain offerings, wine libations, and sacred meals. Only ritually "clean/purified" members of the covenant, whether born an Israelite or a circumcised Gentile convert, were permitted to participate in liturgical worship, the sacred meals, and the sacramental rituals (Ex 12:43-48; Lev 22:3). Only those animals classified as "clean" and approved as food for the covenant people were acceptable to God, thereby making the offeror acceptable (Lev Chapter 11). However, within the group of animals classified as "clean," only five kinds of animals were designated acceptable offerings for sacrifice: cattle, sheep, goats, turtle doves, and pigeons (Lev 1:2, 14). These were the same five animals Yahweh commanded Abraham to sacrifice in his covenant ratification ritual (Gen 15:9).

Despite their failures, Yahweh did not abandon His sinful children. Instead, as in the case of Adam and Eve, He provided the hope of their future redemption and the salvation of humanity. Israel became the means by which God kept His promise in Genesis 3:15 that from the "seed" of a woman, the promised Redeemer would come to undo the work of the serpent, Satan (1 Jn 3:8; Rev 12:9). God provided for the safety of the "promised seed" after His judgment to expel Adam and Eve from Eden (Gen 3:23-24). And He provided for the faithful remnant of humanity that was Noah's family within the safety of the Ark amid the chaos of the flood judgment (Gen 8:15-16). At this point in God's divine plan, the liturgical and sacrificial requirements of the Sinai Covenant and the expanded commands and prohibitions of the Law protected Israel and preserved the people who carried the hope of the "seed of the Woman." The Law served as both Israel's remedy for sin and as a guide for the people to live as a holy nation, teaching the people to recognize their sins and to acknowledge their need for a Redeemer. It also prepared them to receive the promised Redeemer-Messiah's Gospel of salvation when it was time for His arrival upon the stage of human history (CCC 1963-64).

God also continued to honor His unconditional promise to the Patriarchs that their descendants were going to possess the land promised to Abraham (Gen 15:18-21; Ex 33:1-3). While God no longer spoke directly to the people, He communicated with them through the covenant mediator and prophet, Moses, whose radiant face reflected the glory of God after each encounter (Ex 34:34-35). The Israelites also had assurance of God's presence in the Pillar of Cloud and Fire that was seen over the Tabernacle (Ex 40:36-38; Num 9:15-23) and in the rising smoke from the altar of sacrifice in the Tamid worship services in which God accepted their sacrifices and kept His covenant with Israel.

ISRAEL'S COVENANT WITH GOD MAINTAINED THROUGH THE LITURGY OF THE TAMID

The single sacrifice of the *olat ha-Tamid* offered in a morning and afternoon liturgical worship service was the first and only communal sacrifice established for the covenant people before the rebellion of the Golden

Calf. It remained the most important of sacrifices after the children of Israel's covenant failure when God expanded the classes of blood sacrifices. The Tamid was the center of life and liturgical worship for the covenant people and the sacrifice around which all other sacrifices and feast days of the Sinai Covenant revolved. According to the Law of the Sinai Covenant, the holy day sacrifices of the Sabbath, the multiple Passover sacrifices of lambs and goat-kids, and the other monthly, yearly, or periodic feast day sacrifices could not take precedence over the twice-daily offering of the Tamid. All other sacrifices had to be offered within the Tamid liturgical services and only in addition to the Tamid (Num Chapters 28-29). The Tamid was the only offering of a single male lamb as a communal sacrifice except for the single male lamb on the Feast of Firstfruits (*Yom HaBikkurim*) and the Sabbath sacrifice of a male lamb in addition to the Tamid in the morning and afternoon worship services (Num 28:9-10). All other sacrifices of lambs for feast days were multiple male lambs or a single adult ram (i.e., Num 28:11). Outside of these two exceptions on the Feast of Firstfruits and the Sabbath, the morning and afternoon Tamid exclusively required the communal sacrifice of a single, unblemished lamb (not older than a year and not younger than eight days; Ex 29:38, Lev 22:27), for the sins and sanctification of the covenant people.

From the time of the inauguration of the Sanctuary and the first communal sacrifice of the Tamid lamb in the morning liturgical service at Mount Sinai until the destruction of the Jerusalem Temple in AD 70, the focus of the daily prayer life of the covenant people was the single sacrifice of the morning and afternoon Tamid lambs. The liturgical ritual of the daily Tamid was a continual reminder of the Israelites' covenant bond with their God that was to last so long as the Sinai Covenant endured. The Israelites suffered many hardships during the forty years in the wilderness before they took possession of the Promised Land. In the years after they established themselves in Canaan, which became the land of Israel, the Israelites faced many struggles to keep it. But they knew, as long as the sacrifice of the Tamid continued for their atonement and sanctification, they maintained their unique status as Yahweh's faithful covenant people: *Gather to me my faithful, who sealed my covenant by sacrifice* (Ps 50:5).

However, according to Scripture and oral tradition, one day the perpetual offering of the *olat ha-Tamid* on God's sacrificial altar was destined to end (Dan 12:11-13). God's holy prophets warned the covenant people, at a climax in human history, a Davidic Redeemer-

Messiah would usher in a new and eternal covenant (Jer 23:5-6; 31:31-34; 32:40; 50:5; Ez 34:23). It would be a covenant with the promise of a renewed and restored Israel, and with a reinstated covenant relationship through divine adoption (Rom 9:4-5; Gal 4:4-7; Eph 1:3-8) that, like all covenants, was to be celebrated in oath-swearing, sacrifice and a sacred meal of thanksgiving. At that time, according to Jewish tradition, all sacrifices would cease, and the only sacrifice that continued would be the *Todah*, the "Thanksgiving" communion offering and sacred meal reestablishing peace with God, translated as *Eucharistia* in Greek and Latin (Levine, *JPS Torah Commentary: Leviticus*, page 43; Joseph Ratzinger, *Feast of Faith*, Ignatius Press, San Francisco, 1986, pages 58-59; Lev 7:11-15/7:1-5). The destruction of the Jerusalem Temple and the end of the Tamid liturgy in the summer of AD 70 fulfilled this prediction. And the prophecy continues in Jesus Christ's *Todah* of the New Covenant sacred communion meal that He instituted at the Last Supper and which Catholic Christians call the Eucharist—the "Thanksgiving" (Mt 26:26-29; Mk 14:22-25; Lk 22:19-20; 1 Cor 11:23-26).

CHAPTER SUMMARY POINTS: THE SANCTUARY AND THE INSTITUTION OF THE TAMID IN THE SACRED LITURGY OF THE SINAI COVENANT

1. The rendezvous at Sinai was a crossroads in salvation history. It was the intersection between love, law, and liturgy. Yahweh expressed His love for Israel in His gift of the Law and the promised blessings for obedience to the covenant. Israel was to show her love for God in obedience to the Law and the faithful practice of prescribed liturgical worship. Israel's uniquely divine election and covenant formation were to serve as a witness to the other nations of the world.

2. In the liturgy of the Sinai Covenant, human beings reached the deepest expression of divine communion since the fellowship enjoyed by our original parents in Eden. The covenant formation at Sinai inaugurated a new Eden. For the first time since the Edenic Sanctuary, God defined one place on Earth as the meeting place between God and man.

3. Yahweh established a hereditary ministerial priesthood descended through Moses' brother Aaron to serve Him in the earthly Sanctuary and its Tabernacle.

The blood sacrifice of designated animals together with grain and wine offerings in a liturgical service was limited to God's one Sanctuary.

4. The Tamid sacrifice was the center of the liturgical worship of Yahweh. It was the single sacrifice and accompanying blood ritual of an unblemished male lamb slaughtered and burnt entirely on Yahweh's altar twice daily together with the offering of fine wheat flour and the priestly offering of a baked unleavened wafer followed by a libation of wine. The Tamid sacrifice assured the people communal forgiveness, sanctification, and covenant fellowship with Yahweh. The sacrifice of the Tamid lambs was a "standing" or "perpetual" sacrifice as long as the Sinai Covenant endured.

5. The covenant failure of the sin of the Golden Calf separated the Israelites from unlimited access to God in the Tabernacle. The covenant peoples' collective sin in worshipping the Golden Calf was a sign that the Israelites, like all sons and daughters of Adam and Eve, needed a Redeemer-Messiah.

6. The firstborn sons, selected through their redemption experience the night of the first Passover in Egypt, were intended to serve and assist the Aaronic priesthood, establishing Israel as a nation of priests.

They became dispossessed firstborn sons in the rebellion of the Golden Calf, and the tribe of Levi replaced them as God's lesser ministers.

7. Yahweh expanded the Law and the sacrificial system after the sin of the Golden Calf. However, the Tamid sacrifice remained the most important of the classes of blood sacrifice; it was at the core of sacrificial ritual and was the focus of daily life and worship.

8. Humankind's status as a liturgical being, made in the image and likeness of God, separated him from the other living things of creation. In the Fall of Adam, humanity lost the righteousness and divine sonship that gave immortality. In the Sinai Covenant, God extended to Israel a relationship that re-established covenant sonship which was to bear fruit when Israel, the Bride of Yahweh, gave birth to the Davidic Redeemer-Messiah. He was destined to usher in a new covenant with the promise of restored sonship through divine adoption celebrated in sacrifice and a sacred meal of *Todah*/Thanksgiving.

Endnotes: The Sanctuary and the Institution of the Sacred Litergy of the Tamid Sacrifice

1. Heaven was closed after Adam's sin but was opened again at Jesus' baptism (Mt 3:16; CCC 536, 633, 1026). The temporal Old Covenant blessings (Gen 12:1-3; Lev 26:3-13; Dt 28:1-14)

became eternal blessings through the redeeming work of Jesus Christ (Mt 5:1-12; 25:46; Mk 10:29-30; Lk 23:42-43; Jn 3:16; Heb 9:11-12; 1 Jn 5:11-13) when both blessings and punishments became eternal in the New Covenant (Mt 25:31-46; Jn 5:29; Rev 20:11-15; CCC 1033, 1037).

2. The Sanctuary courtyard housed the (1) altar of sacrifice and the (2) water basin for ritual purification. Within the Tabernacle's Holy Place was the (3) Menorah/lamp-stand, (4) the table of the Bread of the Presence and the (5) Incense Altar. Located within the Holy of Holies was the (6) Ark of the Covenant and its (7) Mercy-seat.
3. The two goats offered on the Feast of Atonement/Yom Kippur were also a single sacrifice in atonement for the covenant people's collective sin (Lev 16:5). The two goats represented both death (the sacrificed goat) and life (the goat that carried away the people's sin), a foreshadowing of Jesus' self-sacrifice on the Cross which became death transformed into life in the Resurrection.
4. The Mishnah records that the High Priest offered sacrifice on the Day of Atonement (*Mishnah: Yoma*, 1.2). He also officiated at the offering of the daily Tamid worship services and on all other appointed feasts and Sabbaths. Otherwise, the High Priest officiated when he desired and appointed a priestly representative when he chose not to serve (*Mishnah: Tamid*, 7.3; Antiquities of the Jews, 8.10.3; 8.13.5). Josephus assigned the priestly wafer offering of the Tamid to the High Priest (*Antiquities of the Jews* 3.10.7 [257]). Also see Kurtz, *Offerings, Sacrifice, and Worship in the Old Testament*, page 350-53; *History of the Jewish People in the time of Jesus Christ*, ii, vol.1, pages 255 and 289.
5. For some passages mentioning the 'olat ha-Tamid see Lev 6:8-13 RSV/6:2-6; Num 28:4, 6, 10, 15, 23, 24, 31; 29:6, 11,

16, 19, 22, 25, 28, 31, 34, 38; Ezra 3:5; Neh 10:34. It is also referred to simply as ha-Tamid, "the standing," five times in Dan 8:11, 12, 13; 11:31; 12:12. The Tamid is mentioned as the "morning sacrifice" (i.e., Lev 9:17) and as the "morning and evening sacrifices" (i.e., 1 Kgs 18:29, 36; 2 Kgs 16:15; 1 Ch 16:40; 2 Chr 2:4, 14; 13:11; 31:3; Ezr 3:3; Am 4:4; Ez 46:13-15; and the "evening sacrifice" in Dan 9:21). Also, see *Mishnah: Pesachim*, 5.1; *Mishnah: Yoma*, 6.3; *Mishnah: Taanit*, 4.6; *Mishnah: Menahot*, 4.4 and the entire tractate entitled *Mishnah: Tamid.*

6. The Book of Life and the Books of Deeds are in the heavenly Sanctuary. For references to the Book of Life, containing the names of those destined for salvation, and the Books of Deeds, containing the works or deeds of every man and woman, see Ex 32:32, 33; Ps 40:8; 69:28; 139:16; Is 4:3; Jer 17:1; Dan 7:10; 12:1; Mal 3:16; Lk 10:20; Phil 4:3; Heb 12:23; Rev 3:5; 13:8; 17:8; 20:12, 15; 21:27.
7. The God-ordained pilgrim feasts are Unleavened Bread, Weeks/Pentecost, and Tabernacles/Shelters (Ex 23:14-17; 34:18, 22-23; Dt 16:16, and 2 Chr 8:13). Passover was not a pilgrim feast. The feasts of Hanukkah (1 Mac 4:52-59; 2 Mac 10:5-8) and Purim (Est 9:20-22, 32) are not God ordained feasts but are instead national feasts instituted by the people.

CHAPTER III THE CITY OF JERUSALEM AND A DWELLING PLACE FOR GOD'S NAME

To the place chosen by Yahweh your God as a home for his name, to that place you must bring all the things that I am laying down for you: your burnt offerings and your sacrifices, your tithes and offerings held high, and all the best of your possessions dedicated by you to Yahweh. That is where you will rejoice in the presence of Yahweh your God, you and your sons and daughters, your serving men and women, and the Levite living in your community since he has no share or heritage of his own among you. Take care you do not offer your burnt offerings in all the sacred places you see; only in the place tht Yahweh chooses in one of your tribes may you offer your burnt offerings and do all the things which I have commanded you.

Deuteronomy 12:11–14 (NJB)

THE ISRAELITES BOUND IN COVENANT TO YAHWEH IN SACRED TIME AND SACRED SPACE

Then the Israelites completed construction of Yahweh's Sanctuary at Mount Sinai, God showed His acceptance by taking possession of the Tabernacle during the dedication ceremony in the visible sign of the *Shekinah,* the Glory Cloud (Ex 40:34-35; Num 9:15-16). Aaron and his sons were then ordained as God's ministers to perform the rituals of sacrifice and worship.

Liturgy in the desert Sanctuary began with the celebration of the morning Tamid worship service. Aaron and two of his sons presented the whole-burnt offering of the Tamid on God's sacrificial altar, followed by other whole-burnt offerings, and the fat of communion and sin sacrifices. God graciously showed His approval and accepted the sacrifices in this first liturgical worship service by consuming the sacrificial gifts on the altar with holy fire sent from heaven (Lev 9:1-24).

In the rituals of worship, the people confessed their sins over their sin sacrifices, and the priests, as God's representatives, forgave an individual's sins in a voluntary sin sacrifice and the community's sins in communal sin sacrifices. The priests ate the sin sacrifices (Lev 6:24-26/17-19), and the people ate their communion sacrifices that reestablished peace with God (Lev 7:11, 15/7:1, 5). The communion sacrifices were consumed in a sacred meal in the Presence of God and cooked either in the courtyard of the Sanctuary (the Todah) or the camp of God, depending on the type of communion offering (festival offerings). In each sacrifice, the priests burned the animal's fat on the altar fire, and its blood was either splashed, sprinkled, or poured out at the base of the altar in a blood ritual, according to the type of sacrifice within the Tamid liturgical worship service (i.e., Lev 1:5; 3:8; 4:6, 30).

Grain and wine offerings accompanied some of the sacrifices, and later, when Israel took possession of the Promised Land, grain offerings and wine libations accompanied all the animal sacrifices (Num 15:1-12). While the animals offered in sacrifice represented the vital life-force of the person/persons making the sacrifice, the grain, fruit offerings, and the wine libations represented the fruits of the labors of those vital powers.

The Old Testament represents these sacrifices as "food" or a "pleasing aroma" for Yahweh (Gen 8:21; Ex 29:18; Lev 1:9; Num 28:2). However, the people understood that an omnificent God did not need earthly nourishment or the pleasing smell of sacrifices (Ps 50:12-14; Sir 35:6-7/5-9). It was the spiritual food of the self-surrender of the covenant people that pleased God: *For thou hast no delight in sacrifice; were I to give a burnt offering, thou wouldst not be pleased. The sacrifice acceptable to God is a broken spirit; a broken and contrite heart, O God, thou wilt not despise* (Ps 51:16-17; also see 1 Sam 15:22-23).

In the sacrificial rites, the quality of the sacrifice had to unite with the righteousness of the offeror for the forgiveness of sins and restoration of fellowship between the offeror and God: *If one offers sacrifices from what has been wrongfully obtained, the offering is blemished; the gifts of the lawless are not acceptable. The Most High is not pleased with the offerings of the ungodly; and he is not propitiated for sins by a multitude of sacrifices* (Sir 34:18-19). To be considered valid, animal sacrifices must be offered with the self-sacrifice of a willing and contrite heart together with thanksgiving for the promise of God's mercy. In the Old Covenant of Sinai, as in the New Covenant in Christ Jesus, God deserves the sacrifice of personal surrender and not the empty ritual of the mere material gift of the offeror. A sacrifice offered without prayer and the contrition of a truly repentant heart is like the gift of a body without a soul; it is an empty and lifeless gift not worthy of a holy God.

Israel was now prepared to move forward, to receive the promised blessings God made to the forefathers and to complete her destiny as Yahweh's holy nation by taking possession of the Promised Land (Gen 12:2-3; 15:18-21). In the first month of the second year after leaving Egypt, the Israelites prepared for their departure from Mount Sinai by celebrating the remembrance festivals of Passover and Unleavened Bread (Num 9:1-14). In those God-ordained festivals, every new generation of Israelites relived the events of the Exodus liberation that their ancestors experienced.

Rituals reflect the origins of a people. It was the case in ancient times, and it is true today. Citizens of the United States annually remember their independence from the British in ritual celebrations on the 4th of July. For Catholics, in the ritual of the Mass, they remember the sacred meal, sacrifice, and Resurrection of Jesus Christ that took place two thousand years ago. It is a past event that becomes present in real time on the altar of every Catholic Church. In the unbloody re-presentation of the sacrifice on Calvary, the New Covenant faithful remember and relive their origins.

In the celebration of the Mass, Catholics remember that the origin of their faith founded on the Son of God who began His walk to the Cross on the night of the Last Supper. He offered His disciples His Body, Blood, Soul, and Divinity in an unbloody sacrifice the night on which the Old Covenant Church celebrated the sacred meal of the Passover victims that took place on the first night of the remembrance feast of Unleavened Bread (Mt 26:17, 20–28; Mk 14:12, 17–25; Lk 22:7, 14–20). What took place that night became a world-altering event that marked the beginning of Jesus' Passion. It was on the following morning that Jesus offered Himself in a bloody sacrifice in atonement for the sins of humanity on the altar of the Cross. He then arose from the dead on the third day (as the ancients counted without the concept of a zero-place value), on the annual Jewish Feast of Firstfruits that fell on the first day of the week (Sunday) within the holy week of the Old Covenant Feast of Unleavened Bread. Such origin rituals only change or become devalued or discarded when people lose their understanding of the connection between their rituals and their past experiences as a people (CCC 1356–57).

All the remembrance festivals of the Sinai Covenant, but especially Passover and Unleavened Bread, ensured that the Israelites, year by year and generation after generation, continued to relive their origins in the Exodus experience (Ex 13:14–15). The Israelite's re-enactment of the Exodus liberation and Israel's divine election at Mount Sinai, experienced through the seven annual festivals in their themes of judgment, redemption and divine adoption, provided the catechesis the people needed to remain united to their origins. Reliving the events of the annual festivals kept every generation of the covenant people focused on their divinely appointed mission. It was their mission to reflect the holiness of the God who chose them out the pagan nations of the earth. And it was their divine call to fulfill their destiny as a nation dedicated to serving the invisible God who made Israel His partner in humanity's promised redemption and salvation.

The commands and prohibitions of the Sinai Covenant and the rituals of worship in the Tamid liturgy represented a revolutionary change in the practice of religious expression for the twelve tribes of Israel. The Israelites were now bound to Yahweh in sacred time and sacred space through worship in Yahweh's holy Sanctuary. They were to live in holiness within the covenant by faithfully observing all the ordinances and prohibitions of the Law and by the sanctifying rituals of daily sacrifice.

Yahweh also decreed that His Divine Liturgy of the Tamid and the associated classes of blood sacrifices, grain offerings, wine libations, and the eating of certain sacrifices in a sacred meal must be limited to His one Sanctuary or to the holy camp that surrounded the

Sanctuary of God that was understood as an extension of His Sanctuary (Lev 17:1-9; Dt 12:13-27). Therefore, in the tenth century BC when King Solomon built Yahweh's Temple in Jerusalem, the city became the "camp of God." It was for this reason that the Passover sacred meal and the *hagigah* festival peace (communion) offerings of the pilgrim feasts had to be consumed by the faithful within the walls of the holy city of Jerusalem.

ISRAEL'S FORTY-YEAR JOURNEY TO CANAAN

So they set out from the mount of the LORD three days' journey; and the ark of the covenant of the LORD went before them three days' journey, to seek out a resting place for them. And the cloud of the LORD was over them by day, whenever they set out from the camp.
Numbers 10:35-36

In the second year after leaving Egypt, on the 20th day of the second month, God's Glory Cloud rose from the Ark of the Covenant (Num 10:11). The trumpets sounded, and the twelve tribes of Israel departed from Mount Sinai. Moses, Aaron, and the sons of Aaron who were carrying the Ark of the Covenant were in the front of the procession, leading the march that was intended to end in the conquest of the Promised Land. The people of the tribe of Judah followed them, marching behind their standard. Behind the tribe of Judah, each of the other tribes, preceded by their standards, fell into their assigned places for the march (Num 10:1-2, 11-28, 33-36).

The Israelites constantly complained and continually challenged Moses' authority during the journey. It was probably in the summer when the men, women, children, and herds and flocks of animals of the Israelites arrived at the south-western border of Canaan. The people of the twelve tribes of Israel and the disgruntled rabble from Egypt who joined them in the exodus out of Egypt camped in the desert of Paran at the oasis of Kadesh-Barnea (Num 11:4; 12:16; 13:26).

In preparation for the invasion, God instructed the Israelites to select one man from each of the twelve tribes to reconnoiter the land of Canaan from the southern desert of the Negeb to the lush green of the northern highlands (Num 13:1-3, 17-20). It was late summer (the time of the early fruit harvest) when the twelve men returned from their mission forty days later, bearing samples of the abundant fruits growing in the land (Num 13:21-23). Ten men reported that the country was fertile, but the inhabitants of Canaan were too numerous and too strong for them to conquer. Only

Joshua (Hoshea), a descendant of Joseph from the tribe of Ephraim, and Caleb, a Gentile convert representing the tribe of Judah, demanded that the people trust God and immediately prepare to take possession of Canaan (Num 13:6, 8, 30; 14:6–9).

Despite Moses and Aaron's assurance that with God on their side, they could not fail to conquer the land of Canaan, the Israelites suffered a crisis of faith (Num 13:26–33). They believed the unfavorable reports and refused to consider fulfilling their mission. Many of the Israelites were even in favor of returning to their "safe life" in Egypt (Num 14:1-4). The whole community was talking about stoning Moses, Aaron, Joshua, and Caleb, when God intervened (Num 14:10).

Yahweh suddenly appeared in the form of the Glory Cloud, threatening to destroy the Israelites for their disobedience and disbelief. Once again, Moses intervened in his role as covenant mediator, pleading with God to forgive the people's sinful rebellion. Once again Yahweh, for the sake of His promises to the Patriarchs, forgave the people. However, God denounced the Exodus generation, characterizing them as "a faithless and perverse generation" (Num 14:27, 35). He required atonement for their sin of rebellion and condemned them to wander in the desert wilderness until every member of their generation over twenty years of age died except for faithful Joshua from the tribe of Ephraim and Caleb, the Kenizzite Gentile convert adopted by the tribe of Judah (Num 14:26-35; 32:11-13; Jos 14:6).

It was God's judgment to give Israel's mission to a generation that had not been contaminated by the pagan gods and rituals of Egyptian culture. He sent forth a vigorous new generation, toughened by years of living in the wilderness, and raised on the Law of the covenant and the liturgy of the daily Tamid sacrifice. They became Yahweh's Holy Warriors, obedient to their covenant with Him and worthy to possess the Promised Land. Forty years after leaving Egypt, Joshua and Caleb led the new generation of the twelve tribes of Israel in the conquest of Canaan. These two men, an Israelite and a Gentile, prefigured the composition of the future New Covenant people of God who, in the fullness of time, were to be sent forth as Jews and Gentiles united in the mission to conquer the world for the Kingdom of Jesus Christ (Mt 28:18-20; Rom 2:7, 10). 1

The twelve tribes struggled for years against the inhabitants of Canaan, each tribe fighting to take possession of its allotted portion of Yahweh's Holy Land. After Joshua's death, the struggle continued through the period of the Judges of Israel and then into the Age of the United Monarchy under Israel's kings

Saul and David. Finally, David, the Judahite shepherd boy anointed as King of Israel by the Prophet Samuel, fulfilled God's plan for Israel to subdue the land promised to the Patriarchs (1 Sam 16:13). King David's army drove out Israel's enemies, and he conquered Jerusalem, the city of God's ancient priest-king Melchizedek (Gen 14:18).

David conquered the Jebusite city in c. 1000 BC. Jerusalem (in Hebrew, yi'reh-salem means "Yahweh will provide peace") became the place chosen by Yahweh "as a home for his name" (Dt 12:11-13; 1 Kng 11:36; 2 Chr 6:6). The city of Jerusalem, built on the convergence of mountain ridges at an elevation of from 2400-2500 feet above sea level, became the capital of the United Kingdom of Israel.

David wanted to build a Temple as a permanent "house" for Yahweh in Jerusalem (2 Sam 7:1-3). Refusing David's offer, but acknowledging his desire to provide a permanent dwelling place, Yahweh established a royal-grant covenant (a covenant with no stipulations for covenant continuation) with David and his descendants, promising that his "house," meaning David's sovereign throne and his dynasty, would endure forever (2 Sam 7:8-16; 23:5; 2 Chr 13:5; Sir 45:25). The city of Jerusalem became the "camp of God" and the permanent site of His Holy Temple and sacrificial altar where His ordained priests offered the liturgy of the Tamid twice daily. Jerusalem was the place God chose for His name to dwell (1 Kng 11:36), and from that time forward, Israel's prophets preached that the promised Redeemer-Messiah would be a descendant of the great King David. [2]

THE LOCATION OF MOUNT MORIAH AND THE JERUSALEM TEMPLE IN THE PLAN OF SALVATION HISTORY

Then Solomon began to build the house of the LORD in Jerusalem on Mount Moriah, where the LORD had appeared to David his father, at the place that David had appointed, on the threshing floor of Oran the Jebusite. 2 Chronicles 3:1

Jerusalem, formerly known as the village of Salem in the land of Moriah, was the home of God's first priest-king, Melchizedek, a Hebrew title that means "king of righteousness" (Gen 14:18; Heb 7:1-2). Jewish tradition identifies Melchizedek as Noah's righteous firstborn son Shem (Josephus, *The Antiquities of the Jews*, 1.10.2 [179-180]; *The Jewish Wars*, 6.10, 1; the *Babylonian Talmud, N'darim* 32b). Modern translations of the Jewish Tanach also identify Melchizedek as Shem (*The Jewish Study Bible*, Stone edition, note on page 29 and *The Jewish*

New Testament Commentary, page 679). It was a tradition repeated by early Christian scholars, including Doctors of the Church St. Ephraim in the fourth century AD (*Teaching on Genesis*, 14:18-20) and St. Jerome in the fifth century AD (*Hebrew Questions on Genesis*, 14:18-19).

Shem is the first man identified in Scripture as God's man: *Blessed by the LORD my God be Shem* (Gen 9:26a). Scripture records that the residence of Shem/Melchizedek was Salem, a city located near the Valley of Shaveh ("Valley of the Oath" in Gen 14:17-18). According to the first century AD Jewish priest and historian Flavius Josephus, the valley was a quarter of a mile from Jerusalem. He wrote that before David conquered Jerusalem, it was called Salem and was the residence of God's priest-king Melchizedek (*Wars of the Jews*, 6.10.1 [438]; *Antiquities of the Jews*, 1.10.2 [180]; 7.3.2 [67]).

The inspired writer of the New Testament Letter to the Hebrews identifies Melchizedek as the priest-king of ancient Jerusalem and the one who prefigures the role of Jesus of the Messiah as the priestly King offering sacrifice in the heavenly Jerusalem. Jesus of Nazareth died a self-sacrificial death in atonement for the sins of humanity outside the walls of Jerusalem in AD 30, just below the height of Mount Moriah. Jesus, the heir of King David and the eternal Davidic covenant, then arose from the dead and ascended into Heaven, taking His rightful place as both the King and High Priest of the heavenly Sanctuary (Heb 5:6, 10; 6:20; 7:15, 17, 21; Ps 110:4).

King David, a man of war, completed the conquest of the Promised Land and took Jerusalem as his capital city, establishing Israel as a powerful kingdom in the region. However, it was David's son, Solomon, a man of peace, that God selected to build His Temple in His chosen holy city of Jerusalem (1 Chr 22:7-11; 28:2-7). The Jerusalem Temple replaced the portable desert Sanctuary and its Tabernacle. In the twice-daily liturgy of the Tamid sacrifice, God intended His "house" in Jerusalem to become the center of prayer and worship for all nations (Is 56:7). Unlike pagan temples that served as "houses" for man-made images of pagan deities, the Jerusalem Temple served as a "house" for Yahweh's Divine Name, expressing the concept that human beings cannot confine an omnipresent, omnipotent, and invisible God and His divine will to one place (Dt 12:11; 14:23; 2 Chr 2:1, 4; 3:1).

David brought the Ark of the Covenant and all the sacred furniture for the Sanctuary of God to Jerusalem, making the city the one place on earth where men, women, and children could enter into God's peace (2 Sam 6:12-15; 1 Chr 15:3, 28; 22:1). The liturgy of sacrifice and worship began in Jerusalem when David, by God's command, set up Yahweh's holy altar of sacrifice to receive the daily offerings of the Tamid lambs and other sacrifices. Just as God had instructed Moses in the building of the desert Tabernacle, God also gave instructions to David on the plans he was to share with his son, Solomon, for constructing Yahweh's Holy Temple (1 Chr 22:1-19; 28:11-19). The place God chose for the Temple was the same site where David saw the Angel of the Lord and where he erected Yahweh's altar of sacrifice on an ancient threshing floor at the high point of the city of Jerusalem, on Mount Moriah (2 Sam 24:18-25; 1 Chr 21:18, 26, 28-22:1; Chr 3:1).

The choice of Mount Moriah as the location for the Temple and the site of the liturgy of the Tamid sacrifice was not an arbitrary selection. Sacred Scripture links Mount Moriah to the visionary experiences of Shem's descendant Abraham (Gen 11:10, 26) and Abraham's descendant David, God's anointed king, two ancestors of Jesus of Nazareth (Mt 1:1). The visionary experiences of both the Patriarch Abraham and King David on Mount Moriah involved a "covenant ordeal" in a test of obedience and sacrifice that resulted in a vision of the Angel of the Lord, and also divine intervention. Abraham offered his son Isaac in sacrifice as God commanded, but the angel stopped him. And David, in witnessing a vision of the Angel of the Lord with his sword pointed at Jerusalem, offered to sacrifice his life and his eternal covenant to save his people from a deadly plague. God declined David's offer but intervened to stop the destruction (Gen 22:1-18; 2 Sam 24:16-17; 1 Chr 21:14-30).

Mount Moriah in Jerusalem was where visionary experiences continued for each generation of the sons and daughters of the covenant people of God. The daily liturgy of worship at the Holy Temple on Mount Moriah was an experience of God in the vision of the thick white column of smoke lifting off the altar of sacrifice and rising to Heaven in the burning of the *olat ha-Tamid* and the other sacrifices, signifying God's gracious acceptance of the people's offerings. The white cloud of smoke was also a reminder of the Glory Cloud of the Exodus and gave every new generation the faithful covenant people a vision to support their belief that God's invisible presence was with them, above the Ark of the Covenant within the sacred space of the Temple's Holy of Holies. The visionary experience of God was also part of the life of every son and daughter of the covenant people who experienced spiritual growth, living in peace and fellowship with God, and the covenant community. They lived their unity of faith through obedience to the Laws of the covenant and in the sanctifying power of the sacrifice of the Tamid lambs that signified covenant continuation day by day and year by year from generation to generation.

The Temple on Mount Moriah was where the natural intersected with the supernatural, and it was where generations of the sons and daughters of Israel received their own revelations of God. The Temple served as the point of contact between Heaven and earth and was the center from which the promise of salvation radiated in the sanctifying twice-daily liturgy of the Tamid. However, the day was coming when the vision of God manifested itself in human flesh. In the first century AD, when the beloved Son of God came to Jerusalem to face His covenant ordeal, the people beheld the revelation of God in the promised Redeemer-Messiah who was both fully God and fully man.

On this same mountain, on an elevation just below the summit where the Temple stood, Yahweh provided another sacrifice. In the spring of AD 30, the son of Abraham and the son of David (Mt 1:1) became the unblemished Lamb offered in the blood sacrifice of a New covenant ordeal.[3] But this time God did not stay the hand of the executioner as He had with Abraham and David. The vision of that sacrifice has filled the minds and hearts of sons and daughters of the human family in every succeeding generation and has become the center of liturgical worship for the New Covenant people of God until the end of time.[4]

Significantly, the summit of Mount Moriah was the site of an ancient threshing floor (2 Chr 3:1). A threshing location was a platform or flat area for the separation of the fruit of the harvested grain from the chaff. In the process, the first step was the separation of the grain from the stalks by beating the plant's stems against the floor of the platform or treading them by foot or with cattle. Then, after the heads of the grain were separated from the chaff in the beating process, they were tossed repeatedly into the air (winnowing) either in baskets or with a winnowing fan or rake. As the grain heads and chaff were thrown into the air, the breeze carried away the lighter chaff, leaving the heavier fruit of the grain to fall back into the basket or on to the threshing floor. The final step of the process was to collect the grain from the threshing floor and place it into a storehouse.

The relatively flat, high-point of Mount Moriah was the perfect site for a threshing floor. It was also a fitting symbol for the Jerusalem Temple and the continuing daily liturgy of the Tamid. There, the covenant people's sins were sifted, and the fruit of their souls judged. It was at the Temple, on the site of the threshing floor, that fellowship was re-established with God, the Master of the promised "great human harvest." It was a harvest destined to begin on the day when the promised Redeemer-Messiah offered Himself as a sacrifice of atonement for the sins of humanity and then arose from the dead as the "first-fruits" of the Resurrection, on the "third day" (Mt 20:18-19; Acts 10:40; 1 Cor 15:3-4). It was to be an event that marked a turning point in human history when the gates of Heaven, closed since Adam's sin, were fully opened, and God began receiving the righteous souls of men and women into His heavenly storehouse. It is a harvest that continues and will not end until the return of Christ the King and the Last Judgment (Mt 13:36-43; Rev 20:11-15; CCC 536; 1026; 1038-1041).[5]

YAHWEH'S JERUSALEM TEMPLE

King David's son Solomon built the Jerusalem Temple in seven years and dedicated it on the seventh month of the eighth year during the Feast of Tabernacles/Shelters/Booths, the annual pilgrim feast that remembered the dedication of the desert Sanctuary (Lev 23:33-43; 1 Kng 6:38; 8:2, 65-66; 2 Chr 8:13). Like the desert Sanctuary, the Temple had the same three sacred spaces: the courtyard for the sacrificial altar and the Temple Sanctuary that housed the Holy Place and the Holy of Holies. However, these spaces were twice the size of the desert Sanctuary. The Temple complex also included storerooms, ovens for baking the bread used in the rituals of sacrifice and worship, porticoes for gathering to study the sacred texts, separate courtyards for the women and men worshipers, and another court for non-covenant Gentiles who came to learn about the God of Israel. Unlike the desert Sanctuary, the Jerusalem Temple was a place to which all the peoples of the nations of the earth were welcome to offer sacrifices and to receive instruction concerning the One True God. They were also invited to embrace Yahweh as their God, forsaking all other gods by joining God's covenant family through circumcision for men and ritual immersion for both men and women (1 Kng 8:41-43).

Yahweh's Temple in Jerusalem stood as a symbol of Yahweh, the Master of all Creation, who, in the creation event fashioned the universe as a "house of God" and the earthly Sanctuary in Eden as a cosmic extension of the Heavenly Sanctuary. The Edenic Sanctuary was the place where the God of the universe came down from His heavenly Sanctuary to fellowship with the beings He made in His image and likeness who He created to abide in His love and commune with Him (Gen 1:27).

The Israelites understood this cosmic connection, viewing the heavenly Tabernacle as God's Holy of Holies and the entire universe as God's heavenly Temple. The desert Tabernacle and its successor, the Jerusalem Temple, repeated this pattern as the one place on earth that was God's earthly dwelling-place. The purpose of the desert Tabernacle and its replacement, the Jerusalem Temple, was to serve as a reflection of the Divine Plan. It was a micro-universe with the design of its sacred spaces reflecting the splendor of God's creation both in the heavens and on the earth and celebrated in the consecrating liturgy of the Tamid sacrifice (Levenson, *Sinai and Zion: An Entry into the Jewish Bible*, page 138-145; G.K. Beal, *The Temple*, page 36).

On the day of the Temple dedication, the liturgy of worship began with the communal whole-burnt offering of the *olat' ha-Tamid* as the Glory Cloud filled the Sanctuary. It was the visible manifestation of the presence of God taking possession of His Temple, and it was the same way the visible form of God's presence in the Glory Cloud took possession of the desert Tabernacle (Ex 40:34; Lev 9:17, 23; 1 Kng 8:10-11; 2 Chr 5:13-14). God also signaled His pleasure by sending holy fire from Heaven to consume the burnt offering of the Tamid and the other sacrifices on the bronze sacrificial altar in the Courtyard of the Priests. It was a visible sign of God's acceptance of His people's liturgy of sacrifice and praise, just as He had signaled His approval at the first liturgical service of the morning Tamid at Mount Sinai and when David first built the sacrificial altar at His command on Mount Moriah (Lev 9:23-24; 1 Chr 21:26; 2 Chr 7:1-2).

In the Temple's continuing morning and afternoon liturgical services, all other sacrifices had to take place within the ritual of the perpetual sacrifice of the morning and the afternoon Tamid, with all other sacrifices offered "in addition" to the continual whole-burnt offering of the Tamid (mentioned fifteen times in Num 28:10, 15, 23, 24, 31; 29:6, 11, 16, 19, 22, 25, 28, 31, 34, 38). Seven days a week, morning worship began with the sacrifice of the first Tamid lamb, and the worship service of the afternoon Tamid lamb concluded the sacrificial offerings for each day for the atonement and sanctification of Yahweh's chosen covenant people.

WAITING FOR THE MESSIAH

Yet the LORD warned Israel and Judah by every prophet and every seer, saying, "Turn from your evil ways and keep my commandments and my statutes, in accordance with all the law which I commanded your fathers, and which I sent to

you by my servants the prophets." But they would not listen, but were stubborn, as their fathers had been, who did not believe in the LORD their God. They despised his statutes, and his covenant that he made with their fathers, and the warnings which he gave them.
2 Kings 17:13-15

The Temple on Mount Moriah in Jerusalem was the one place on earth designated for offering sacrifices for sins and sacrifices of praise to Yahweh in liturgical worship. The law of the Sinai Covenant was unequivocal on the point that legitimate, God-ordained worship must be limited to Yahweh's one holy dwelling place (Lev 17:1-9; Dt 12:2-7; 11-14; 1 Chr 22:1, 17-19; 2 Chr 3:1). However, the temptation for the Israelites to offer sacrifice at high places other than the Temple was a continuing problem as splinter groups of apostate Israelites separated themselves from the unified covenant hierarchy in Jerusalem.

After a civil war split the United Kingdom of Israel into the two kingdoms of Israel in the north and Judah in the south, King Jeroboam (reigned 930-910 BC) of the Northern Kingdom of Israel feared the influence that centralized worship at the Jerusalem Temple (located in the rival Kingdom of Judah) might have on his ability to control his kingdom. Jeroboam, a descendant of Joseph son of Jacob and prince of the tribe of Ephraim, rejected the Jerusalem Temple and the liturgy of worship established in the Sinai Covenant. Under the guise of a nationalistic reformation, King Jeroboam rejected the God-ordained priestly descendants of Aaron, expelled them and the Levitical lesser ministers from the Northern Kingdom, and formed a separate priesthood to minister in his kingdom. He built rival altars of sacrifice in his territory and established illicit rituals of worship including worship of images of the Golden Calf (1 Kng 12:26-33; 2 Chr 11:13-17).

Worshiping images of the Golden Calf violated the first of the Ten Commandments and propelled the Israelite political schism into a tragic religious chasm. Ten of the twelve tribes of the Northern Kingdom embraced political unity over covenant unity and became separated from the Tamid liturgy and the covenant with Yahweh (1 Kng 12:20-33; 2 Chr 11:13-16; 13:1-3, 8-9). God's prophets condemned the rejection of the Jerusalem Temple, calling a covenant lawsuit against the Northern Kingdom of Israel. Later, God's prophets also called a covenant lawsuit against the Southern Kingdom of Judah when there were Judahite Davidic kings also violated the covenant.6 God's holy prophets warned the people that when God lifted His hand of protection, the sin of the people's apostasy was going to fall heavily on both Israelite kingdoms (i.e., 1 Kng 13:1-3, 33-34; 2 Kng 17:7-19; Am 3:13-15).

In the eighth century BC, Yahweh's judgment came in the form of the Assyrians who conquered the Northern Kingdom of Israel, disbursing the people of the ten northern tribes into the Gentile lands to the east. The Assyrians replaced the ten tribes of the Israelites with five Gentile communities, settling them in the former territory of the ten tribes that became the Assyrian province of Samaria. The superstitious immigrants adopted the worship of what they considered to be the land's regional deity, developing their liturgical worship of Yahweh mingled with their devotion to their pagan gods. These people came to be known as the Samaritans (2 Kng 17:3-6, 26-41). The people of the Southern Kingdom of Judah despised the Samaritans as heretics. 7

With the deportation of the ten northern tribes, the tribes of Benjamin and Judah were all that remained of the original twelve tribes of Israel. David's descendants continued to rule as kings of Judah, but some of the Davidic kings, like the rulers of the nine different dynasties of the Northern Kingdom, fell into apostasy and built altars to idols. God was patient in extending His mercy to Judah because of His covenant promise to David that his throne would endure forever (2 Sam 7:16; 23:5; 2 Chr 13:5; Ps 89:2-5). Righteous Davidic kings like Hezekiah (716-687 BC) and Josiah (640-609 BC) instituted religious reforms by tearing down the altars of pagan gods and affirming that worship must be limited to Yahweh at the Jerusalem Temple, temporarily holding back God's judgment on the people of the Southern Kingdom of Judah (2 Kng 18:1-4; 22:1; 23:15).

Unfortunately, King Josiah's sons and grandson who succeeded him were not faithful to Yahweh. The Babylonians defeated the armies of the Assyrians and the Egyptians in the late seventh century BC, becoming the regional world power and taking members of the royal families of conquered vassal states as captives, including the children from Judah's royal and noble families in 605 BC (Dan 1:1-7). In 597 BC, the nation of Judah's refusal to continue to submit to Babylonian dominance resulted in the Babylonian capture of Jerusalem. The Babylonians deposed young Davidic King Jehoiachin (grandson of Josiah) and exiled him and his mother to Babylon along with part of the population of Judah, while his uncle, Zedekiah, ruled in his place as their vassal king (2 Kng 24:8-17).

In 589 BC, Zedekiah, the last Davidic king of Judah, revolted against the Babylonians by forming an alliance with the Egyptians. On the 9th of Ab, 587/586 BC, the Babylonian army conquered Jerusalem and destroyed the beautiful Temple built by King Solomon. As punishment for the revolt and to deter future rebellions, the Babylonians exiled the majority of the population of Judah into the land of Babylon. Their exile was a judgment God imposed on the people of the Southern Kingdom for their apostasy; it was an exile God told the prophet Jeremiah would continue for seventy years (Jer 52:28-30; 2 Chr 36:19-21).

From the heights of jubilation in the revelation of God at Sinai to the depths of despair in the destruction of Yahweh's Temple and the Babylonian exile, a remnant of the children of Israel struggled to live in covenant unity with Yahweh. This faithful remnant of Israel labored like an expectant mother to bring forth the promised Messiah—the one the prophets called the righteous "Branch" from the House of David who was destined to restore and shepherd Israel, and be a light to the nations of the Gentile world (Is 9:2; 11:1-3; 49:5-6; Jer 23:5; 33:15; Ez 34:23).

During the years of exile and suffering, Yahweh's prophets continued preaching the promise of redemption for the faithful remnant of Israel who remained committed to Yahweh through the commands and prohibitions of the Sinai Covenant. An added tragedy during the period of the seventy-year exile was that there was no Holy Temple of Yahweh and no Altar of Burnt Offerings where they could keep the twice-daily liturgy of the Tamid, the sacrifice that was required to burn day and night continually on Yahweh's holy altar. They could not offer this holiest sacrifices for the forgiveness of their communal sins and the sanctification of a covenant people living in fellowship with Yahweh.

The Babylonian's destruction of the Jerusalem Temple may have suspended the Tamid sacrifice, but it was not forgotten. Even in exile in pagan lands, the people remembered the 'olat ha-Tamid every morning and afternoon in their daily prayer life (Dan 9:20-21). And it figured in the prophecies of the return from exile and the coming of the Messiah. The people clung to the promises of the prophets. They looked forward to the day of restoration to their homeland when they could rebuild the Temple, and when the sanctifying sacrifice of the Tamid burned again on God's holy altar (Is 44:21-23, 28). Living in exile, it was through the seven annual remembrance feasts that the covenant people relived the judgment of Israel's oppressors and the liberation of the Exodus experience. They remembered God's promise that one day, He would raise up a prophet like Moses to lead His people in their time of great distress (Dt 18:15-19).

Before the Babylonian exile, the prophets Isaiah and Jeremiah taught the people that the future Redeemer-Messiah, born of a virgin from King David's lineage, was promised to restore and reunite Israel into one holy kingdom (Is 7:14; 11:10-12, 16; Jer 23:3-8). The priest-prophet Jeremiah and the priest-prophet Ezekiel who accompanied his people into exile in Babylon prophesied that the Redeemer-Messiah was to come forth from the house of David as His people's liberator. He was going to spiritually restore and reunite the lost ten tribes of Israel (referred to as "Ephraim") to the remnant of Judah in an everlasting, new covenant of peace (Jer 31:31-33; 32:40; 50:5; Ez 34:23-25a, 37:1- 28). And prophesying from his captivity in Babylon and later in the capital of the Persian conquerors of Babylon, the prophet Daniel linked the coming of the Redeemer-Messiah to the end of the Tamid sacrifice (Dan 7:13-14; 12:11).

King Cyrus of Persia conquered the Babylonians in 539 BC. In fulfillment of the prophecy of Isaiah, King Cyrus issued a decree allowing the Judean captives to return to their homeland and rebuild their Temple (Is 44:28; 45:1-4, 13; 2 Chr 36:22-23; Jer 29:19; Ezra 1:1-4). Upon returning to Jerusalem, the faithful remnant of Judah immediately built an altar on Mount Moriah. They reinstated the morning and afternoon Tamid, and the other sacrifices offered within the ritual of the daily liturgies of the Tamid worship service: They erected the altar on its old site, despite their fear of the people of the country, and on it, they presented burnt offerings to Yahweh, burnt offerings morning and evening (Ezra 3:1-3).

CHAPTER SUMMARY POINTS: THE CITY OF JERUSALEM AND A HOUSE FOR GOD'S NAME:

1. National and religious rituals reflect the origins of a people, sustaining a national identity and spiritual unity.

2. Israel's election as a holy nation and the successful conquest of the Promised Land was a result of God's promises to the Patriarchs. God's continued protection depended upon Israel's obedience to the covenant.

3. The city of Jerusalem became the camp of God, where He established His sacrificial altar. It was the place where God told the covenant people *there you shall offer your burnt offerings, and there you shall do all that I am commanding you* (Dt 12:14).

4. David's son, King Solomon, built the Temple of Yahweh on the summit of Mount Moriah. It was the place where Abraham passed his covenant ordeal when he submitted himself to God in offering his beloved son Isaac in sacrifice until the Angel of God stayed his hand. Mount Moriah was also where King David saw the vision of the Angel of the Lord and offered himself in sacrifice for the salvation of his people.

5. The Temple was a house for God's name where the natural intersected with the supernatural, and it was where generations of the sons and daughters of Israel experienced spiritual union with Yahweh. The Temple served as the point of contact between Heaven and earth, and the point from which the promise of salvation radiated.

6. The Temple of Yahweh in Jerusalem symbolically represented in miniature the vast universe over which God ruled from His heavenly Temple. The Jerusalem Temple was God's threshing floor where men and women were separated from the chaff of their sins so that their souls could bear the good fruit of promised salvation.

7. When the Babylonians destroyed the Jerusalem Temple and exiled the covenant people into the lands of Babylon, the people did not forget the daily liturgy of

the Tamid. The people remembered the two worship services of the Tamid lamb in their twice-daily prayer life.

8. As soon as the people were permitted to return to Judah, they immediately reinstituted the perpetual burnt offering of the Tamid.

Endnotes: The City of Jerusalem and a House for God's Name

1. Moses changed Joshua's name from Hosea ("salvation") to Yah'shua/Yeshua, meaning "Yahweh is salvation" or "Yahweh saves" (Num 13:16). In Scripture, a change in a name reflects a change in mission or destiny. Joshua succeeded Moses as the leader of the covenant people. He led the people of God into the Promised Land of Canaan, foreshadowing Yah'shua/Yeshua (Jesus' name in Hebrew or Yehoshua in Aramaic) who led the people of God into the true "Promised Land" of Heaven.
2. The prophets promised God would send a Redeemer-Messiah who was a descendant of the great King David (Is 7:14; 11:1-5, 10; Jer 23:5; 30:8-9; 33:14-15; Ez 34:23-24; 37:24-25; Hos 3:4-5; Am 9:11-12; Zec 12:7-10; 13:1). The Gospel of Matthew proclaimed the fulfillment of the Davidic covenant in Jesus' genealogy in Mt 1:1, 6, 17, and in the promise of the virgin birth (Is 7:14) in Mt 1:20-23, and in Lk 1:31-33.
3. Some scholars identify Jesus' death in AD 30 and others in AD 33. St. Luke records that Jesus and John the Baptist began their ministries when they were about 30 years old (Lk 3:23).

John the Baptist began his ministry in the fifteenth year of Tiberius Caesar's reign (Lk 3:1-3) and was born six months before Jesus (as the ancients counted; see Lk 1:24-26). Tiberius became emperor on August 19th, AD 14. As the ancients counted, without the concept of zero as a place-value, the 15th year of Tiberius' reign extended from August 19th, AD 28 to August 19th, AD 29. However, if following the Syrian method of counting a regnal year, the 15th year is from September/October AD 27 to September/October AD 28. The Syrians had a slightly different way of calculating a regnal year than the Romans and Judeans, beginning that year not on the year the successor assumed the throne but by beginning with the new calendar year. Therefore, if St. Luke is using the Syrian method of calculating the years of Tiberius' reign, the 15th year of Tiberius is from September/October AD 27 to September/October AD 28. St. John's Gospel marks the years of Jesus' ministry in the cycle of the annual feasts in three different Passovers in Jn 2:13; 6:4; 11:55, which spanned three years as the ancients counted, probably from year #1 in AD 28 to year #3 in AD 30.

4. Our "meeting with God" in the liturgical expression of worship is our experience with the supernatural. For those of us in the New Covenant, our visionary experience is in witnessing the miracle of Transubstantiation when we have the "faith vision" of Christ made present in the Eucharist. Hopefully, our vision continues to expand as we grow spiritually and come to know and love Christ more deeply in our faith journey. Worship, to have meaning, has to be a visionary experience.
5. The Fall of Adam closed the gates of Heaven (CCC 536; 1026). The beginning of the opening of the gates of Heaven occurred at Jesus baptism (Mt 3:16; Mk 1:10; Lk 3:21). Jesus

spoke of the gathering in of righteous souls into Heaven using the imagery of a great harvest (c.f. Mt 13:39-42; Lk 10:2; Jn 4:35-36; also see Rev 14:14-20). The first of the great human "harvest" was composed of the souls Jesus rescued from Sheol (the abode of the dead) after His death on the Cross when He descended to the realm of the grave to preach the Gospel of salvation (1 Pet 3:18-20; 4:6; CCC 633, the Apostles' Creed).

6. A covenant lawsuit was the official declaration of a broken covenant and the warning of God's impending divine judgment. For examples of prophets declaring covenant lawsuits see Is 1:2-9 (against Israel); Jer 1:16-2:37 (against Judah); 11:1-14 (against Judah); Ez 17:19-24 (Judah and her king); in Hos 2:1-13 (against Israel and Judah); 4:1-14 (against Israel and Judah); 5:1-7 (against failed priests).
7. At best, the Jews considered the Samaritans to be half-breed apostate Israelite-Gentiles, and at worst, heretics who corrupted the true faith. The Samaritans rejected the Jerusalem Temple and the ordained priesthood of Aaron. They established a separate form of worship, ordained their own priests, built their own temple, and accepted only the Torah (first five books of Moses) in their canon of sacred Scripture. Jewish priest-historian Flavius Josephus records that the Samaritans both denied and sometimes professed themselves as kinsmen of the Jews (*Antiquities of the Jews*, 12.5.5[257]). St. Paul may have been referring to the Samaritans when he made the statement in Romans 9:6 that not all those who claim to be born Israelites belong to Israel.

CHAPTER IV
DAILY WORSHIP IN JERUSALEM'S SECOND TEMPLE (517/6 BC–AD 70)

Accordingly, it is commanded that every day the priests should offer up two lambs, one at the dawn of the day, and the other in the evening ...
Philo of Alexandria (c. 20 BC–AD 50), Special Laws I XXXV [169].
(For the Israelites, "evening" was from noon until sunset when the next day began).

THE TIME DIVISIONS OF THE JEWISH DAY AND NIGHT IN THE FIRST CENTURY AD

The Jewish day in Biblical times was divided into twelve seasonal daylight hours from dawn to sunset (Jn

11:9). The daily life of the people was centered on God's holy Temple, whether in attending the twice-daily worship service of the Tamid or in observing the times of Temple worship in private prayer. During the eras of the first Jerusalem Temple (c. 970-587/6 BC) and the second Jerusalem Temple (c. 517/6 BC-AD 70), there were three "hours" (periods) of individual prayer times that were officially observed by the covenant people wherever they were residing. Those prayer times coincided with the morning and afternoon Tamid liturgical worship services (Acts 3:1; Telushkin, Jewish Literacy, pages 47 and 715; Eisenberg, The JPS Guide to Jewish Traditions, page 399; Schurer, A History of the Jewish People in the Time of Jesus, II, vol. 1, pages 290-291, n. 248; the Talmud, Berakoth iv.1). For example, while living in exile, the prophet Daniel observed prayer time (Dan 6:10), and he was praying and confessing his sins and the sins of his people at what would have been the hour of the afternoon Tamid sacrifice, when the angel Gabriel appeared to him (Dan 9:20-21). Saints Peter and John made their way to the Temple at the hour of afternoon prayer and sacrifice in Acts 3:1. And St. Peter, while visiting in the city of Joppa, observed his private prayer time in association with the liturgical worship schedule in Acts 10:9, as did Roman God-fearer

Cornelius, a Gentile who professed belief in Israel's God, in Acts 10:3, 30.

Today, Rabbinic Judaism observes three "hours" of prayer: Shacharit, "Morning Prayer"; Minhah/Minchah, "Gift-offering" or afternoon prayer; and Ma'ariv, "Evening Prayer" which begins at sundown, the beginning of the next day. Shacharit and Minhah, morning and afternoon prayer coincides with the ancient Temple's Tamid liturgy. However, the Jewish Talmud records the late addition of the third "hour" of prayer after the Temple's destruction in AD 70. Ma'ariv is therefore not connected with the ancient sacrificial system (*Mishnah: Berakhot* and *The Jewish Book of Why*, volume I, page 148).

From the time of Solomon's Temple until the eras before the Greek and Roman occupation, the covenant people observed three equal time divisions or "Watches" of the nighttime hours. After the Roman conquest, the Jews adopted the Greek and Roman custom of dividing the night into four watches. In our time, the divisions equated to: (1) "evening/night watch" from sundown to 9 PM; (2) "midnight watch" from 9 PM to midnight; (3) "cockcrow watch" from midnight to 3 AM; and (4) "dawn watch" from 3 AM to dawn. Jesus listed the same four night-watches in Mark 13:35 when He said: "Watch, therefore; you do not know when the lord of the house is coming, whether in the evening, or at midnight, or at cockcrow, or in the morning." Matthew 14:25 and Mark 6:48 also mention the fourth watch in association with Jesus' miracle of walking on the Sea of Galilee. A trumpet signaled the end of each watch. The trumpet blast that announced the end of the third watch and the beginning of the fourth and final watch was known as the "cockcrow." 1

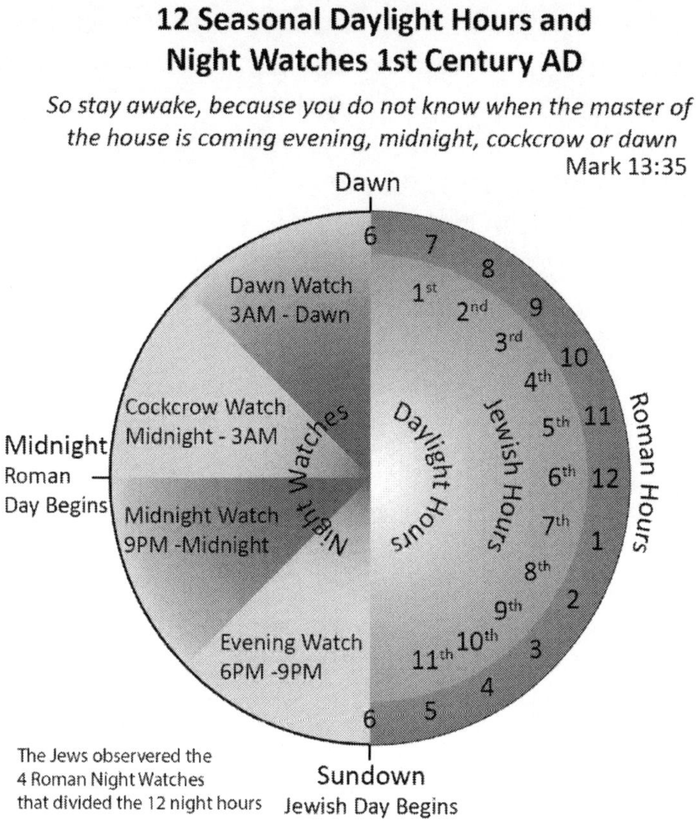

THE TAMID MORNING LITURGICAL WORSHIP SERVICE IN THE SECOND TEMPLE PERIOD

The Book of Sirach gives a description of the High

Priest Simon II (high priest 220-195 BC) celebrating the morning Tamid worship service in the Jerusalem Temple:
The leader of his brethren and the pride of his people was Simon the high priest, son of Onias ... When he put on his glorious robe and clothed himself with superb perfection and went up to the holy altar, he made the court of the sanctuary glorious. And when he received the portions from the hands of the priests, as he stood by the hearth of the altar with a garland of brethren around him, he was like a young cedar on Lebanon; and they surrounded him like the trunks of palm trees, all the sons of Aaron in their splendor with the Lord's offering in their hands, before the whole congregation of Israel (Sirach 50: 1, 11-13).

The sacrificial system was at the heart of the Temple ritual. Public and private offerings were made daily. A public sacrifice was brought each morning and afternoon.
The Jewish Book of Why, volume I, page 148 (referring to the Tamid sacrifice)

SCHEDULE OF THE TAMID SACRIFICE AND THE TEMPLE LITURGICAL SERVICE *This is the order of the daily whole offering in the liturgy of the house of our God.* *Mishnah: Tamid,* 7:3R The sacrifice of the two Tamid lambs was a single sacrifice (Exodus 29:42 and Numbers 28:3).
DAWN After the preparation of the altar, the first male lamb was brought out at dawn (at approximately 6 AM) from the Lamb Chamber. The High Priest inspected the lamb and gave it a drink from a golden cup. The priests kept the lamb in the Court of the Priests (inner courtyard) near the altar for everyone to observe its perfection from dawn until the third-hour Jewish time/9 AM (*Mishnah: Tamid,* 2:1-3:4; Philo, *Special Laws XXXV* [169]).

THIRD HOUR
When the sacrifice of the first Tamid lamb took place, the Temple gates opened for the Morning Prayer service at the third hour/9 AM (Acts 3:1; Edersheim, *The Temple: Its Ministry and Services*, pages 72-75), as a priest collected the lamb's blood in a chalice (*Mishnah: Tamid* 3:7H; 4:1A-F). The first "hour" of individual prayer, in Hebrew *Shacharit*, "morning prayer," could be recited from the third to the sixth hours/9 AM to noon (*Mishnah: Berakhot*, 4:1A). At about the fifth hour (11 AM), the liturgical service ended, the Levites cleansed the courtyard, and preparations for the second prayer service began at noon (Edersheim, *The Temple: Its Ministry and Services*, page 108).
SIXTH HOUR
The second lamb was brought out from the Lamb Chamber at the sixth hour (noon). A priest inspected it and gave it a drink from a golden cup. The lamb remained in the Court of the Priests until the time for the second daily liturgical service (*Mishnah: Tamid* 3:4; 4:1G-N; Josephus, *Against Apion*, 2.8[105]).
NINTH HOUR
The sacrifice of the second lamb signaled the beginning of the afternoon prayer service (Philo, *Special Laws I*, *XXXV* [169]). According to the first century AD Jewish priest-historian, Flavius Josephus, this service began at about the ninth hour/3 PM (*Antiquities of the Jews*, 14.4.3 [65]). It was the second hour of prayer, in Hebrew *Minhah*, "gift-offering," lasting from the sixth hour (noon) to the eleventh hour/5 PM, the length of the time from tying the second lamb near the altar to the conclusion of the afternoon service (*Mishnah: Berakhot*, 4:1C; Acts 10:9). The afternoon prayer service and all sacrifices ended by about the eleventh hour, 5 PM (Josephus, *The Wars of the Jews*, 6.9.3 [423]).
Michal E. Hunt Copyright © 2011

Worship in the Jerusalem Temple was an exhilarating assault upon the senses. There was the sound of trumpets blaring, the melodious voices of the Levitical chorus and the congregation, and the bleating and bellowing of animals of the herd and flock. There was the smell of blood, incense, smoke, and roasting flesh, and there was the feel of the animal upon which one placed one's hands before confession and sacrifice. There was also the sight of the altar fire with its great column of white smoke rising toward Heaven. And there was the smell and taste of the boiled meat of sacrificial victims, consumed by the priests in the sin and guilt sacrifices and by the faithful in the sacred meal of the *Todah*, the "Thanksgiving" communion offering.[2]

Of the different classes of blood sacrifice offered on Yahweh's Altar of Burnt Offerings, none was as important as the whole-burnt offering of the Tamid lambs, the sacrifice around which the daily Temple liturgy, the prayer life of the covenant people, and the entire sacrificial system revolved. In the Jewish Talmud, in the Fifth Division of the *Mishnah*, entitled "Holy Things," is the sub-section "Tamid." Section 1:2-7:4 of the *Mishnah: Tamid* lists the detailed requirements for the daily offering of the Tamid in the Second Temple's liturgical services, ministered by the ordained priests who were the descendants of Aaron, Israel's first High Priest.

The chief priests, descended from Moses' brother Aaron, served as Yahweh's ordained ministers (Ex 28:1; 40:12-15), and the Levitical lesser-ministers were members of the three clans of the tribe of Levi who served the chief priests (Num 3:5–10; 1 Chr 23:27–32). The Levites assisted the chief priests in the Court of the Priests. However, they could not offer sacrifice at the altar, touch the sacred vessels, forgive sins, or take on any other duties assigned to the chief priests; and they could not enter the sacred spaces of the Sanctuary (Num 3:10; 18:1, 6–7; *Mishnah: Kelim,* 1:8I–L).

During the slaying of the thousands of lambs and kids on the Feast of Passover, the Levites collected the blood of the victims in the Court of the Priests, but they passed the chalices of blood to the chief priests who applied the blood to the sacrificial altar (2 Chr 30:15–16). In addition to assisting the chief priests in the liturgy of worship, the Levitical duties included guarding the Temple, keeping the night watches, playing instruments for the Temple orchestra, singing in the Temple choir, cleaning and maintaining the Temple, serving in the Temple bakery, and instructing the faithful in the commands and prohibitions of the Law (1 Chr 9:33; 15:16; 23:28–32).

King David established the division of the families of the priests and the Levites into twenty-four "courses" or family clans. Each clan of priests and Levites performed duties in the Temple for eight days from Sabbath to Sabbath, twice a year during non-festival times in their liturgical calendar (1 Chr 23:3–6,

24-32). However, for the holy day festivals, all the chief priests and Levitical ministers were required to attend the Temple's liturgical services.[3]

On the Sabbath, the previous week's priestly ministers and Levitical clans presided over the morning Tamid worship service. The priests and Levitical ministers who arrived to serve in the next week's worship schedule began their week of service on the same Sabbath by presiding over the afternoon Tamid worship service (2 Chr 23:8). With the exception of the High Priest, the drawing of lots determined the daily duties of the chief priests serving in the Temple liturgy (Neh 10:34; Lk 1:8-9; *Mishnah: Tamid,* 3:1).[4]

The liturgical day began before dawn. The chief priests and the Levites assigned to Temple service for that day arose at the trumpet signal called the "cockcrow," at 3 AM (*Mishnah: Tamid* 1:2E). The priests who wanted to participate in the first lot drawing cleansed themselves by immersion in the Temple's ritual purification pool called a *mikvah* (*Mishnah: Tamid,* 1:1Q; 1:2H; *Mishnah: Yoma,* 3:3A). After bathing, they dressed in their white linen priestly tunics, waistbands, headdresses, and under-drawers (Ex 28:40-43). The priests only wore their priestly garments when they were performing their liturgical duties (*Mishnah: Tamid,* 5:3; Ez 42:14). They were also required to remove their sandals and to walk barefoot when they performed their ministerial duties (*Mishnah: Tamid,* 5:3).[5] The Temple was holy ground; therefore, God's instructions to Moses and Joshua when they were in His Divine Presence also applied to the Court of the Priests and the Temple Sanctuary: *put off your shoes from your feet, for the place on which you are standing is holy ground* (Ex 3:5 and Josh 5:15).

Before dawn, the chief priest who served as the Superintendent of the Temple took the key that opened the door to the Temple courtyard via the Chamber of the Hearth where the priests slept. The other priests charged with the "dawn patrol" followed him, dividing into two groups with two lighted torches in their hands. One group went eastward along the colonnade and the other to the west, inspecting that everything was in order until they converged at the Bakery where a priest instructed the Levites who were the bakers to fire the ovens (*Mishnah: Tamid,* 1:3A–I).

The other priests assembled in the Chamber of Hewn Stones, one of the large rooms at the south side of the Court of the Priests (the location of the Bronze Altar of Sacrifice). It was the responsibility of the Superintendent of the Temple to oversee the casting of the lots for each day's ceremonial duties. During the morning, the priests assembled there three times to draw four rounds of lots to determine their priestly duties for the morning Tamid worship service (*Mishnah: Tamid*,1:2H-J; 3:1A; 5:2).

The priests selected by lot performed the same duties assigned in the morning service again in the afternoon Tamid service. The exception was the priest chosen to burn the sacred incense in the Sanctuary's Holy Place if the High Priest decided to delegate that duty. The honor of burning the incense as the High Priest's representative was a once-in-a-lifetime event for a priest. Only those who had never previously served in the burning of the incense could participate in the drawing, and so another priest was selected by lot for that honor in the afternoon worship service (*Mishnah: Tamid*, 5:2).

The burning of the incense took place in the Sanctuary's Holy Place on the golden Altar of Incense. It was a small altar that stood in front of the embroidered curtain shielding the entrance to the Temple's most sacred space, the Holy of Holies, where the presence of God once resided between the figures of the two golden cherubim on the Mercy-seat of the Ark of the Covenant (Ex 25:18-22). In the Second Temple, there was no Ark of the Covenant in the Holy of Holies. Before the destruction of Solomon's Temple by the Babylonians in the 6th century BC, the prophet Jeremiah rescued the Ark and hid it on Mount Nebo to prevent Israel's most sacred shrine from falling into the hands of pagans (1 Mac 2:1-8). But the people still believed that God's Divine Presence dwelt among them in the Holy of Holies, having returned with His people from exile.

The first-round of the drawing of lots occurred immediately after the priests assembled in the pre-dawn hours. This drawing determined which priests were to prepare the sacrificial altar in the Temple's inner courtyard for that day's sacrifices. The first priest selected was assigned the duty of removing the ashes from the previous day's sacrifices and depositing the ashes at a designated site outside the city walls. Other priests assisted him in cleansing the sacrificial altar and in selecting and laying the wood for the altar's holy fire that burned continually was never extinguished (Lev 6:10-12-13; *Mishnah: Tamid,* 2:1-2:5). Before going about their duties, each priest sanctified his hands and feet by washing them in the laver in the Court of the Priests (*Mishnah: Tamid,* 1:4H; *Mishnah: Kelim,* 1:9D).

The people's daily sacrifice of the Tamid came from flocks of firstborn lambs that were kept about five miles south of Jerusalem in fields near the village of Bethlehem (Ex 13:1-2, 11-15). The village's name, which in Hebrew meant "house/place of bread," was the ancestral home of the revered King David. The prophet Micah foretold that David's town of Bethlehem would be the birthplace of the promised Davidic Messiah (Mic 5:1). The selected Tamid lambs could not be younger than eight days and not older than a year; they had to be male, and they had to be without a single blemish or defect (Lev 22:20, 27).

Five days before every Tamid service (as the ancients counted with the first day counting as day #1), the male lambs were examined by the priests as possible candidates for the Tamid. The priests brought the selected lambs to Jerusalem and kept them in a special enclosure only for the Tamid lambs and no other animals within the Temple precincts known as the Lamb Chamber or Lamb Office. There were always at least six acceptable lambs in the Lamb Chamber at one time. The chief priests inspected each lamb several times, including the night before and on the day of the service to ensure the requirement that the Tamid lamb was in a state of ritual perfection (Num 28:3–5; *Mishnah: Tamid,* 3:3A–C, 3:4C).

Many preparations took place prior to the morning Tamid liturgy. Before dawn, the Levites set the fires in the Temple ovens for baking the bread offerings in preparation for the day's liturgical ceremonies. There was also the requirement for griddle cakes of wheat flour mixed with pure olive oil and formed into flat, unleavened rounds cooked in a pan. These wafer-like cakes were the High Priest's *korban*, also called the High Priest's required tribute/*minhah* offering to God the Great King (Lev 6:19-23/6:12-16; *Mishnah: Yoma,* 2:3IIC).

In addition to the priestly wafer, if it was the Sabbath, twelve new loaves of bread, representing each of the twelve tribes, were baked in the Temple ovens to replace the past week's twelve loaves. These loaves were a permanent (*tamid*) covenant offering called the "Bread of the Presence [of God]" or literally, the "Bread of the Face [of God]." The new loaves were placed on the golden table in the Sanctuary's Holy Place after removing the previous week's bread, which the outgoing priests and incoming priests ate if they were in a state of ritual purity (Ex 25:30; Lev 24:5-9; *Mishnah: Seqalim,* 6.4; Edersheim, *The Temple Its Ministry and Services,* page 144).

While the Temple ovens were heating, the Levites collected the ninety-three silver and gold utensils used in the liturgical service from the Chamber of Vessels along with the salt, olive oil, and the sacramental wine used in the libation ceremony (*Mishnah: Tamid* 3:4A). The oil and the wine were in the Chamber of Oils in the southwest corner of the Women's Court (*Carta's*

Illustrated Encyclopedia of the Holy Temple in Jerusalem, page 81). The oil was used for mixing with the grain offerings and as fuel for the lamps of the golden *Menorah* (lamp-stand) in the Sanctuary's Holy Place. The sacramental wine was for the libation ceremony at the conclusion of the worship service and was carefully measured out into a special silver flagon (Ex 29:40-41; Num 28:7-8).

While some Levites collected the oil and the wine libation, others brought salt from the Salt Chamber. The salt, a sign of purification and incorruption, signified the preservation of the faithful who offered sacrifice to God in obedience to His covenant. The priests salted all grain offerings and animal sacrifices before placing them on the altar fire (Lev 2:13; Ez 43:23-24; *Mishnah: Tamid*, 4:3S). This practice and its related symbolism probably explain Jesus' comment when He spoke of everyone being "salted with fire" on Judgment Day (Mk 9:49-50).

After the completion of the preparation of the altar, the priests gathered a second time in the Chamber of Hewn Stones for the drawing of the second-round of lots. This drawing was "to determine who executes the act of slaughter, who tosses the blood, who removes the ashes of the inner altar [Altar of Incense], who removes the ashes of the candlestick [Menorah], who carries up the limbs to the ramp" (*Mishnah: Tamid,* 3:1). The priest selected by lot to collect the blood of the Tamid lamb and perform the Blood Ritual also offered the wine libation and performed the ritual of pouring out the wine against the altar in the concluding rites of the morning service (*Mishnah: Tamid,* 5:2D; 7:3A–K).

A priest was also chosen by lot to perform the act of slaughter for the Tamid if a ritually pure "Tamid man," was not available. Since the Tamid was a sacrifice of atonement and sanctification for the entire covenant community, men of good reputation within the covenant community volunteered to serve in the Temple as Tamid men lay ministers. These laymen were chosen to offer the sacrifice as the community's representatives and to perform the laying-on-of-hands, the confession of the people's sins, and the rite of the sacrifice (Kurtz, *Offerings, Sacrifice and Worship in the Old Testament*, page 349). They accompanied the clan of priests who had the obligation for Temple service that week, traveling from wherever that week's priestly community was residing. However, only a priest could catch the blood of the Tamid lamb in a consecrated vessel and apply it to the altar in the prescribed Blood Ritual. He also drew a lot for this sacred honor as the High Priest's representative

(*Mishnah: Tamid,* 3:1; Edersheim, *The Temple: Its Ministry and Services*, page 108 and 123).

The second-round lot drawing also determined which nine priests were to take part in the procession that carried the congregation's gifts of sacrifice to the altar. They placed the gifts of sacrifice on the lower half of the altar ramp on the west side where the salting of the victim's parts and the grain offerings took place. Five priests were also selected to perform the rituals of service within the Holy Place. Those priests were assigned the duties of preparing the golden Menorah and removing the ashes from the inner altar called the Altar of Incense, the golden column for the burning of the holy incense (*Mishnah: Tamid,* 2:5; 3:1; 3:6; 3:9; 6:1).

The golden Menorah was the seven-branched lamp-stand with seven oil lamps that signified the presence of the spirit of God among His people and Israel's mission as a "light" to the other nations of the world. The priests selected to prepare the lamp-stand were required to trim the wicks, refill the bowls with pure olive oil, and relight those that had gone out during the night, using the fire from the center bowl. The central bowl was to be kept burning continually and could only be re-lit with the sacred fire from the bronze Altar of Sacrifice—a fire that was kept perpetually burning (Lev 6:12/6:5; 24:1-4; *Mishnah: Tamid,* 3:9E-H). After the second round of lots, the priests were dismissed to prepare for their duties.

As priests prepared the Menorah, other priests saw to the golden Altar of Incense that stood in front of the richly embroidered curtain (as thick as a man's hand), shielding the entrance to the Holy of Holies where the presence of God dwelt in the midst of His people (Ex 25:8, 21-22; 30:1-8). The Altar of Incense had to be cleaned and made ready to burn the incense at a precise moment in the order of the liturgical service. The mixture of sweet-smelling herbs and spices was a secret recipe only used in the worship services (Ex 30:34-37).

After the second-round of lots, the Superintendent of the Temple assigned a Levite to go the pinnacle of the Temple to watch for the sun to rise over the Mount of Olives directly to the east of the Temple Mount. Yahweh's liturgy of worship commenced at dawn. When the assigned Levite sighted the first rays of light, he shouted "Barkai!", "Morning has arrived" (*Mishnah: Tamid*, 3:2)! This signal announced that the sacred ritual of the Tamid sacrifice could begin. It was time for the first lamb of the Tamid to be led from the Lamb Chamber into the inner courtyard. The first lamb could not be brought out to the altar until "the whole eastern horizon is light" (*Mishnah: Tamid*, 3:2C).

The High Priest or his representative inspected the lamb for the last time, judging the perfection of the victim offered for the atonement and sanctification of the entire covenant community by announcing "I find no fault." Then the lamb received a drink from a golden cup before it was tied to a post on the north side of the sacrificial altar where it remained until it was time for the sacrifice (*Mishnah: Tamid,* 3:4B-C; *1 Clement,* 41:2). The victim had to be visible from just after dawn until the time of sacrifice for everyone present to witness the male lamb's perfection, while the chief priests and Levites continued the necessary preparations for the morning's liturgical worship service.

The third hour from dawn (about 9 AM), the Superintendent gave the order for the priests who stood on the west side of the altar to blow three blasts on the silver Sanctuary trumpets (Num 10:1-3). Only the priests blew the silver trumpets which sounded no fewer than twenty-one notes on ordinary days: three to signal the opening of the Temple gates, nine at the offering of the morning Tamid, and nine at the offering of the afternoon Tamid (*Mishnah: Sukkah,* 5:5; Edersheim, *The Temple: Its Ministry and Services,* pages 49-50).

The three trumpet blasts in the morning signaled the Levites to open the Temple gates to admit the faithful and summon the other Levites to their various duties. Then there were nine blasts for the peoples' representative, the Tamid man, to begin the ritual of sacrifice (*Mishnah: Sukkah,* 5:5H). Some accounts said that people could hear the loud trumpeting as far away as Jericho. The sound announced to the covenant people that the morning Tamid was about to be sacrificed, and the worship service that signified the continuation of the covenant was beginning. The deep, rich tones of the Sanctuary trumpets also symbolized Yahweh summoning His covenant people, just as He did at the first divine encounter with the children of Israel at Mount Sinai (Ex 19:16, 19-20).

As the gates to the Temple swung open, it was the beginning of the Morning Prayer service: *The one who was going to execute the act of slaughter did not perform the act of slaughter until he heard the sound of the great gate opening* (*Mishnah: Tamid,* 3:7H). At the moment the Temple gates swung open, the designated Tamid layman placed his hands firmly upon the head of the Tamid lamb and then, facing west toward the Holy of Holies, confessed the sins of his people over the victim and quickly slit the throat of the innocent lamb with a ritual knife. The assigned priest then collected the blood that flowed out of the victim into a golden chalice called a *mizrak* (*Mishnah: Tamid,* 4:1F-M). The slaying of the Tamid lamb was also the signal for the opening of the doors to the main Sanctuary that housed the Holy Place and the Holy of Holies to allow the selected priests to commence with their assigned duties.

In the ritual of sacrifice, it was necessary to separate the blood of the victim from the body, the blood representing the soul or life-force of the animal. It was the blood of the victim that expiated the people's sins (Lev 17:11; Heb 9:22), and the flesh of the victim consumed in the fire of the altar represented the covenant people yielding their lives in submission to the will of God. It was the humble surrender of His people that Yahweh desired, not the material value of the animal's life (1 Sam 15:22; Ps 51:16-17; Hos 6:6). A sacrifice offered without prayer and repentance from the contrite heart of the offeror or the humbled and repentant hearts of the community was a meaningless and lifeless gift without substance: *Thus says Yahweh: ... But my eyes are drawn to the person of humbled and contrite spirit, who trembles at my word* (Is 66:1a, 2b NJB).

For the holy people of God, the morning Temple liturgy had begun. After entering the Temple gates, the ritually purified men of the covenant community gathered in the Court of Israel; a colonnaded area separated from the Court of the Priests by a low balustrade. The opened colonnade faced the Court of the Priests, and the men had an unobstructed view of the altar of sacrifice and the main Sanctuary. The women remained in the Court of the Woman that had an upper gallery where they could look down upon the Court of the Priests (*Mishnah: Middot,* 2:5P). A doorway connected the Court of the Women to the Court of the Priests where the Levitical choir and the musicians assembled on fifteen semi-circular steps, each step representing one of the fifteen "Songs of Ascent" in Psalms 120-134 (*Mishnah: Middot,* 2:5Q-T; *Mishnah: Sukkah,* 5:4-F). The "God-fearers," Gentiles seeking have a relationship the God of Israel but who had not taken the final step of conversion through ritual immersion and circumcision (for men), were restricted to a large outer court known as the Court of the Gentiles, located on the outer limits of the Temple complex.

The community of the faithful (including the Levitical lesser ministers) was not allowed to enter the sacred space of the Sanctuary's Holy Place, and only the chief priests were permitted to minister at the Bronze Sacrificial Altar (Num 18:2-3). Individual covenant members were only admitted to the Court of the Priests and allowed to approach the altar when they had personal sacrifices to offer after the sacrifice of the morning Tamid and after the High Priest or his priestly representative laid the bread offering on the altar fire.

Everyone who entered the Court of the Priests had to have previously sanctified themselves in a *mikveh*, a ritual purification pool (*Antiquities of the Jews*, 15.11.5 [418-419]; *Mishnah: Yoma 3:3; Mishnah: Kelim* 1:8; Jeremias, *Jerusalem in the Time of Jesus*, page 209). Gentiles who were not converts to the covenant could present their offerings to the priests, but they were forbidden to go beyond the Court of the Gentiles. The penalty for an unauthorized person trespassing beyond the barrier was death (Acts 21:27-28; *Mishnah: Kelim*, 1:8F; Josephus, *Jewish Wars*, 5.5.2 [193-194]).

The priests assigned to prepare the Holy Place entered the Sanctuary doors to carry out their duties as the blood of the morning Tamid lamb flowed into a golden chalice. The High Priest or his designated priestly representative carried the chalice with the blood of the lamb and approached the altar. According to the instructions God gave at Mount Sinai, the High Priest was to officiate during the morning and afternoon Tamid service. However, at some point in the first century AD, it became acceptable for the High Priest to officiate only on the Sabbath and during the holy feast days, and at other worship services, he could appoint a chief priest as his representative (Josephus, *Wars of the Jews* 5.5.7 [230].

The same officiating priest who collected the blood of the Tamid lamb at the moment of sacrifice performed the Blood Ritual by splashing the blood against the foot of the altar in the northeastern corner and then in the southwestern corner. The blood that remained was then poured out on the southern base of the Bronze Sacrificial Altar. According to the Jewish Mishnah: *At the southwestern corner [of the Altar] there were two holes like two narrow nostrils by which the blood that was poured over the western base and the southern base used to run down and mingle in the water-channel and flow out into the brook Kidron* (*Mishnah Tamid* 4:1; *Mishnah: Middoth*, 3:2).

The Kidron Brook was a stream that flowed in the valley between the Temple Mount and the Mount of Olives. In the Blood Ritual, the covenant people and their priestly representatives offered the blood of the unblemished Tamid lamb to Yahweh in atonement for the sins and sanctification of the entire covenant people. The contact between the blood of the sacrificial victim and the altar became a channel of grace for all classes of sacrifices, signifying the humble submission of the offeror's life to God through the life-force of the sacrificial offering. As Yahweh told His covenant people: *For the life of the flesh is in the blood; and I have given it to you upon the altar to make atonement for your souls; for it is the blood that makes atonement by reason of the life* (Lev 17:11-12; also see Ex 29:42-43; *Mishnah: Tamid*, 4:1I-N).

As the Blood Ritual was taking place, the body of the Tamid lamb was skinned, cut into parts and cleansed with water in preparation for the altar. When the body of the Tamid lamb was ready, the priests chosen by lot received its body parts along with the other offerings. Bearing the community's gifts, they solemnly processed to the altar. Six priests carried the pieces of the Tamid lamb, a seventh brought the offering of fine flour, an eighth the baked griddle wafer that was the tribute offering (*minhah*) of the High Priest, and a ninth priest carried the silver flagon with the wine libation (*Mishnah: Yoma*, 2:5C). Arriving at the foot of the west side of the altar ramp, the priests carrying the lamb parts and the grain offerings laid down their burdens on the ramp for the ritual salting the offerings (Lev 2:13; Ez 43:24; *Mishnah: Tamid*, 4:3Q-T).

At this point in the morning worship service, the priests gathered for the third and last time in the Chamber of Hewn Stones for the solemn ritual of the liturgical prayers and the final drawing of lots. Together, as of one voice, the priests offered up prayers of praise and thanksgiving to God. They recited the Ten Commandments (Ex 20:3-17; Dt 5:6-21) and the *Shema Israel*, the first communal profession of faith (Dt 6:4-9;

11:13-21; Num 15:37-41), followed by the daily benedictions (*Mishnah: Tamid* 5:1).

If it was the Sabbath, there was also a blessing for the outgoing priestly clan (*Mishnah: Tamid,* 5:1). After the prayers, it was time for the drawing of the third and fourth round of lots (*Mishnah: Tamid,* 5:2). The third drawing determined which priest had the honor of burning the holy incense on the golden Altar of Incense that stood in front of the curtain covering the entrance to the Holy of Holies. The burning of the incense had initially been the duty of the reigning High Priest (Ex 30:7-8); however, if the High Priest so elected, he could allow a chief priest to be chosen by lot as his representative. The exception was on the Day of Atonement (Yom Kippur) when only the High Priest offered the incense (Lev 16:12-13).

The burning of the incense during the Tamid service was a once-in-a-lifetime honor for a priest. No priest could take part in the drawing for the burning of the incense if he previously received the honor of this service (*Mishnah: Tamid,* 5:2A). The priest selected by the lot then chose two brother priests to assist him in his duties. On one significant future day in salvation history, God was going to appoint an elderly, childless priest named Zechariah to draw the lot for burning the incense. During the ritual incense offering on the golden Altar of Incense in the Holy Place of the Sanctuary, the life of that elderly priest and the destiny of humanity would be altered forever (Lk 1:5, 8-9).

The final drawing was the fourth round of lots that designated which priests were to carry the people's gifts from the ramp up to the altar. At the top of the altar, the High Priest (or his officiating representative) waited to receive the sacrifice and to lay the divided body of the lamb and the grain offerings on the altar fire. With the conclusion of the drawing of the third and fourth lots, the priests selected for service exited the chamber. They ritually purified their hands and feet in the large water basin in the Court of the Priests before going about their duties, as had all the priests who drew the previous rounds of lots (Ex 30:17-21; *Mishnah: Tamid,* 2:1B; *Mishnah: Kelim,* 1:9; *Mishnah: Yoma* 4:5).

After leaving the Chamber of Hewn Stones, the High Priest (or his priestly representative) ritually sanctifying his hands and feet before ascending to the altar platform where he stood ready to receive the sacrifices and gift offerings. As the High Priest ascended the ramp up to the altar, the priest who received the honor to burn the incense and the priests he chose to assist him left the Chamber of Hewn Stones and, after ritually washing their hands and feet, approached the sacrificial altar. One assisting priest used a shovel to take some of the burning coals from the altar fire and placed them in a fire-pan, a golden vessel called a *teni*. The second assisting priest held the vessel containing the incense as the incensing priest spooned it into a golden censer (*Mishnah: Tamid*, 5:4-5:5). The incensing priest and his assistants then turned and slowly walked toward the Sanctuary doors.

When they reached a point midway between the altar and the porch of the Sanctuary, one of the assisting priests took the shovel he used to fill the fire-pan and threw it down. The sharp sound made by the metal shovel against the stones of the courtyard served three purposes. First, it alerted the priests in the Sanctuary that the incensing priest was approaching. Second, it alerted a Levite whose duty it was to run to the leader of the Levitical choir to tell him it was time to begin the singing. And third, it alerted the Levitical guard to have those men of the covenant who were ritually unclean and could not enter the Court of Israel to stand at the eastern gate of the Temple where they could hear the singing and the prayers (*Mishnah: Tamid*, 5:6).

As the Levitical choir began to sing, the incensing priest and his assistants, preceded by two of the priests who cleansed the incense altar and tended the Menorah, climbed the steps of the portico that led into the Holy Place of the Temple. Meanwhile, in the courtyard, the

High Priest (or his representative) stood near the altar, ready to receive the sacrifice. When the incensing priest and his assistants entered the Sanctuary, a priest struck a large gong-like instrument called the *magrefah*. The beautiful, deep tones of the *magrefah* reverberated throughout the Temple and echoed far into the city of Jerusalem, announcing that the prayers of the covenant people were about to be offered in the ceremony of the burning of the sacred incense (Edersheim, *The Temple: Its Ministry and Services*, page 127).

With solemn dignity, the incensing priest and his two assistants walked the entire length of the Holy Place while their brother priests stood at the altar in the courtyard. At the west end of the Holy Place, the golden Altar of Incense stood in front of the curtain that covered the entrance to the Holy of Holies where God's presence was believed to reside. The incense altar was a gold-covered square column that stood about chest high with a small, ornate golden fence around its top (Ex 30:1-8). Arriving at the Altar of Incense, the assisting priests prepared the altar to receive the incense. When given the signal by the priestly Superintendent standing at the entrance to the Holy Place, the incensing priest stepped forward to place the incense on the coals of the altar. A dense white smoke immediately began to billow upward, covering the ceiling of the Holy Place. The people believed that the rising smoke of the burning incense carried the covenant people's prayers and petitions up to God in the heavenly Sanctuary (Rev 8:3-4; *Mishnah: Tamid*, 6:3).

In the courtyard, the High Priest or his representative sanctified his hands and feet in the water font before ascending the altar ramp to receive the people's offerings from the priests who were assigned to present them (*Mishnah: Yoma*, 4:5IID). The priest watching at the Sanctuary door gave a signal when the cloud of smoke from the incense filled the Sanctuary and floated out of the entrance. At this point, the trumpets were sounded to announce that the same sign of the Glory Cloud that the Israelites of the Exodus generation observed of God's Divine Presence in the desert Sanctuary. It was also the same sign of the Glory Cloud witnessed at the dedication of God's Temple built by King Solomon (Ex 40:34; 1 Kng 8:10). The same sign was now taking place as the covenant with Yahweh continued in their generation. At the trumpet signal, the priests handed the body parts of the Tamid lamb to the High Priest standing at the Altar of Burnt Offerings.

The High Priest (or his representative) took each part of the victim that was handed to him and placed it on the altar fire along with the offering of fine flour mixed with oil. The wafer-like unleavened wheat cake, which was the High Priest's tribute gift (*minhah*) in "drawing near" (*korban*) to Yahweh, was held up before the people and broken into pieces before being covered with oil and incense and then placed on the altar fire. According to Jewish tradition, the High Priest's offering of the unleavened wafer came after laying the body of the Tamid lamb on the altar with the regular Tamid grain offering of flour mixed with oil but before the wine libation (Kultz, *Offerings, Sacrifices and Worship in the Old Testament,* page 353). Immediately, a cloud of white smoke, called in Hebrew the *'Olah* ("burning"), rose high into the morning sky. The smoke signified that God graciously accepted the covenant community's offering of atonement for their sanctification and the continuation of the covenant in the perpetual ritual of the Tamid sacrifice.

PLAN OF THE TEMPLE'S INNER COURTYARD AND THE SANCTUARY:

Notice the three-section division of the courtyard, the Holy Place, and the Holy of Holies which, from the New Covenant perspective, suggests the three divine persons of the Most Holy Trinity. In the desert Sanctuary, the arrangement of the furniture formed a cruciform, foreshadowing the altar of the Cross and the site of the offering of the final and perfect victim of sacrifice, but in the Temple the basin of water was moved to the right (the southeast) in the courtyard (Ex 30:17-21; 1 Kng 7:39; 2 Chr 4:10).

Inner Court of the Priests

- Bronze Altar of Sacrifice
- Bronze holy water basin for purification

Holy Place

- L = Golden Lampstand (menorah)
- T = Golden Table containing the Bread of the Presence
- I = Golden Altar of Incense in front of the curtain separating the Holy Place from the Holy of Holies
- the curtain separating the Court of the Priests from the Holy Place

Holy of Holies

- A richly embroidered curtain separated the Holy Place from the Holy of Holies. The Ark of the Covenant, covered with the solid gold Mercy Seat that was the dwelling place of Yahweh among His people, used to reside in this space before the destruction of Solomon's Temple in 587/6 BC.

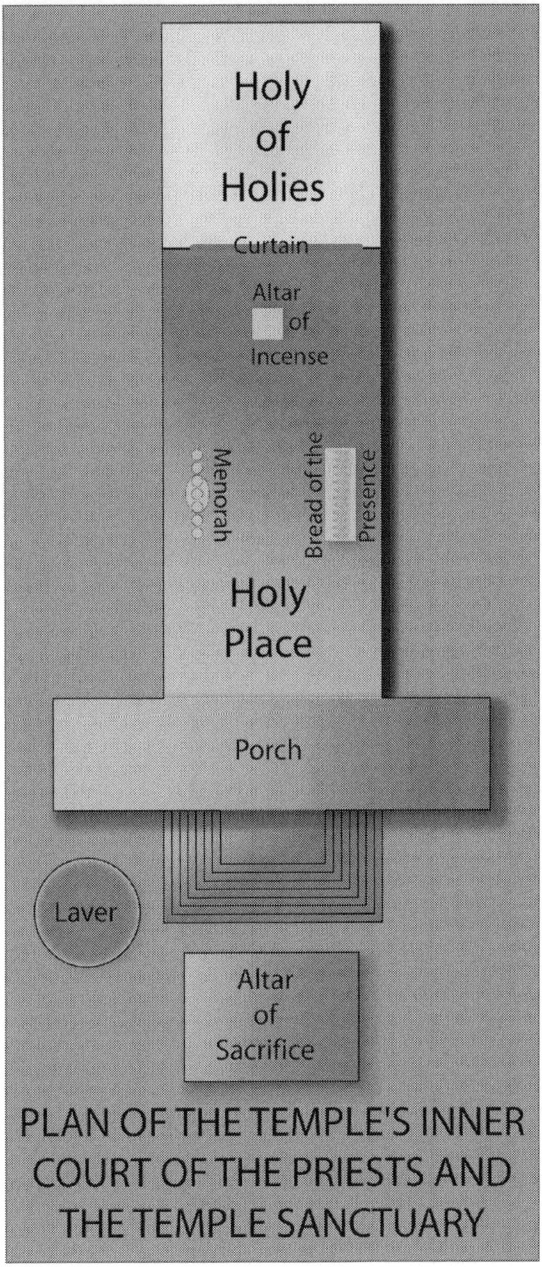

PLAN OF THE TEMPLE'S INNER COURT OF THE PRIESTS AND THE TEMPLE SANCTUARY

THE CONCLUDING RITES OF THE MORNING TAMID LITURGY

The conclusion of the morning Tamid worship service, celebrated by the High Priest, Simon II, c. 220-195 BC: Finishing the service at the altars and arranging the offering to the Most High, the Almighty, he reached out his hand to the cup and poured a libation of the blood of the grape; he poured it out at the foot of the altar, a pleasing odor to the Most High, the King of all. Then the sons of Aaron shouted, they sounded the trumpets of hammered work, they made a great noise to be heard for remembrance before the Most High. Then all the people together made haste and fell to the ground upon their faces to worship their Lord, the Almighty, God Most High. And the singers praised him with their voices in sweet and full-toned melody. And the people besought the Lord Most High in prayer before him who is merciful, till the order of worship of the Lord was ended; so they completed his service. Then Simon came down and lifted up his hands over the whole congregation of the sons of Israel, to pronounce the blessing of the Lord with his lips, and to glory in his name; and they bowed down in worship a second time, to receive the blessing from the Most High.
Sirach 50:14-21

At this point in the worship service, the people could bring forward their individual whole-burnt offerings, sin sacrifices, communion offerings, or the prescribed holy day sacrifices after laying the body of the Tamid lamb on the altar fire (Kurtz, Offerings, Sacrifices and

Worship in the Old Testament, page 349). Sometimes the additional sacrifices continued until the hour for the afternoon Tamid worship service, at which time, all other sacrifices ceased (Josephus, The Wars of the Jews 6.9.3 [423].

An exception in the order of the worship service occurred in the case of the Passover sacrifices on the 14th of Abib/Nisan. After the morning Tamid, the priests suspended the offering of other sacrifices, and the afternoon Tamid took place earlier to allow enough time for the sacrifices of thousands of Passover lambs and goat kids. Moving the afternoon Tamid worship service to an earlier hour allowed the time needed to complete the multiple Passover sacrifices, to cleanse the courtyard of the blood afterward, and for the people to roast the meat of their Passover goat kids and lambs within the city of Jerusalem for the sacred meal that took place at sundown (Ex 12:8). If the day of the Passover sacrifice fell on a Friday, which was the day of preparation for the Sabbath, according to the Talmud, the afternoon Tamid lamb was sacrificed even earlier at half past the sixth hour (12:30 PM) and the Passover sacrifices began within the next hour (*Mishnah: Pesahim*, 5:1B–D).

After the additional sacrifices offered in the morning service (the voluntary sin, reparation, and communion sacrifices for a non-festival day), it was time for the wine libation which signaled the concluding rites of the morning service. As the anointed High Priest (or his priestly representative) stepped down from the altar to pour out the wine libation, the Temple Superintendent waved a white flag. It was the signal that it was time for the musicians to sound the cymbals and for the choir to offer up their hymns of praise. At this signal, the trumpets sounded a prolonged wavering sound, and a great shout of thanksgiving went up from among the priests as the wine libation was poured out at the foot of the altar (Num 10:10; Sir 50:16; *Mishnah: Tamid*, 7:3K-O).

The musicians played their cymbals, lyres, and harps, and the Levitical cantor and the chorus burst into song. As the smoke rose from the sacrifice burning on the altar, the orchestra accompanied the chorus of Levites, and the congregation joined in with hymns of praise to Yahweh, God of Israel (1 Chr 15:16; 25:1; 2 Chr 29:25-28; *Mishnah: Sukkah*, 5:5C). At every break in the singing, there was a prolonged blast from the trumpets, and the people knelt and bowed their heads (*Mishnah: Tamid*, 7:3P-Q). As they sang, their voices rose up to Heaven along with the pillar of cloud above the sacrificial altar. They sang the psalms of the day, and when the High Priest called out God's Divine Name,

"Yahweh," the people prostrated themselves and cried out, "Blessed be the name and the glory of His kingdom forever and ever!" (*Mishnah: Tamid*, 7:2F; 7:4; *Mishnah: Yoma*, 6:2D).

The Hebrew/Old Testament text of Sacred Scripture uses the four consonants YHWH for God's Divine Name more than any other name/title for the God of Israel. Sometime in the first century BC, the Pharisees introduced a prohibition against speaking God's Divine Name aloud and replaced God's covenant name with the word Adonai, meaning "Lord," ordaining the speaking aloud of the Divine Name could only occur in the daily services of the Tamid: In the sanctuary they would pronounce the divine name as it is written, and in the provinces, by an epithet (*Mishnah: Tamid*, 7:2F).

The singing of the psalms in the daily liturgy rotated according to the day of the week. On the first day of the week (Sunday), the Levitical choir sang Psalm 24, commemorating the first day of Creation when God created and then took sovereign possession of the cosmos (*Mishnah: Tamid*, 7:4A-B):

> *To Yahweh belongs the earth and all it contains,*
> *the world and all who live there;*
> *it is he who laid its foundations on the seas,*
> *on the flowing waters fixed it firm* (Ps 24:1-2 NJB).

On the second day of the week, they sang Psalms 48, on the third day Psalm 82, on the fourth day Psalm 94, on the fifth day Psalm 81, and on the sixth day Psalm 93. At the end of the week, on the Sabbath (Saturday), two Sabbath lambs were offered as whole-burnt offerings in addition to the morning and afternoon Tamid lambs (Num 28:9-10), and the Levites and the congregation sang Psalm 92. It was a hymn of praise for God's mercy and justice and *for the world that is to come, for the day which is wholly Sabbath rest for eternity* (*Mishnah: Tamid* 7:4H, I):

> *It is good to give thanks to Yahweh,*
> *to make music for your name, Most High,*
> *to proclaim your faithful love at daybreak,*
> *and your constancy all through the night,*
> *to the murmur of the harp* (Ps 92:2-3 NJB).

At every break in the singing, the people knelt again in prayer as the white cloud of the *Olah* rose higher and higher into the morning sky from the roasting flesh of the Tamid lamb, the other sacrifices, and the grain offerings burning on the sacrificial altar in the courtyard of the Temple. The pillar of white cloud rising from the altar not only assured the people of God's gracious acceptance of their sacrifices in obedience to His commands, but it also reminded the people of

Yahweh's continuing presence that began on the Exodus journey when He traveled with them in the great white pillar of the Glory Cloud (Ex 13:21-22). The visible manifestation of His presence in the *Olah* was a daily symbol that Yahweh's *hesed,* His faithful and merciful covenant love, was still with them on their journey through life as individuals and with Israel, His covenant people, on their journey through history.

Just before the priest placed the body parts of the Tamid, the priestly wafer, and the grain offering on the altar fire, the Temple Superintendent gave a signal, and the faithful standing in the Court of Israel turned their attention from the sacrificial altar in the courtyard and looked toward the west, directing their gaze toward the Temple Sanctuary where the cloud of the burning incense came spilling out of the entrance to the Sanctuary. At this moment in the morning liturgy, the assembled congregation knelt, spread their hands in prayer and then bowed their heads, facing toward the Temple's Holy of Holies just as they had on the very first morning Tamid service at the foot of Mount Sinai when God miraculously consumed their altar sacrifices in holy fire (Lev 9:24).

A profound silence fell upon the congregation and spread across the entire Temple complex. The people were offering Yahweh the essence of their lives in submission and humility in the smoke from burning flesh of the Tamid lamb that rose off the altar in the white cloud of the *Olah*. And they were offering their prayers and petitions in the smoke of the burning incense spilling out of the Sanctuary doors into the courtyard and rising from the earthly Temple to God's heavenly Temple. The people, filled with gratitude and love for the God of Israel as they witnessed what they believed were the visible signs of God's Divine Presence and His faithful covenant love for His people (*Mishnah: Tamid*, 7:3O-Q; Lk 1:8-10; Edersheim, *The Temple: Its Ministry and Services*, page 128).[6]

Before the destruction of the First Temple, the Holy of Holies housed the Ark of the Covenant and its golden lid, the Mercy-seat (Seat of Atonement), the footstool of God's heavenly throne and His earthly throne of mercy (1 Chr 28:2; 99:5). The Ark did not return when the exiles and the other pieces of sacred furniture returned after the seventy years of exile in Babylon. It remained lost to the covenant people, and the Holy of Holies became an empty room (2 Mac 2:4-5). However, the covenant people still believed God's unseen presence resided in the sacred space that provided a supernatural connection between Heaven and earth.

It was then time for the concluding blessing of the morning worship service. The chief priests assembled on the porch steps that led into the Holy Place to bless the congregation. The five priests who had the duty of preparing the Holy Place stood to the south of their fellow priests, holding the five sacred vessels used in their ministrations. The other priests lifted their hands in preparation for the final blessing as the people knelt again in prayerful worship. The priestly blessing intoned a three-time repetition of God's Divine Name, obedient to the command God gave Aaron and his sons in pronouncing His Divine blessing over the covenant people (*Mishnah Tamid*, 7:2; Sir 50:20-22):

> *May Yahweh bless you and keep you.*
> *May Yahweh let his face shine on you and*
> *be gracious to you.*
> *May Yahweh show you his face and*
> *bring you peace* (Num 6:24-26 NJB).

THE AFTERNOON TAMID LITURGY

Let my prayer be counted as incense before thee, and the lifting up of my hands as an evening sacrifice!
Psalms 141:2
(their "evening" equates to our "afternoon")

The priests are appointed to go into the temple but at certain hours: for, in the morning, at the opening of the inner

temple, those that are to officiate receive the sacrifices, as they do again at noon.
Flavius Josephus, *Against Apion 2.8 [105]*

The afternoon liturgical service of the second Tamid lamb repeated the ritual of the morning sacrifice but with a few modifications. The purification of the Bronze Altar of Sacrifice in the Court of the Priests was omitted; they did not remove the ashes from the altar until the next morning. The priests chosen by lot for the morning service repeated their duties in the afternoon, except for the priest who drew the lot to offer the incense if the High Priest was not presiding. Another priest was selected by lot to offer the holy incense on the golden Altar of Incense in the Sanctuary for the afternoon service. It was the only lot drawn for the afternoon service. In addition, more wood was needed for the altar to provide for the fire to burn throughout the night. It was the practice according to Yahweh's command: Yahweh spoke to Moses and said: "Give these orders to Aaron and his sons: 'This is the ritual for the burnt offering that is, the burnt offering that stays on the altar brazier all night until morning and is consumed by the altar fire'" (Lev 6:1-2 NJB [6:8-10 RSV]).

The only other change in the afternoon service was the order for burning the incense and offering of the Tamid victim on the altar fire. In the morning service, the burning of the incense took place before the Tamid lamb's body parts, the grain offerings, and the other sacrifices were placed on the altar's fire. These were then followed by the pouring out of the wine libation which signaled the beginning of the concluding rites of the service. But in the afternoon worship service, the incensing priest burned the incense on the Altar of Incense in the Holy Place after placing of the body of the Tamid lamb on the altar (*Mishnah: Yoma*, 2:5; 3:5; Edersheim, The Temple: Its Ministry and Services, page 132). In this way, the offering of the prayers of the covenant people in the burning of the holy incense embraced the two parts of the single communal sacrifice of the Tamid, coming before the burning of the morning Tamid lamb and after the afternoon Tamid lamb was laid on the altar fire (Philo, Special Laws I, 171).

The ritual of service for the afternoon sacrifice began by bringing the second unblemished, male Tamid lamb into the courtyard. The time was fixed by the Law of the Covenant as "between the twilights (plural) of the day," which was noon or the sixth hour Jewish time (Ex 29:41; Num 28:4, 8; *Mishnah: Tamid* 4:1F-G; Josephus,

Against Apion, 2.8 [105]). At noon when the sun was directly overhead, the second lamb was brought out from the Lamb Chamber. It was inspected for the last time by the priests and given a drink from a golden bowl before tying it near the altar and remained there for everyone to judge its perfection until the hour of sacrifice.

Flavius Josephus (AD 37-100), a Jewish priest who ministered in the Temple's Tamid liturgy during the last years before the Temple's destruction in AD 70, wrote that the sacrifice of the second lamb took place when the Temple doors opened at about the ninth hour Jewish time (3 PM). The ninth hour was the appointed time for the second hour of prayer, known as Minhah (gift/tribute-offering). Writing about the liturgical sacrifice of the Tamid lambs that took place during the Roman army's historic assault on Jerusalem in 63 BC, Josephus recorded that the dedication of the priests to this holy covenant sacrifice was so great that even when their brother priests were dying around them in the Roman attack: the priests were not at all hindered from their sacred ministrations by their fear during this siege, but did still twice each day, in the morning and about the ninth hour, offer their sacrifices on the altar (Josephus, *Antiquities of the Jews*, 14.4.3 [65]; emphasis added).

It is important to note that Josephus' identification of the time of the afternoon worship service that began at three in the afternoon agrees with Scripture's identification of the hour of afternoon prayer:

- Acts 3:1 ~ Saints Peter and John were going up to the Temple at the hour of prayer, the ninth hour (3 PM).
- Acts 10:3 ~ The Gentile "God-fearer" Cornelius was saying his prayers at about the ninth hour (3 PM) when an angel visited him.
- Acts 10:30 ~ St. Peter says: At this time three days ago I was in my house saying the prayers for the ninth hour (3 PM).

In these passages, Scripture identifies the ninth hour as the time for "evening"/afternoon private prayer (Acts 3:1) that coincided with the afternoon Temple worship service of the Tamid.

For the sacrifice and liturgical service to have begun on the half hour as *Mishnah: Pesahim* 5:1 records, in contradiction of Josephus' statement that the afternoon Tamid lamb was sacrificed at the ninth hour (3 PM), does not fit with the even hourly division that is evident in the order of both services. The first ritual commenced at dawn (about 6 AM), the first sacrifice at the third hour from dawn (9 AM), the second ritual began at noon, which was the sixth hour, and the second sacrifice at the ninth hour (3 PM), with each division at the beginning of the hour. It does not seem reasonable that the orderly division that marked the morning ritual was not present in the afternoon service with the sacrifice and the beginning of the worship service occurring two and a half hours from the beginning of the ritual that started at noon. The time order of the daily liturgical services, beginning at dawn and ending at approximately five in the evening, is reflected in Jesus' parable in Matthew 20:1-16 in which the "Master" (God) seeks laborers at dawn, the third hour (9 AM), the sixth hour (noon), the ninth hour (3 PM), and finally at the eleventh hour (5 PM). There is a reason the Mishnah, written approximately seventy years after Jesus' resurrection (c. AD 200) during the period of the reshaping of Jewish religious practices without a Temple and in conflict with early Christianity, disagrees with earlier accounts concerning the time of the afternoon Tamid sacrifice, which will be addressed later.

As in the morning service, the priests blew the silver trumpets announcing the concluding rites of the afternoon worship service as the wine libation was poured out at the altar. At this time, the Levitical chorus and all the faithful gathered in the Temple came together to lift their voices in prayer and praise for

God's blessings. They sang songs of thanksgiving like Psalms 134, designated in Scripture for the afternoon liturgy: *Come, bless Yahweh, all you who serve Yahweh, serving in the house of Yahweh in the courts of the house of our God. Through the night watches stretch out your hands toward the sanctuary and bless Yahweh* (Ps 134:1-2, NJB).

The afternoon service was often shorter than the morning liturgy since most individuals brought their voluntary sacrifices to the Altar of Burnt Offerings in the morning. The afternoon worship service concluded at about five in the evening (the eleventh-hour Jewish time) when all aspects of Temple worship and sacrifice ceased. It was necessary to end by the eleventh hour to permit the priests and Levites enough time to cleanse the Court of the Priests before sundown (Josephus, *The Wars of the Jews* 6.9.3 [423]). The second Tamid lamb was left slowly burning on the Altar of Burnt Offerings all through the night (Lev 6:8-9/6:1-2). There were no worship services at night except during the Feast of Tabernacles (Sukkot) in the "Ceremony of Lights" which was in addition to the morning and afternoon Tamid worship services (*Mishnah: Sukkah*, 5:2-5:4).

The only exception to the liturgical time requirements in the daily sacrifice of the Tamid lambs at nine in the morning and three in the afternoon occurred during the Passover Sacrifice when the afternoon sacrifice was advanced to accommodate for the large number of lambs and goat-kids sacrificed for the Passover. However, even on the holy feast days, including the Sabbath, the three pilgrim feasts, the other annual feasts of "remembrance," and the monthly Feast of the New Moon, the daily Tamid was not allowed to be omitted but had precedence over all the other festival sacrifices (Num 28-29).

THE IMPORTANCE OF THE TAMID AND THE RITUAL OF SACRIFICE IN SALVATION HISTORY

It was through the purity rites of the covenant, the rituals of the sacrificial system, the shared sacred meals, the holy festivals, and the liturgy of the daily Tamid worship services that Yahweh prepared His people for the coming of the Redeemer-Messiah. It was during the annual remembrance feasts that generations of Israelites relived the themes of judgment and death in contrast to Yahweh's blessings in the gift of the redemption and salvation of Israel (Ex. 12:13). The reliving of these themes was especially significant during the Feast of Unleavened Bread where the faithful consumed the Passover sacrifice in a sacred meal, remembered Egypt's death judgment and the children of Israel's redemption under the "sign" of the blood of the sacrificed Passover victims smeared in a cruciform across the doors of their houses from the threshold to the lintel above the door, to both door-posts (Ex 12:12-14, 21-25).

These liturgical services, rituals, and festivals became the backdrop for the momentous climax of God's plan of redemption for His covenant people's liberation from slavery to sin and death. Through a new exodus, inaugurated by the promised Redeemer-Messiah as the new Moses, God planned to one day lead His people out of slavery to sin and free them from the curses of their ancestors' disobedience to the covenant. Jesus' mission, as the new Moses, was to save His people under the "sign" of the blood sacrifice in a new exodus liberation from sin and death. At the appointed time in salvation history, the promised "seed of the Woman," Jesus, the Son of God, stepped across the threshold of time to battle Satan for the souls of humanity. He came to willingly offer Himself as the one perfect sacrifice for the sins of the world within the timeframe of the sacred Old Covenant Passover sacrifice, the pilgrim feast of Unleavened Bread, and in fulfillment of the communal blood sacrifice of the Tamid Temple liturgy.

It was at Mount Sinai that Yahweh established the formal ritual requirements of liturgical worship united to sacrifice. The first blood sacrifice ordained by Yahweh for the covenant people collectively until the sin of the Golden Calf was the single sacrifice of the daily burnt offering (holocaust) known as the *'olat ha-Tamid*, "the burnt standing" as in a continual/perpetual whole sacrifice. The repeated link between covenant formation and blood after the Fall of man established that the blood of sacrifice had a threefold purpose in God's plan for humanity:

- Blood is the chief agent in covenant making and covenant continuation.
- Blood is the chief agent in expiation for sins.
- Blood is the chief agent in re-establishing fellowship with Yahweh.

These functions were continually present in the rhythm of worship celebrated in the liturgical calendar of Temple liturgy. But the Tamid remained the first and most holy sacrifice of the Sinai Covenant, a single sacrifice offered on Yahweh's sacred altar twice daily and perpetually for the atonement and sanctification of the covenant people and the future salvation of humanity. The covenant people believed that the Tamid was to endure until the end of the Sinai Covenant and the coming of the Redeemer-Messiah (*The JPS Torah*

Commentary: Leviticus, page 43; Dan 12:11). In the fullness of time, there was going to be a new exodus and the formation of a new covenant on another holy mountain. At that time, the unblemished Lamb of God, prefigured by the Tamid sacrifice, was to become the stone that shattered the Old Covenant holy mountain to build a new and eternal covenant and a new Kingdom that could never be destroyed (Jer 31:31-34; Dan 2:44-45).

CHAPTER SUMMARY POINTS: DAILY WORSHIP IN THE JERUSALEM TEMPLE

1. The daily liturgical life of the covenant people and the focus of the entire sacrificial system revolved around the Tamid sacrifice.

2. As the first sacrifice ordained for the covenant community, the Tamid was to be a perpetual sacrifice offered on God's holy altar so long as the Sinai Covenant with Israel endured.

3. Biblical covenants are formed and maintained within the context of sacrifice, blood ritual, oath swearing, and the eating of a sacred meal. All the

classes of blood sacrifice presented on the altar of the Jerusalem Temple affirmed that without the shedding of blood, there was no remission of sin and no re-established fellowship with God.

4. The sacrificed animal was a substitution for the offeror; therefore, the confession of sin accompanied a sin sacrifice just as communion sacrifices included a confession of praise and thanksgiving. The members of the ordained priesthood heard the peoples' confessions as God's representatives and had the authority to forgive unintentional sin in God's name (Num 15:27-31).

5. The repeated link between covenant formation and blood sacrifice after the Fall of Adam established blood sacrifice as the chief agent in covenant making and covenant continuation, the chief agent in expiation for sins, and the chief agent in re-establishing fellowship with Yahweh.

Endnotes: Daily Worship in the Jerusalem Temple

1. The trumpet signal of the "cockcrow" is mentioned several times in the Jewish Talmud (e.g., *Mishnah: Sukkah*, 5.4; *Mishnah: Tamid*, 1:2E; and *Mishnah: Yoma*, 1:8). Other references to the trumpet signal of the "cockcrow" appear in the writings of St. Hippolytus (c. AD 170-235). He referred to the early hour of prayers by the faithful after "cockcrow" in Canons 27 and stated that at

"cockcrow" prayers were always said in worship services in obedience to evangelical counsel). The hour of "cockcrow" is also mentioned in the Apostolic Constitution (an early document of the Church compiled from even earlier writings and dated to c. AD 325). The Apostolic Constitutions, item 8, records six hours of Christian prayer: (1) at dawn, (2) at the third hour (9 AM), (3) the sixth hour (noon), and (4) the ninth (3 PM) hour; (5) in the evening, and (6) at the "cockcrow" (3 AM). St. Jerome (d. 420) mentions the same six hours of prayer and includes a reference to the time-marker signal of "cockcrow" (Fr. Raymond Brown, The Gospel According to John, page 828; Jeremias, Jerusalem in the Time of Jesus, pages 47-48, note 44). Also see Ancient Christian Writers, vol. 38 which identifies the "cockcrow" as a trumpet signal: "Introduction," pages 47 and 30; the fourth-century account of Egeria, a nun's pilgrimage to the Holy Land: Ancient Christian Writers: Diary of a Pilgrimage, translated and annotated by George E. Gingras, Newman Press, 1970 (see pages 89, 91, 92, 97, 98, 103, 105, 107, 108, 117, 118, 121 and chapter notes on pages 154 and 215). In Jerusalem during the Roman occupation, there were two "cockcrow" signals at 3 AM: one trumpet announced "cockcrow" by the Watch of the Temple Levites within the Temple precincts and the other by the Roman soldiers in the Antonia fortress (see Mk 14:30 where Jesus mentions the two "cockcrow" signals).

2. There were three types of voluntary communion sacrifices: the Todah "Thanksgiving" offering, the Neder vow offering, and the Nedavah voluntary offering, which on feast days was called the Hagigah/Chagigah, literally the "festival" communion offering (Lev 7:11/7:1-17/7; 19:5-8; 22:18-25; Num 6:13-20; JPS Commentary: Leviticus, pages 42-44; *Mishnah: Hagigah*).

3. Goldhill, *The Temple of Jerusalem*, page 73; Josephus, *Antiquities of the Jews*, 7.14.7 [363-67]. Accounts estimate that from 300-700 priests served at the Temple every week from Sabbath to Sabbath

during non-festival weeks, not counting Levites (Josephus, Antiquities of the Jews, 7.14.7 [365]; Jeremias, Jerusalem in the Time of Jesus, pages 198-207). For the three pilgrim feasts, all twenty-four courses of the priesthood and the twenty-four courses of the Levites were present at the Temple (Jeremias, Jerusalem at the Time of Jesus, page 160, 163-65).

4. For the use of lots, see Josephus, *Antiquities of the Jews*, 7.14.7 [366] and Acts 1:23-26 for the Apostles' selection of Matthias as Judas' replacement by drawing lots.

5. For the prohibition against priests and Levites wearing sandals during ministerial service in the Temple, see Edersheim, *The Temple: Its Ministry and Services*, page 109; A History of the Jewish People in the Time of Jesus Christ, Division ii, vol. I, page 278.

6. The silence of reverent prayer at the time of the incense offering recalls St. John's vision in Revelation 8:1-4 when he saw the heavenly Altar of Incense and heard the prayers of the saints, followed by a profound silence that filled the heavenly Sanctuary. Those who celebrate the sacrifice of the Catholic Mass experience the same profound silence immediately after receiving the Eucharist and before the concluding rites.

CHAPTER V
THE ADVENT OF THE MESSIAH

"Behold, the days are coming, says the LORD, when I will make a new covenant with the house of Israel and the house of Judah, not like the covenant which I made with their fathers when I took them by the hand to bring them out of the land of Egypt, my covenant which they broke, though I was their husband, says the LORD. But this is the covenant which I will make with the house of Israel after these days, says the LORD: I will put my law within them, and I will write it upon their hearts; and I will be their God, and they shall be my people. And no longer shall each man teach his neighbor and teach his brother, saying 'Know the LORD,' for they shall know me, from the least of them to the greatest, says the LORD; for I will forgive their iniquity, and I will remember their sin no more."

Jeremiah 31:31–34

My little children, I am writing this to you so that you may not sin; but if any one does sin, we have an advocate with the Father, Jesus Christ the righteous; and he is the expiation for our sins, and not for ours only but also for the sins of the whole world.

1 John 2:1–2

At the precise moment in salvation history determined by God for the opening chords of the Messiah's symphony of salvation and His repeated refrain of faith and repentance to mark the future of all human history, an angel appeared to a priest named Zechariah. The elderly priest was burning the incense on the golden Altar of Incense in the Holy Place of the Jerusalem Temple during the liturgy of the Tamid sacrifice (Lk 1:9-10). Earlier that week, Zechariah traveled to Jerusalem with his brother priests who were descendants of Aaron from the clan of Abijah (1 Chr 24:1, 10, 19; Lk 1:5). They came from their village in the Judean hill country to fulfill their week-long obligation to serve God in the offering of the twice-daily Tamid and the other sacrifices in the Jerusalem Temple (Lk 1:8). The last time Zechariah served in the Temple was during the most recent pilgrim feast when all the priestly clans gathered in Jerusalem to offer ministerial service to the God of Israel. Zechariah had reached a venerable old age, and he knew his years of serving God in His holy Temple were coming to an end.

ZECHARIAH'S REVELATION DURING THE RITUAL OF THE TAMID SACRIFICE

Behold, I will send you Elijah the prophet before the great and terrible day of the LORD comes. And he will turn the hearts of fathers to their children and the hearts of children to their fathers, lest I come and smite the land with a curse.
Malachi 4:5 (3:23-24)

While I was speaking and praying, confessing my sin and the sin of my people Israel, and presenting my supplication before the LORD my God for the holy hill of my God; while I was speaking in prayer, the man Gabriel, whom I had seen in the vision at the first, came to me in swift flight at the time of the evening [afternoon] sacrifice.
Daniel 9:20-21

The first sight of the Temple, gleaming on the heights of Mount Moriah, must have filled Zechariah and his brother priests with pride and awe. Herod, the Roman vassal king, was despised by orthodox Jews as an interloper whose rule was contrary to the covenant command that only a descendant of Jacob-Israel could rule as the king of the covenant people (Dt 17:15). Herod was not a Jew. He was an Idumaean, a descendant of Esau, the son of Isaac and the twin brother of Jacob-Israel who was the ancestral father of the twelve tribes of Israel. However, Herod deserves credit for taking the humble little structure that was the Second Temple built by the faithful remnant of the exiles that returned from Babylon and turning it into one of the most beautiful buildings in the world. Hoping to win over the hearts of the people, Herod began the rebuilding project of the modest post-exile Temple in c. 20/19 BC, doubling the area covered by the former Temple complex.1 After finishing the central part of the Sanctuary, the ordained ministerial priesthood consecrated the Temple, but the embellishments of the outer courts, cloisters, and storerooms remained a work in progress for many decades (Jn 2:20). Word of its beauty spread across the Roman world, and it became a saying that he who has not seen Herod's building has never seen anything beautiful (Schurer, The History of the Jewish People in the Time of Jesus Christ, Division i, vol. I, page 438).

Built with exquisitely polished white stone, the Temple glittered in the bright morning sun and glowed in the soft light of sunset. A huge golden grapevine embellished with grapes and leaves covered the entrance of the Sanctuary and hung from beams above the Sanctuary doors (*Mishnah: Middot*, 3:8F). Behind the doors that led into the Sanctuary hung the first of two embroidered curtains, interwoven with threads of linen, blue-violet, purple and crimson. The second embroidered curtain hung within the Sanctuary and separated the Holy Place from the Holy of Holies. The

Jews believed that the Holy of Holies was the supernatural link between the earthly Temple and Yahweh's heavenly Temple. Large cloisters encompassed the entire Sanctuary, and there were several inner courts, including the Court of the Priests (where the sacrificial altar stood), the Court of Israel, and the Court of the Women. There was also the large outer court called the Court of the Gentiles. It was within this space that the other peoples of the earth were welcomed to come to offer their sacrifices and to learn about the One True God, allowing the covenant people to perform their mission as the "light" of Yahweh to the pagan Gentiles (Is 42:6).

The preparation for the day's morning Tamid worship service began before dawn. Like the other priests, the drawing of lots would determine Zechariah's duties that day. Those who wanted to participate in the first round of lots had to rise before the "hour of cockcrow," at the beginning of the Fourth Watch (3 AM). They had to purify themselves by ritual immersion in the pool of the Temple mikveh before dressing in under-drawers and the priestly linen tunic, sash, and headpiece. Sometimes the younger priests were kind enough to add heated water to the pool for elderly priests like Zechariah.

At about 3 AM, alerted by the trumpet signal of the "cockcrow," the Temple Superintendent called the priests of Abijah who were assigned to that day's service to come to the Chamber of Hewn Stone. The drawing of the first-round of lots selected the priests who were to remove the ashes from the fire that had been burning throughout the night on the bronze sacrificial altar in the inner courtyard and to cleanse and prepare it for the morning sacrifice. The older priests like Zechariah often left the first-round of lots to the younger priests.

After the priests prepared the sacrificial Altar of Burnt Offerings, Zechariah and his brother priests, who had ritually bathed and dressed in their liturgical garments, reassembled in the Chamber of Hewn Stones for the drawing of the second round of lots. The priests who drew the lots in the second drawing were assigned duties at the Altar of Burnt Offerings. Priests were also selected to prepare the Sanctuary's Holy Place. Zechariah did not receive an assignment in this drawing.

While the priests were meeting in the Chamber of Hewn Stones, the Levitical lesser ministers, who served the chief priests in the Temple and whose clan was also in service for their weekly duty, saw to the firing of the Temple ovens and preparing the dough for the unleavened wafer offering of the high priest. The men serving in the Levitical choir and orchestra were awakened to rehearse the choral arrangements for the day's service, and other Levites carried out the many necessary preparations that did not require the attention of the chief priests. The Levites, however, were not allowed to enter the main Sanctuary or the Chamber of Hewn Stones, nor were they permitted to touch any of the sacred vessels or serve at the Altar of Sacrifice.

When a Levite positioned on the pinnacle of the Temple announced that the first rays of dawn were visible, a priest led the first unblemished, male Tamid lamb out from the Lamb Chamber. After the High Priest (or his representative) inspected the Tamid lamb one last time and announced "I find no fault" with the victim, it received a drink from a golden cup and a priest tied it to a post on the north side of the sacrificial altar. Zechariah did not know it, but this was the beginning of the most momentous day of his long life.

At about 9 AM, the silver trumpets announced the beginning of the morning liturgy. As the morning Tamid lamb was sacrificed, Levites threw open the gates to admit the faithful to the Temple complex. The doors that led into the Temple Sanctuary were also opened to allow the priests who were assigned various duties to prepare the Holy Place. It must have warmed the old man's heart to see so many of the covenant faithful streaming through the gates into the Temple precincts for the morning worship service.

When the designated Tamid man confessed the sins of the people and slit the throat of the lamb of the morning Tamid, a priest immediately collected the blood of the lamb in a golden chalice and splashed it against the altar. The priests then hung the body of the lamb on a pole and skinned it before placing the body on a marble table where it was cut into pieces and washed in preparation for the sacrificial altar. In the meantime, Zechariah's brother priests, those who drew the lots to minister in the Sanctuary's Holy Place, went about their duties.

After the preparation of the Holy Place (lighting the Menorah and cleaning the Altar of Incense), other priests in the courtyard skinned the body of the Tamid lamb and cut it into sections. Then, after the priestly procession of the gifts, it was laid on the ramp that led up to the altar to where priests salted all the offerings. At this point in the service, Zechariah and all the priests assigned to that day's service assembled once again in the Chamber of Hewn Stones. The assembled priests of the clan of Abijah, together with the High Priest, the Superintendent, and the other permanent Temple priests joined together in reciting the prescribed prayers. After the opening blessing, Zechariah and his brother priests repeated the Ten Commandments followed by the Shema (Dt 6:4-9, 11:13-21, and Num 15:37-41), and then they blessed the people with three blessings.

If this was the afternoon service, at the end of the priestly ceremony, it was time for the drawing of the lot that selected the priest who was to have the great honor of burning the incense in the Holy Place. The lot for burning the sacred incense was the only lot drawing repeated in the afternoon worship service, and only priests who had never had this honor before were eligible to participate (unless every priest present had previously had the honor). Since Zechariah had never drawn the lot for burning the incense, he stepped forward to take his turn.

According to the ordinances of the Sinai Covenant, only men descended from Aaron, the first High Priest, were permitted to burn the sacred incense for the morning and afternoon worship services (Ex 30:6-7). The High Priest burned the incense on festival days, but it was acceptable for a brother priest to serve as the High Priest's representative on non-festival days. To offer incense improperly, or to offer incense without authorization was to incur the wrath of God. In the past, men died for committing such offenses, including two sons of Aaron, rebellious lesser ministers of the tribe of Levi, and God even inflicted a Judahite king with leprosy for attempting to usurp the priestly prerogative of burning the incense (Lev 10:1–2; Num 16:1–7, 16–19, 35, 40; 2 Chr 26:16–21).

Now while he was serving as priest before God when his division was on duty, according to the custom of the priesthood, it fell to him by lot to enter the Temple of the Lord and burn incense (Lk 1:8–9). When Zechariah drew the lot to burn the incense, he must have gasped in shock. For many years, he had been unsuccessful in drawing the third lot. He knew that it was during the offering of the sacred incense during the Tamid worship service that a priest was most apt to receive a revelation from God. About a century earlier, the High Priest John Hyrcanus was blessed with a divine revelation as he offered the incense during the Tamid liturgy (Josephus, *Antiquities of the Jews* 8.10.3).

Except for the High Priest who entered the Holy of Holies once a year during the Feast of Atonement (Lev 16:2, 34), no other priest came so close to the Divine Presence of God. The priest who offered up the prayers of the people in the burning of the sacred incense in the morning and afternoon Tamid services stood at the entrance to the Holy of Holies, the dwelling place of God among His people. To be selected to burn the incense for the Tamid sacrifice was a once-in-a-lifetime event, and the pious, elderly Zechariah must have felt both humbled and especially blessed to be chosen by God through the lot drawing for this very holy act of priestly service. The covenant people believed that an angel carried the prayers of the people, enveloped by the sweet-smelling incense, into the heavenly Sanctuary, laying the people's petitions before the throne of Yahweh (Rev 5:8; 8:1-4).

Zechariah immediately selected two other priests to assist him in this most sacred of priestly duties, most likely choosing members of his immediate family as was the custom. As he conferred with the priests who would assist him, brother priests in the clan of Abijah not selected for service removed their liturgical garments and hung them on hooks in the chamber. They would leave in their underpants and dress in secular clothing before joining other worshipers in the Court of Israel (Ez 44:19).

Zechariah and the other priests selected for service followed the High Priest from the Chamber of Hewn Stone into the Court of the Priests. They ritually sanctified their hands and feet, washing them in the Temple water purification laver located between the altar and the Sanctuary porch before approaching the altar of sacrifice to continue the offering of the Tamid sacrifice. The ritually clean men of the covenant watched from the colonnades to the sides of the courtyard, and the women watched from the balconies above the Court of the Women as one of the priests Zechariah selected to assist him walked up the ramp to the sacrificial altar. Zechariah's assisting priest took embers from the altar fire and placed them in a golden vessel while the second assisting priest spooned the sacred incense into Zechariah's golden censer. Then Zechariah and his brother priests turned and slowly walked, with great reverence and dignity, from the Court of the Priests toward the steps of the portico that led into the Sanctuary.

When they reached the half-way point between the altar and the Sanctuary, Zechariah glanced at the assisting priest carrying the fire-pan and its shovel. Immediately he threw down the shovel that made a loud clang upon the stone pavement of the courtyard. The sound was the signal that the incensing priest was approaching the Sanctuary. As he climbed the steps of the Sanctuary's portico, Zechariah may have looked up to admire the beautiful golden vines full of gold leaves and grapes that decorated the outer wall of the Sanctuary's entrance and the equally beautiful golden oil lamp suspended from the porch ceiling. The oil lamp burned continually, acknowledging the presence of God within the Sanctuary. It was a gift from a righteous Gentile convert, Queen Helena of Adiabene (*Mishnah: Yoma* 3:10; *Antiquities of the Jews* 20.2.1-6; 20.4.3).

Zechariah and his brother priests walked through the double doors, past the beautifully embroidered curtain, and entered into the Holy Place of the Temple. As they walked into the Holy Place, a priest struck the magrefah. Its deep tone reverberated far into the city of Jerusalem and across the Mount of Olives to the east, announcing that the incense was about to be offered and the people's prayers, enveloped in the holy smoke, was to be carried by an angel to God in His heavenly Sanctuary.

Zechariah and his two assisting priests walked the length of the Holy Place to the golden Altar of Incense that stood at the end of the room in front of the magnificent curtain that separated the Holy Place from the Holy of Holies. As they walked to the west end of the Holy Place, they must have admired the curtain, richly embroidered on the front and the back with crimson, blue and purple wool threads and with fine twined linen. The curtain, hung by golden rings, was as thick as a man's hand.

When the three priests arrived at the end of the room, they stopped in front of the Altar of Incense. The priest carrying the live coals from the sacrificial altar stepped forward and reverently placed the embers on the Altar of Incense. After the first priest positioned the burning embers, the second priest stepped forward to spoon the incense on to a corner of the altar's recessed top but not on the glowing embers. The two assisting priests prostrated themselves in front of the incense altar, facing the Holy of Holies, and then rising they stepped back and turned around to retrace their steps to the entrance. The other priests still in the Holy Place accompanied them, leaving Zechariah utterly alone in the sacred space.

As he waited for the signal to offer the incense, Zechariah must have admired the beautiful inner altar that was a copy of the heavenly incense altar Moses saw when God instructed him to build the furnishings for the earthly Sanctuary (Ex 25:9). The incense altar was a small gold-covered column with a square top. It was twice as tall as it was wide, and it stood about the height of his chest. Its recessed gold top had four horn-like protrusions at each of its four corners, and the top was trimmed with a golden fence to contain the coals and the incense (Ex 30:1-10). In those moments, Zechariah prayed; he must have prayed for the deepest desire of his heart. Zechariah and his wife had no children, but he continually prayed for a child to carry on his name. It was an impossible petition for an old man with a barren old wife, but his God was the God of impossible petitions (Lk 1:5-7).

The chief priest who served as the Temple Superintendent stood at the door to the Sanctuary, waiting to give the command that it was time to offer the incense. If this was the morning service, he gave the command before the presiding chief priest placed the body of the Tamid lamb and the grain offerings on the altar fire. If it was the afternoon service, he did not give the command until after the placing of the body of the lamb and the grain offerings on the fire. The sacrifice of the Tamid offered to God on His holy altar, morning and afternoon, had to fall within the two offerings of the incense, identifying the two Tamid lambs as a single sacrifice. As the choir was singing and as the people were praying outside in the Sanctuary, the priest standing at the door of the Sanctuary signaled to Zechariah that it was time to burn the incense. Zechariah stepped forward to complete a service to God that was the climax of his priestly life.

The old priest solemnly approached the Altar of Incense and carefully spooned the incense upon the burning embers. Immediately, sweet-smelling white smoke rose from the incense altar and began to fill the Sanctuary. The congregation in the courtyard was facing the Altar of Burnt Offerings, watching the High

Priest or his representative place the body of the Tamid lamb and the people's other offerings to God upon the sacrificial altar (if it was the afternoon Tamid service). However, when the smoke of the incense began to spill out of the Sanctuary doors, they turned toward the Sanctuary and the Holy of Holies. The people fell to their knees, and then lifting up their hands, they prostrated themselves in prayer and submission to Yahweh, their God.

The choir ceased their songs, and a profound silence enveloped the entire Temple complex. In that moment of silence, as the old priest prepared to prostrate himself in front of the Altar of Incense, he was startled by a sudden movement. As he looked up, he saw an angelic being standing beside the Altar of Incense. The angel may have come from behind the curtain that covered the Holy of Holies, the sacred space that united God's heavenly Sanctuary to His earthly Sanctuary. On this day, the divine messenger had another mission in addition to carrying the prayers of the faithful to Heaven: And the whole multitude of the people were praying outside at the hour of incense. And there appeared to him an angel of the Lord standing on the right side of the altar of incense (Lk 1:10-11). The angel stood to the right of the incense altar, the same position in which he stood by the incense altar in the heavenly Sanctuary (Rev 8:1-3).

The old priest must have been trembling with fear, and so the angel calmed him, telling him there was no reason to be afraid because God heard Zechariah's prayer. The liturgical service of the Tamid continued in the courtyard, and as the music of the Levitical choir and orchestra drifted into the Sanctuary, the angel told Zechariah that he and his wife were to become the parents of a son. The angel commanded Zechariah to name the child Ye'hohanan (rendered in English as "John") which means "Yahweh is gracious." He told the priest that the child, filled with His Spirit in the womb of his mother, was going to be dedicated to God's service in the spirit and power of the great prophet Elijah. Elijah was the holy prophet who called the people of Israel to repentance in the ninth century BC (1 Kng chapters 17-19; Lk 1:12-17).

This revelation was more than the old man could comprehend. In shock and disbelief, he protested saying, "How shall I know this? For I am an old man, and my wife is advanced in years" (Lk 1:18). The angel answered the old man's question by revealing his name as he said, "I am Gabriel, who stand in the presence of God" (Lk 1:19). Then the angel silenced the priest, striking him dumb and telling him that his inability to speak was to continue until the birth of the child. The name of the angel, coupled with the name of the prophet Elijah that the angel used in his prophecy for the child was all Zechariah needed. With his knowledge of Sacred Scripture, the old priest could comprehend the significance of the announcement of the birth of his son and the promise of the One who was to follow.

Zechariah must have remembered that this angel's name was only revealed twice in the sacred scrolls, and that was in the Book of the Daniel (Dan 8:16 and 9:21). Gabriel was the same angel who appeared in the sixth century BC to the prophet Daniel while he was in exile in Babylon. Daniel, like Zechariah, also experienced paralyzing fear at the sight of this powerful angelic being who explained to him, "the coming of the end" (Dan 8:15-17). The old priest must have recalled that on the second visit from the angel Gabriel, when Daniel was at prayer, that it was the hour of the afternoon Tamid sacrifice (Dan 9:20-21). Perhaps it was the same time in which the same angel visited Zechariah.

When Gabriel visited Daniel the second time, he revealed that the seventy years of exile were fulfilled for the people of God to return from Babylon to their homeland in Judah and to rebuild the Temple (Dan 9:24). Zechariah must have remembered that it was Gabriel who gave Daniel the prophecy of three momentous events: the coming of an Anointed One (Messiah) destined by God to die, the end of the Tamid sacrifice, and the destruction of God's Sanctuary (Dan 9:25-27). Zechariah must also have remembered Daniel's vision of the heavenly court and the divine Messiah, rising on a cloud into the presence of the Most Holy God. It was a vision of one who looked like "a son of man" (a human being) who received dominion and kingship over all the nations of the earth, establishing the promised everlasting kingdom (Dan 7:13-14).

The name of the angel must have caused Zechariah to recall the passages in the Scriptures concerning the angel Gabriel, Daniel's prophetic visions, and the mission and the prophecies concerning the prophet Elijah in the scroll of Malachi, the last of the prophets. Knowing there was a link to the birth of his son, Zechariah must have understood the importance of his son's birth in the unfolding events of God's Divine Plan for the covenant people and the salvation of humanity. In the spirit of Elijah, Zechariah's son would call Israel to repentance, and he would herald the coming of the Messianic Age as prophesied by the prophet Malachi (Mal 3:1-5; 4:5-6/3:23-24).

According to the prophecies, the Messiah was coming as Yahweh's premier prophet, priest, and Davidic king to keep the promises made to the

Patriarchs and fulfill the Sinai and Davidic Covenants. He knew it was the Davidic Redeemer-Messiah's destiny to bring the eternal covenant with David to fulfillment and establish the new covenant prophesied by the prophet sixth century BC prophet, Jeremiah (2 Sam 7:16; 23:5; Jer 23:5-6; 31:31-34; 32:39; 50:5). He would be the King of the everlasting kingdom that God revealed to the prophet Daniel (Dan 2:44; 4:3; 7:14, 18, 27) in which all flesh shall see the salvation of God (Is 40:5 NJB). It was surely another miracle that the elderly priest survived such an astounding revelation!

THE ANGEL GABRIEL'S REVELATION TO MARY OF NAZARETH

Six months later (as the ancients counted but five months as we count with a zero place-value), the angel Gabriel made another visitation and another announcement.[2] He appeared to a virgin of the lineage of King David, living in the Galilean village of Nazareth and betrothed to a man of the same Davidic heritage named Joseph (Mt 1:20; Lk 1:26-27). The angel greeted Mary quite differently from the way he greeted the priest Zechariah. Gabriel did not approach Zechariah with the same degree of respect and status as he did with Mary, using an unusual title and without the typical Semitic greeting of shalom *(peace)*. Instead, he greeted her in the Greek text using the word *chare*, which English Bibles usually translate as "hail" or "rejoice," and then he announced Mary's special status, often translated as "full of grace," but that is not the literal Greek rendering of his words to Mary. The angel's first words in the Greek text are *Chare, kecharitomene* [kah-ray kay-kah-ree-toe-may-nay]. He addressed Mary by a title that was a past perfect participle of the Greek noun *charis*, meaning "grace," which renders his greeting *kecharitomene* as "has-been-graced" (Fitzmyer, *Gospel of Luke*, page 345). This tense indicates a condition that existed in the past and continues in the present. In the past as in the present, Mary exists in a state of divine grace. To be "graced" in the past perfect tense is never to have been lacking in God's grace, and it is an indication of Mary's unique conception without original sin. This Greek phrase appears in only one other place in the New Testament in Ephesians 1:6 where St. Paul describes how God's grace has been granted to all Christians in Christ Jesus.

In this way, Gabriel announced to Mary of Nazareth that she was "the Woman" chosen from among all women to give birth to the Son of God (Lk 1:28-33). It was her destiny to fulfill God's promise that a virgin daughter of Isreal would give birth to the Davidic Redeemer-Messiah (Is 7:14; Mt 1:23). It was a promise and prophecy God first made when He cursed the serpent after Adam and Eve's fall from grace and pronounced this judgment: *I will put enmity between you and the woman, and between your seed and her seed; he shall bruise your head, and you shall bruise his heel* (Gen 3:15).

The angel's greeting was not *pleres charitos,* "full of grace," as translated in most versions of Luke 1:28. "Full of grace" is a transliteration of Jerome's Latin Vulgate translation of the Greek text. However, while "full of grace" certainly describes Mary's condition, it is not what was expressed in the Greek past perfect participle *kecharitomene.* John 1:14 describes Jesus Christ as "full of grace," and the same Greek phrase describes St. Stephen in Acts 6:8. Mary's title, *kecharitomene,* indicates a state which is beyond filled. In addressing Mary with this unique title, the angel is signifying that she possesses, and has always possessed, a plentitude of Divine grace (Keating, *Catholicism and Fundamentalism,* page 268-69). That Mary was *deeply disturbed by the angel's greeting* (Lk 1:29) is evidence that someone of her humble station had received a highly unusual salutation.

The Fathers and Doctors of the Church have taught what Pope Pius IX expressed in the encyclical *Ineffabilis*

Deus: "this singular, solemn and unheard-of greeting showed that all the divine graces reposed in the Mother of God and that she was adorned with all the gifts of the Holy Spirit." This singular condition meant that Mary was never subject to the curse of original sin and was preserved from all sin. The theologically explosive words of the angel Gabriel constitute one of the critical text sources which reveal the dogma of Mary's Immaculate Conception (Pius IX, *Ineffabilis Deus*; and Paul VI, *Creed of the People of God*).

The angel told Mary to name God's Son Yahshua/Yeshua (in Hebrew but Yehoshua in the Aramaic of the first century AD), which means "Yahweh saves" or "Yahweh is salvation" (Lk 1:31). It is a name that reflected the child's destiny and rendered as "Iesous" in Greek and "Jesus" in English versions of the New Testament. The angel Gabriel told Mary that the child would inherit the throne of his ancestor David and a kingdom of which there would be no end (Lk 1:31–33). God granted Mary the opportunity to participate in the salvation of humanity in saying "yes" to His divine plan to undo the knot of disobedience wrought by the virgin Eve in a rebellious act which bound humanity in slavery to sin and death down through the centuries.

In exercising her free will, just as the virgin Eve employed her free will, the Virgin Mary courageously spoke her *fiat* in her formal declaration: *"Behold, I am the handmaiden of the Lord, let it be done to me according to your word"* (Lk 1:38). At the moment of her submission to the will of God the Father, God the Holy Spirit overshadowed her just as God's presence overshadowed the Ark of the Covenant when He took possession of the desert Sanctuary (Ex 40:34; Lk 1:35). [3] In the Incarnation of Jesus, Mary's womb became the Ark of the New Covenant, bearing the enfleshed Living Word of God.[4]

In the sixth century BC, the prophet Jeremiah prophesied that in the Messianic Age the Ark of the Covenant that held the word of God in the covenant document of the Ten Commandments would no longer be the focus of faith (Jer 3:16). God promised through His prophet that He would create something new on earth: *For Yahweh is creating something new on earth: a woman shall enclose a man* (Jer 31:22; literal Hebrew translation IBHE vol. III, page 1817) and bring about a new and eternal covenant (Jer 31:31; 32:40; 50:5). Jeremiah's prophecy that "a woman will enclose a man" is a reversal of the "something new on earth" in the time of Adam when the woman Eve was born from Adam's body (Gen 2:21-22). Mary's womb became the well-spring of the New Creation.

As the late sixth century BC prophet Micah foretold, Mary gave birth to the promised Messiah in the hometown of his ancestor, King David, the Judean village of Bethlehem (Rt 1:1-2; 4:13-18; Mic 5:2; Lk 2:4-7). It was within walking distance of Jerusalem and where the herds of the Tamid lambs grazed before their selection for sacrifice. Perhaps the shepherds who were the first to receive the angelic announcement of the birth of the Messiah were the same shepherds who guarded the flocks of the Tamid lambs.

It was ironic that shepherds were the first humans chosen to receive this divine birth announcement (Lk 2:8-20). The legalistic religious and political sect of the Pharisees considered shepherds to be in a continual state of ritual impurity because of the demands of their profession. Herdsmen were one of the "despised trades," and they could not give testimony in a Jewish court of law (*The Works of Philo: On Husbandry*, 61; Jeremias, *Jerusalem in the Time of Jesus*, pages 304, 311). Once again, God affirmed His love for the poor and disadvantaged in choosing not kings but simple shepherds to receive the announcement of the birth of the King of kings.[5]

The prophets foretold that the Redeemer-Messiah would come from the lineage of father Abraham and the great King David. The legal genealogy of Jesus' adopted father, Joseph in the Gospel of Matthew, and the physical link in Mary's genealogy in the Gospel of Luke establish the fulfillment of those prophecies (Mt 1:1; Lk 3:31, 35). St. Matthew's Gospel begins Jesus' genealogy by naming the two men from Jesus' family line who had visionary revelations of the divine on Mount Moriah in Jerusalem: Abraham and David. The visions of both men are unique, and both men had a profound impact on salvation history:

1. God formed unconditional and everlasting covenants with both Abraham and David before their visionary experiences (Gen 15:18; 17:2, 4, 7; 2 Sam 23:5).
2. Both men experienced visions and divine intervention on Mount Moriah (Gen 22:1–18; 2 Sam 24:16–17; 1 Chr 21:14–19, 28).
3. Both men passed the test of a covenant ordeal (Gen 22:2; 2 Sam 24:1, 17; 1 Chr 21:17).
4. The tests of both men involved sacrifice (Gen 22:2; 1 Chr 21:17).
5. The sons of both men (Isaac and Solomon) had prominent roles in salvation history because of their fathers' visionary experiences (Gen 22:2; 1 Chr 22:1–11).
6. The visions of Abraham and David resulted in the selection of Jerusalem as God's holy city of

sacrifice and worship, the building of Yahweh's altar on the summit of the mountain, and later the building of God's "house," the Jerusalem Temple (Gen 22:9; 2 Sam 24:18-19; 1 Chr 21:18-19, 26; 2 Chr 3:1).

7. Both men are Jesus of Nazareth's ancestors, as revealed in the first line of St. Matthew's Gospel: *The book of the genealogy of Jesus Christ, son of David, son of Abraham* (Mt 1:1).

In the birth of Jesus of Nazareth, the covenant promises God made to Abraham and David, which remained unfulfilled in their lifetimes, came to fulfillment in Jesus the promised Davidic Redeemer-Messiah. God promised Abraham a kingdom, descendants as numerous as the stars, and a worldwide blessing (Gen 12:1-3; 15:5; 22:17-22). The Lord promised David an eternal covenant and everlasting kingdom ruled by his descendant (2 Sam 7:13-16; 23:5). Jesus is the eternal Davidic King of the Kingdom of Heaven on Earth (the Church). He welcomes every generation of sons and daughters into the family of God, and through His universal gift of eternal life, He becomes a worldwide blessing to the peoples of all nations in every age across the face of the earth (Jn 5:24; 6:40; 11:25-26; Gal 3:14, 29; 1 Jn 2:25).

Forty days after giving birth to her son, it was time for Mary's ritually purification in obedience to the Law (Lev 12:1-4, 6-8). Mary, along with her husband Joseph (Jesus' foster father), and baby Jesus traveled the five miles from Bethlehem to the Jerusalem Temple. During the liturgy of the morning Tamid, Mary presented her sacrifice. It was the sacrifice prescribed for the poor (two young pigeons or two turtledoves) presented as an offering to God by a holy family that was spiritually rich beyond measure (Lev 12:8; Lk 2:22-24).

CHAPTER SUMMARY POINTS: THE ADVENT OF THE MESSIAH

1. It was during the liturgy of the Tamid that the angel Gabriel appeared to the priest Zechariah to announce the future birth of his son, John (the Baptist), the precursor to the Messiah.

2. Zechariah's visionary experience at the Temple on Mount Moriah recalls the visionary experiences of Abraham and David on the same mountain.

3. Zechariah's vision while burning the sacred incense during the liturgy of the Tamid sacrifice set in

motion events that resulted in the fulfillment of the promises of the prophets relating to the birth of the Davidic Redeemer-Messiah.

4. After announcing the birth of a son to Zechariah, the angel Gabriel appeared to a virgin named Mary to tell her that God chose her to bear His Son. The angel told her to name her son Jesus, and His destiny was to receive the throne of his "father" David and to rule an everlasting kingdom.

5. In submitting to the will of God, the Virgin Mary of Nazareth fulfilled the prophecy God made of a future Redeemer in Genesis 3:15. Mary's obedience to the will of God resulted in the Incarnation of God the Son.

Endnotes: The Advent of the Messiah

1. Jewish priest-historian Flavius Josephus wrote that King Herod began construction on the Temple in the eighteenth year of his reign in *Antiquities of the Jews* 15.11.1 [380], but in Wars of the Jews 1.21.1 [401] he wrote that Herod rebuilt the Temple in the fifteenth year. The difference can be accounted for by whether one counts from 37/36 BC when the Romans installed Herod as King of the Jews or from 34/33 BC when Herod finally subdued opposition to his rule. According to Josephus, construction began in the year 20/19 BC with the Sanctuary completed in one year and six months in 18/17 BC (Antiquities 15.11.6 [421]). However, the

construction on the Temple complex continued for another 46 years, as the Jews reminded Jesus in John 2:20.

2. The ancients did not have the concept of zero as a place-value in counting. Counting a series from zero did not make a significant appearance in the west until the eleventh and twelfth centuries AD (*Christianity and the Roman Empire*, page 282; *Calendar: Humanity's Epic Struggle to Determine a True and Accurate Year*, page 189; *Mapping Time: The Calendar and its History* page 77-78, 81). The first day, or month, or year in a series counted as #1; therefore, Jesus was in the tomb three days from Friday to Sunday as the ancients reckoned the number of days but only two days according to the modern count.
3. The Greek word translated "overshadow" in Luke 1:35 is the verb episkiazo. It is the same word used in Matthew 17:5, Mark 9:7, and Luke 9:34 during the Transfiguration event. It is also the same verb used in the Septuagint Greek translation of the Old Testament in Exodus 40:35 when the Glory Cloud "overshadowed" and then indwelled the Tabernacle (The Septuagint with Apocrypha, page 125). See # 1982 in *Strong's Exhaustive Concordance*; IBGE, vol. IV, Lk 1:35, page 153.
4. The inspired writer of the Letter to the Hebrews wrote that the Ark of the Covenant at one time contained a jar of the heavenly manna, Aaron's staff (the dead branch that came back to life and grew buds), and the words of God written on the tablets of the Ten Commandments (Heb 9:4). The Blessed Virgin Mary can rightly be said to be the Ark of the New Covenant since her womb held: He who is the Living Bread come down from Heaven (Jn 6:51), the Branch (a Messianic title) which was dead but came back to life (Is 11:1, Jer 23:5), and He who is the Living Word of God (Jn 1:1).

5. God has a special love for shepherds. Shepherds who figured prominently in salvation history include Abel, Abraham, Jacob, Moses (in Midian), David (in his youth), and the prophet Amos. Scripture often refers to God as the "Shepherd" of His people (Ps 23:1; 80:1; Is 40:11). Old Testament Scripture records that the promised Messiah will guide His people like a shepherd does his sheep (Ez 34:23; 37:24), and Jesus referred to Himself as "the Good Shepherd" (Jn 10:11).

CHAPTER VI
BEHOLD THE LAMB KING

And he will turn many of the sons of Israel to the Lord their God, and he will go before him in the spirit and power of Elijah, to turn the hearts of the fathers to the children, and the disobedient to the wisdom of the just to make ready for the Lord a people prepared.
Luke 1:16–17

John [the Baptist] bore witness to him, and cried, "This was he of whom I said, 'He who comes after me ranks before me, for he was before me.'"
John 1:15

THE PROPHECY OF MALACHI FULFILLED

In AD 28, in the fifteenth year of the reign of the Roman Emperor Tiberius, Pontius Pilate was the Roman governor of Judea, and Joseph Caiaphas was the reigning High Priest of Yahweh's holy Jerusalem

Temple (Lk 3:1-2). At that time, a young priest named John son of Zechariah received the call from the Holy Spirit to begin his ministry in the power and spirit of the great 9th century BC prophet Elijah (Lk 1:17; 3:2b-3).[1] John, who was six months older than his kinsman Jesus (as the ancients counted but five months in modern counting), started his ministry of baptizing for the repentance of sins in the same year that Jesus began His ministry when they were both thirty years old (Lk 3:23). An ordained priest completed his training and began his service in the Temple when he was thirty years old, and Jesus' ancestor, David, became King of Israel when he was thirty (Num 4:3-4; 2 Sam 5:4; Lk 1:36; 3:23).

Instead of beginning his priestly service at the Jerusalem Temple in the daily offering of the Tamid, the Gospel of John records that it was at "Bethany beyond the Jordan," on the east side of the Jordan River, where John began his ministry (Jn 1:26-28). His mission was to call the covenant people to submit to a ritual baptism (water emersion for spiritual purification) of repentance in preparation for the coming of the Kingdom of God (Mt 3:1; Mk 1:4-5; Lk 3:3; Jn 1:28). It is unknown what month St. John began his ministry in the year of AD 28, but forty days before the Feast of

Atonement, celebrated in the early fall, was the traditional period of repentance, fasting, and prayer.

It came to the attention of the religious hierarchy in Jerusalem that a young priest who belonged to the Abijah section of the priesthood had recently emerged from the Judean wilderness and was drawing large crowds of people to the Perea side of the Jordan River. It concerned them that many of the people claimed this young priest came in fulfillment of the words of the prophets relating to the Age of the Messiah.

The 8th century BC prophet Isaiah foretold that a prophetic voice, preaching in the wilderness, would proclaim the coming of the Messianic Era: *A voice cries: "In the wilderness prepare the way of the LORD, make straight in the desert a highway for our God. Every valley shall be lifted up, and every mountain and hill be made low; the uneven ground shall become level, and the rough places a plain. And the glory of the LORD shall be revealed, and all flesh shall see it together, for the mouth of the LORD has spoken"* (Is 40:3-5; quoted as fulfilled in John in Mt 3:1-4, Mk 1:1-4, Lk 3:2b-6, and Jn 1:23). And, in the 5th century BC, the prophet Malachi prophesied the day when God would send the prophet Elijah as His messenger to announce the coming of the Messiah that would reach a climax in the Lord's Day of Judgment. Malachi wrote: *Behold, I send my messenger to prepare the way before me, and the Lord whom, you seek will suddenly come to his Temple; the messenger of the covenant in whom you delight; behold, he is coming, says the LORD of hosts ... Behold, I will send you Elijah the prophet before the great and terrible day of the LORD comes* (Mal 3:1; 4:5/3:23).

Israel's collective sins had resulted in the inability to produce a holy prophet to guide the people (Ps 74:9; Lam 2:9; Ez 7:26; Mic 3:6). No prophet of God had come forth from among the people for about five centuries. One of the last of the post-exile prophets was the holy man known as Malachi, whose Hebrew name meant "my messenger," prophesying the coming of God's herald in the spirit of the prophet Elijah to prepare the way for the promised Davidic Messiah. For centuries the covenant people mourned the loss of God's voice spoken through His prophets (1 Mac 9:27; 14:41). However, they still held out hope for the day when God remembered His promise to send a "prophet like Moses" (Dt 18:15-18) to purify the covenant people of their collective sins and to reclaim a new, spiritually restored Israel.

Everyone was talking about the young priest who offered a baptism of repentance and preached the coming of the Redeemer-Messiah dressed like the prophet Elijah in a camel hair tunic with a leather belt around his waist (2 Kng 1:8; Mt 3:4). Therefore, a delegation of priests and Levites from the Temple in Jerusalem traveled the twenty miles to the site of John's purification ceremonies on the east side of the Jordan River across from the ancient city of Jericho. They asked John three questions: "Who are you?", "Are you Elijah?", and "Are you the Prophet?" They wanted to know by what authority John ritually purified the people and if he claimed to be the Messiah or the promised prophet like Moses, the one God promised to raise up from among his brothers to speak the words of Yahweh to the covenant people (Dt 18:18-19; Jn 1:19-22).

It was prudent for the priests and Levites to investigate if John was the promised prophet like Moses. A significant passage from the prophecy included the warning that God would hold anyone who refused to listen to the words of the promised prophet accountable for that failure (Dt 18:19). In answer to their questions, John denied that he was the promised prophet or the Messiah or Elijah (Jn 1:20-21). Although John preached "in the spirit of Elijah," he did not claim to be a reincarnation of Elijah. [2] John only identified himself as the fulfillment of the prophet Isaiah's prophetic voice calling for the people's repentance (Mt 3:3; Mk 1:2-3; and Jn 1:23 quoting Is 40:3).

Instead of calming the concerns of the religious hierarchy from Jerusalem, John agitated them further by insulting their dignity. When a group of Pharisees and Sadducees tried to present themselves for baptism, John called them a "brood of vipers" (children of the great Serpent, Satan). He then told them to first "produce fruit in keeping with repentance," meaning they needed to show a change of attitude that demonstrated their sincerity before they presented themselves for a baptism of repentance (Mt 3:7–8).

John continued to call the people to repentance and conversion in preparation for the coming of the Messiah, but he did not perform miracles. The priests, Levites, Pharisees, and people were looking for the promised new Moses who could demonstrate by signs and wonders that he had come with authority from God to liberate the people and to inaugurate a new Israel. True to His role as God's promised supreme prophet, priest, and Davidic king, Jesus did not disappoint them.

THE BAPTISM OF THE SON OF GOD

...we have an advocate with the Father, Jesus Christ the righteous; and he is the expiation for our sins, and not for ours only but also for the sins of the whole world.
1 John 2:1b–2

Jesus of Nazareth came to receive St. John's ritual immersion on the east side of the Jordan River. Early Christian writers identified this site as Bethabara, meaning "place of the crossing." They believed it was the site where Joshua and the children of Israel crossed the Jordan River from east to west when they began the conquest of Canaan (Josh 3:14-16; 4:19). Joshua and Jesus bore the same Hebrew name. If this was the same place where the Israelites crossed the Jordan River to take possession of the Promised Land, it was near to where God took the ninth century BC prophet Elijah into Heaven with His chariots of fire from the east side of the river (2 Kng 2:4-12). It was also where Elijah's successor, Elisha, who became an even greater prophet, crossed back to the Jericho side of the River (crossing from east to west) to begin his ministry after receiving a double blessing of Elijah's spirit of power (2 Kng 2:13-14). Perhaps St. John the Baptist selected this site because of the historical importance of the location in both the conquest of the Promised Land and in the ministry of the prophet in whose spirit he was called to carry out his mission. Like Elijah and his successor Elisha who worked twice as many miracles, it was John's destiny to be succeeded by an even greater prophet and miracle-worker, Jesus of Nazareth.

St. John hesitated to baptize Jesus, recognizing Him as the promised Messiah, but Jesus told John that it was necessary for Him to submit to John's baptism (Mt 3:13-15). Jesus' baptism was not a baptism of repentance like the other baptisms John performed (Mt 3:6; Lk 3:3). Jesus was without sin (2 Cor 5:21). His baptism was His anointing as the true Davidic King by the hand of a priestly descendant of Aaron, Israel's first High Priest.

When Jesus willingly submitted to John's baptism as a sign to the people, He awoke all of creation to the opening of the gates of Heaven that had been closed since the Fall of Adam (CCC 536, 1026). God the Holy Spirit descended from Heaven in the form of a dove, and the voice of God proclaimed Jesus of Nazareth the Son of God. St. Mark records: It happened in those days that Jesus came from Nazareth of Galilee and was baptized in the Jordan by John. On coming up out of the water, he saw the heavens being torn open and the Spirit, like a dove, descending upon him. And a voice came from the heavens, "You are my beloved Son; with you I am well pleased" (Mk 1:9-11 NAB; also see Mt 3:16-17 and Lk 3:21-22). At that moment, for the first time in salvation history, the covenant people witnessed a revelation of the Triune God: The Son was present, submitting to the will of the Father, God the Holy Spirit descended upon God the Son enfleshed, and God the Father proclaimed His pleasure in the Son.

As Jesus crossed the Jordan River back to the western shore of Judea, the symbolic significance of this act must have struck some of the Jews in the crowd who heard God's thunderous voice identifying the man Jesus as God's Son. Jesus/Yahshua (Yehoshua in the Aramaic of the first century AD) then crossed the Jordan River in the same way, from the east to the west, as the first Joshua/Yahshua crossed the Jordan River when he led the armies of the covenant people in the conquest of the Promised Land of Canaan (Jos 3:14-4:19). The new Yahshua was also ready to lead a conquest, but His conquest was against sin and death, and His victory would come when He led His victorious army of saints across the river of death into the Promised Land of Heaven (Jn 3:16; 1 Jn 2:25). The name both men shared identified their mission—Yahshua means "Yahweh saves" or "Yahweh is salvation."

After His baptism, the Holy Spirit led Jesus into the Judean wilderness on the west side of the Jordan River where Jesus spent forty days without food or water before He faced His first covenant ordeal in His temptation by Satan (Mt 4:1-11; Mk 1:12-13; Lk 4:1-13). Jesus was the new Adam of a new creation (1 Cor 15:45-49). Like the first Adam, He was tested by Satan in the same way the first Adam fell into sin and the temptations in the world that tested all humans. Satan tempted Jesus just as He tempted Adam and Eve by the pleasing appearance with the promise of food and power from the fruit of the tree that was forbidden (Gen 2:16-17; 3:3-6). First, Satan tempted Jesus to satisfy His physical hunger at Satan's command (Lk 4:3). Next, Satan tempted Jesus with earthly power (Lk 4:5-6). Finally, Satan tempted Jesus to place His human will over the will of God for His life (Lk 4:9-11), just as Satan tempted Adam and Eve in their desire for power and knowledge apart from God (Gen 3:5). Jesus, the second Adam, triumphed over Satan who withdrew until he could find a more opportune time to launch an attack upon the Son of God (Lk 4:13).

THE LAMB OF GOD WHO TAKES AWAY THE SINS OF THE WORLD

A few days after His ordeal, Jesus was walking near the site of St. John's baptisms on the east side of the river when the Baptist directed the crowd's attention to Jesus, calling out: *"Behold, the Lamb of God, who takes away the sin of the world! This is he of whom I said, 'After me comes a man who ranks before me, for he was before me.'*

I myself did not know him; but for this I came baptizing with water, that he might be revealed to Israel" (Jn 1:29–31). And the next day, John identified Jesus in the same way: *"Behold the Lamb of God!"* (Jn 1:36). In this declaration, John, who according to Scripture was several months older than Jesus (Lk 1:36), testifies that Jesus is the divine Messiah by proclaiming His pre-incarnate existence ("he was before me") and also by announcing Jesus to the crowd using the shocking statement: "Behold, the Lamb of God, who takes away the sin of the world!"

On the Resurrection side of salvation history, it is often difficult for us to imagine the impact that John the Baptist's words and Jesus' teachings had on first century AD Jews. We are familiar with the symbol of the Cross and with words that describe Jesus as the "Lamb of God." We are also familiar with concepts like the essential elements of the new Law instituted by Jesus Christ and communicated to New Covenant believers in invisible grace and visible sanctification through the Sacraments that are necessary for our salvation. However, when first introduced, these were radical concepts. How often do we realize that the cross was a feared instrument of torture and death and that the statement by John the Baptist that Jesus is the "Lamb of God" (Jn 1:29, 36) identifies Jesus of Nazareth as a human sacrifice? The Baptist's statement was a radical pronouncement to the crowd assembled on the banks of the Jordan River the day he pointed out Jesus. John stated that Jesus was like a lamb offered up in the communal sacrificial rites of the Sinai Covenant whose death expiates not only the sins of the covenant people but remarkably the whole of humanity when he said: *"Behold, the Lamb of God, who takes away the sin of the world!"*

But what blood sacrifice in the rituals of the Sinai Covenant would have come to mind for the Jews who heard John's declaration? Surely it was not the Passover sacrifice that occurred only once a year and in which multiple male lambs or goat-kids were the required sacrifice for the households of the faithful (Ex 12:5). Nor did they probably think of a sin sacrifice. In sin sacrifices, the wealth of the offeror determined the type of animal offered on God's altar of sacrifice: a bull for a priest or the community, a male goat for a ruler, a female goat or ewe for an ordinary citizen, or two turtledoves or two young pigeons for the poor (Lev 4:3, 13-14, 22-23, 27-32; 5:7). It is possible that some in the crowd might have thought of an individual's guilt offering/reparation sacrifice, where the requirement was an adult male ram (Lev 5:15-18). However, since the majority of each day from dawn to the hour before sunset was spent in the Tamid liturgical worship service or in the observance of the individual prayer time associated with the sacrifice of the Tamid, the people listening to the young priest's declaration must have immediately thought of Jesus in the context of the Tamid lamb.

It was the single sacrifice of an unblemished male lamb offered in the twice-daily liturgy of the *'olat ha-Tamid* that burned on the altar continually during the day and all through the night (Ex 29:39-42). The Tamid liturgical service was either taking place at the moment of St. John's declaration or the Tamid lamb was burning on the altar fire. The Tamid lamb was a sacrifice offered in atonement for the covenant people's sins, the restoration and sanctification of the covenant people as a whole and, according to the first century AD Jewish theologian Philo of Alexandria, for the salvation of <u>the entire human race</u> (Philo, *Special Laws I*, XXXV.169).[3] For the Jews, it was the most important sacrifice of the entire sacrificial system; it was the perpetual sacrifice which was to last so long as the Sinai Covenant endured.

In St. John the Baptist's announcement concerning Jesus recorded in the Gospel of John 1:29 and 36, the Greek word for lamb is *amnos* (IBGE, vol. IV, page 250; *Strong's* Greek Lexicon #286). It is the same word used four times in the Greek Septuagint translation of Exodus in the instructions for the offering of the daily sacrifice of the Tamid: twice in Exodus 29:39, and again in verses 40, and 41 (Benton, *The Septuagint with Apocrypha,* page 110, #286). A sacrifice for the atonement of sins, the restoration and sanctification of the entire covenant community, and (as Philo claimed) "for all of humanity" as described in John's statement proclaiming Jesus as "the lamb of God who takes away the sin of the world" finds fulfillment only in a link between Jesus and the sacrifice of the *'olat ha-Tamid.* If this was John's intention, then he was identifying Jesus, He who is fully man and fully God, as the living, human embodiment of the **Tamid**: two lambs offered as a single sacrifice (Ex 29:42; Num 28:3).

JESUS PROCLAIMS THE KINGDOM OF GOD

And in the days of those kings the God of heaven will set up a kingdom which shall never be destroyed, nor shall its sovereignty be left to another people. It shall break in pieces all these kingdoms and bring them to an end, and it shall stand forever; just as you saw that a stone was cut from a mountain by no human hand, and that it broke in pieces the iron, the bronze, the clay, the silver, and the gold.

A great God has made known to the king what shall be hereafter.
Daniel 2:44-45

After Herod Antipas arrested St. John the Baptist, Jesus returned to the northern territory of the Galilee and began to preach, *"Repent, for the Kingdom of Heaven is at hand"* (Mt 4:17; Mk 1:15). He was about thirty years old; it was the same age when His ancestor David became King of Israel (2 Sam 5:4; Lk 3:23). Jesus began reunifying the Kingdom of the covenant people from the same location where Israel was torn asunder when the Assyrians began exiling the first of the ten northern tribes into the Gentile nations in the eighth century BC (2 Kng 15:29). It was a prophetic and historical connection that St. Matthew identified in his Gospel. Matthew cited the prophetic fulfillment of the prophet Isaiah's promise of Israel's future restoration in the era of the Messiah. In the eighth century BC, Isaiah wrote: *The land of Zebulun and the land of Naphtali, toward the sea, across the Jordan, Galilee of the Gentiles—the people who sat in darkness have seen a great light, and for those who sat in the region and shadow of death light has dawned* (Mt 4:15-16 quoting Is 9:1-2a LXX).

In the Galilee, Jesus began to gather the "lost sheep" of the house of Israel as foretold by the sixth century BC prophet Ezekiel. It was through Ezekiel that Yahweh promised He would come Himself to gather His scattered sheep, and He would appoint one shepherd, the Messiah, a descendant of King David, to pasture them and to rule over a restored Israel with whom He would make an eternal covenant of peace (Ez 34:11-24; 37:24-28; Mt 1:1; 15:24; Jn 10:14).

Jesus is the Incarnation of God's Kingdom. As the Davidic heir and rightful king (Mt 1:1; Lk 1:32-33), Jesus embodies the Kingdom which He makes present on the earth as He stated when He told the people: *Behold, the kingdom of God is in the midst of you* (Lk 17:21). But there is also a spiritual dimension in which God's Kingdom is understood to be present in the believer. For the Old Covenant people, the presence of God the Divine King dwelt above the Mercy Seat of the Ark of the Covenant, but in the New Covenant in Jesus the Christ ("the Anointed/Messiah") our King dwells through the Holy Spirit in the hearts/lives of His disciples (Eph 3:16-19). Finally, there is also an ecclesiological dimension to the Kingdom expressed in the covenant union of the people of God in the sacred assembly of the Church that is the Body of Christ (Rom 12:4-5). It is in the liturgical life of believers that Jesus Christ makes His presence known and in which He indwells His Church and shares His divine life in the New Covenant *Todah* (sacred "thanksgiving" communion meal) of the Eucharist (1 Cor 10:16–17).

In the Sermon on the Mount, Jesus, the new Moses, called His holy people to a new holy mountain to give them a new Law for a new covenant (Mt Chapters 5–7). His mission was to transform a faithful remnant of the old Israel to become the spiritually revitalized new Israel and the vehicle to carry the good news (gospel) of God's gift of salvation to the ends of the earth (Mt 28:19–20; Acts 1:8). The commissioning of His Jewish emissaries before His Ascension to take His Gospel of eternal life to all nations fulfilled what the prophet Isaiah foretold when he wrote that *all flesh shall see the salvation of God* (Is 40:5 LXX quoted in Lk 3:6). And the founding of Jesus' New Covenant Kingdom of the Church fulfilled the prophecy of the prophet Daniel that a fifth Kingdom after Babylon was to have everlasting authority over all nations (Dan 2:44; 7:27). Jesus did not tell those He called to stay away, as God warned the Israelites at Mount Sinai (Ex 19:20–25). He encouraged them and us to draw near to Him and to become radically transformed in His image.

In each of the public and private "signs" of His authority, Jesus declared by His actions that He was the promised Messiah who came to fulfill the Law and the prophets, which means all of Old Testament revelation

(Lk 24:44). When Jesus performed His first miracle at the wedding at Cana, He turned water in stone vessels into wine, a miracle that recalled Moses' first water miracle when he turned water to blood, even water in stone vessels (cf. Ex 7:19 and Jn 2:6–10). The Cana miracle and Jesus' other miracles were prophetic "signs," proclaiming that the Messianic Kingdom promised by the prophets was at hand. His teaching and healing ministry continually addressed the needs of the people spiritually, physically, and emotionally, fulfilling the Messianic prophecies of the prophets:

- He healed physically, giving sight to the blind, hearing to the deaf, health to the sick, and healing the lame and dumb (e.g., Is 29:18; 35:5–6; 42:7 → fulfilled in Mt 9:27–30, 32–33; 11:4–5; 21:14; Mk 7:32–35; Lk 5:12–13; 11:14; 13:11–13; Jn 9:1, 7).
- He healed spiritually, including purifying those who were unclean in spirit by casting out demons (e.g., Is 52:1–3; 53:4–5; Mal 3:2–3 → fulfilled in Mt 8:16–17, 28–32; Lk 4:33–35; 11:14).
- He raised the dead (e.g., Is 26:19 → in Mt 9:23–25; Lk 7:14–15; Jn 11:43–44).

- He proclaiming glad tidings to the poor and broken-hearted (e.g., Is 29:19; 35:4; 61:1-3 → fulfilled in Mt 11:5b; Lk 6:20-23).
- He forgave sins and gave the gift of peace with God (e.g., Is 53:12; Jer 31:34 → fulfilled in Mt 9:2; Lk 5:20, 24; 7:47-48).

However, Jesus coupled the forgiveness of sins with the warning to turn away from transgressions contrary to the Law and to become reconciled with God (Jn 8:11).

It is also significant that Jesus applied the title "Son of Man" to Himself. It was how the prophet Daniel described his vision of the Divine Messiah. The figure in Daniel's vision looked "like a son of man," meaning he resembled a human being, but he was divine. After ascending to Heaven to take his seat at the right hand of God, the "man" in Daniel's vision "*received dominion, glory, and kingship; nations and peoples of every language serve him. His dominion is an everlasting dominion that shall not be taken away, his kingship shall not be destroyed* (Dan 7:13-14). Jesus applied this passage from Daniel to Himself, and those who heard Him could not miss the implications of the connection He was making. He even identified Himself as the "Son of Man" from this passage during His trial before the Jewish Sanhedrin when the court found Him guilty of blasphemy and sentenced Him to death (i.e., Mt 24:30; 26:64-66).[4]

Everything Jesus did and said declared to the people that He was the Anointed One promised by the prophets and sent by God to redeem Israel. Many people came to believe He was the Redeemer-Messiah.

As Jesus' ministry continued, the religious hierarchy in Jerusalem grew increasingly uneasy about His growing support among the people. Jesus' radical teaching, the miracles He performed, the sinners He forgave, His persistence in healing the sick on the Sabbath, and His claim to divine authority sparked a growing animosity (Mt 9:3; 12:14; Mk 11:27-28; Lk 5:21). His actions increasingly drew both the attention and jealousy of the Pharisees, Scribes, Sadducees, and chief priests. These men were the religious leaders who sat in authority on the "chair of Moses" in the Temple and the synagogues throughout the land (Mt 23:2). They should have been the first to recognize Jesus' fulfillment of the promises of the prophets, but their pride blinded their eyes and hardened their hearts against God's Anointed. Their animosity fermented into a hatred that reached its boiling point in the last year of Jesus' ministry in the spring of AD 30 (Lk 19:47; Jn 11:53, 55-57). It was during the Passover and the pilgrim Feast of Unleavened Bread that their hatred reached its climax in a drama that unfolded during the liturgical worship service and sacrifice of the Tamid lambs in the Jerusalem Temple.

CHAPTER SUMMARY POINTS: BEHOLD THE LAMB KING

1. St. John the Baptist, son of the priest Zechariah, was born with the spirit of the prophet Elijah to herald the coming of the Redeemer-Messiah. The angel Gabriel announced St. John's birth; he was the same angel who interpreted for the 6th century BC prophet Daniel the visions of the coming of the "Anointed One." Gabriel prophesied the advent of the Redeemer-Messiah and a period of intense tribulation accompanied by the end of Tamid and the founding of an everlasting kingdom.

2. St. John the Baptist began his ministry of repentance and ritual purification of the covenant people in preparation for the arrival of the Messiah when he was thirty years old.

3. Jesus began His ministry when He was thirty years old. He proclaimed that the Kingdom of Heaven,

the everlasting kingdom prophesied by the prophet Daniel, was at hand.

4. St. John the Baptist baptized Jesus on the east side of the Jordan River. For the first time since the fall of Adam and Eve, the gates of Heaven opened. It was the first revelation of the Triune God: God the Son was present submitting to the will of the Father, God the Holy Spirit descended upon the Son enfleshed, and God the Father proclaimed His pleasure in the Son.

5. St. John the Baptist identified Jesus as a living sacrifice offered for the forgiveness of humanity's sins and the embodiment of the single sacrifice of the Tamid lambs.

6. Jesus began to fulfill the promises of the prophets by proclaiming the Kingdom of God. Jesus began His ministry in the Galilee, fulfilling the prophecy of Isaiah that the Messiah was to establish the reunification of Israel from the region where the Assyrians dispersed the covenant people into the Gentile world in the eighth century BC.

7. The religious leaders and the authorities in Jerusalem became increasingly hostile toward the Galilean Rabbi who called for a revolutionary rebirth into the family of the Kingdom of God.

Endnotes: Behold the Lamb King

1. The ancients counted without the concept of a zero place-value. Therefore, the 15th year of Tiberius (who began his rule in August of AD 14) is AD 28 (see Lk 3:1). Pontius Pilate was the Roman governor of Judea from AD 26-36.
2. John the Baptist, in the womb of his mother Elizabeth, received the spirit of Elijah in much the same way that Elijah's successor Elisha received the prophet's spirit in 2 Kng 2:9-15. John was not a reincarnation of Elijah. Reincarnation is contrary to the doctrine of the Old and New Testaments and the teachings of the Church (Heb 9:27; CCC 1013).
3. Philo of Alexandria (c. 20 BC to AD 50) was a contemporary of Jesus of Nazareth (c. 3/2 BC-AD 30). He was a leader of the Jewish community in Alexandria, Egypt and one of the most important Jewish theologians of the Second Temple Period.
4. In the Gospels, Jesus refers to Himself as the "Son of man" 78 times: Mt 8:20; 9:6; 10:23; 11:19; 12:8; 12:32, 40; 13:37; 16:13, 27, 28; 17:9, 12, 22; 18:11; 19:28; 20:18, 28; 24:27, 30 (twice), 37, 39, 44; 25:13, 31; 26:2, 24 (twice), 45, 64; Mk 2:28; 8:38; 9:12, 31; 10:33, 45; 13:26, 34; 14:21 (twice), 41, 62; Lk 5:24; 6:5, 22; 7:34; 9:22, 26, 44, 56, 58; 11:30; 12:8, 10, 40; 17:22, 24, 26, 30; 18:8, 31; 19:10; 21:27, 36; 22:22, 48, 69; Jn 1:51; 3:13, 14; 5:27; 6:27, 53, 62; 8:28; 12:23; 13:31. In the underlined verses, Jesus is either quoting or referring to the Prophet Daniel's vision of the "son of man" in Daniel 7:13-14.

CHAPTER VII
THE LAST JOURNEY TO JERUSALEM

Behold, I send my messenger to prepare the way before me, and the Lord whom you seek will suddenly come to his temple; the messenger of the covenant in whom you delight, behold, he is coming, says the LORD of hosts. But who can endure the day of his coming, and who can stand when he appears?
Malachi 3:1-2

Throw out the old yeast so that you can be the fresh dough, unleavened as you are. For our Passover has been sacrificed, that is Christ; let us keep the feast, then, with none of the old yeast and no leavening of evil and wickedness, but only the unleavened bread of sincerity and truth.
1 Corinthians 5:7-8 (NJB)

The Gospel of John charts the journey to Jesus' sacrificial death through three successive Passover celebrations, stretching from the year AD 28 to the year AD 30. The covenant people celebrated the Feast of the Passover in the early spring, in the Hebrew month of Abib (Ex 13:4). After the Babylonian exile, the Jews adopted the Babylonian name for this month, and it came to be known as the month of Nisan (Neh 2:1; Est 3:7). In the first year of His ministry, in His first public miracle, Jesus changed water into wine at a wedding in the town of Cana, in the Galilee. Afterward, in obedience to the Law of the covenant, Jesus traveled to Jerusalem to attend the Feast of the Passover and the week-long pilgrim feast of Unleavened Bread (Jn 2:13; Dt 16:16).

Jesus was the perfectly obedient Jew of the Sinai Covenant, expressing in His words and actions the true meaning and intention of all the commands and prohibitions of God's covenant with Israel. The second Passover was near the time when Jesus miraculously fed more than 5,000 men and demonstrated His divinity by walking on the Sea of Galilee. During the same week, He gave the Bread of Life Discourse, prophesying that one day those who believed in Him would eat His Body and drink His Blood to receive the gift of eternal life (Jn 6:4-59).

The third and last Passover of Jesus' public ministry was the prelude to His Passion: Now the Passover of the Jews was at hand, and many went up from the country to Jerusalem before the Passover, to purify themselves. They were looking for Jesus and saying to one another as they stood in the temple, "What do you think? That he will not come to the feast?" Now the chief priests and the Pharisees had given orders that if anyone knew where he was, he should let them know, so that they might arrest him (Jn 11:55-57).

THE COUNTDOWN TO THE PASSION

In the late winter/early spring of AD 30, in the final year of His ministry, Jesus traveled down the east side of the Jordan River and preached in Perea (Jn 11:40-42). When Jesus' disciples, the sisters Martha and Mary of Bethany, sent word to Him that their brother was deathly ill; however, Jesus intentionally delayed crossing the river to go to them in the village of Bethany until Lazarus had died. Then, as one final sign for the people of His divine authority, Jesus raised Lazarus from the dead (Jn 11:11-44). When some Jews brought news of His latest miracle to the Pharisees and chief priests, the High Priest, Joseph Caiaphas, decided Jesus' influence over the people was too dangerous to continue, and Jesus must die. It was at this time that Jesus withdrew to a town bordering the Judean desert (Jn 11:45-54).

When it was time for the feasts of Passover and Unleavened Bread, Jesus and His disciples traveled to Jerusalem. Jesus stopped in the village of Bethany, east of Jerusalem on the eastern slope of the Mount of Olives, to visit with His dear friends Martha, Mary, and Lazarus. Jesus had stayed with this family on other pilgrimages to Jerusalem (Lk 10:38-42). The Gospel of John establishes the day Jesus visited the family and the day of the final Passover of Jesus' ministry: *Six days before the Passover, Jesus came to Bethany, where Lazarus was, whom Jesus had raised from the dead. There they made his supper; Martha served, and Lazarus was one of those at table with him* (Jn 12:1-2).

The day after the supper at Bethany, Jesus rode into the city of Jerusalem on the foal of an ass (Jn 12:12). It is the event Christians celebrate as Palm (Passion) Sunday. Therefore, the dinner at Bethany, on the day before Jesus' entry into Jerusalem, was a Saturday Sabbath meal that Jesus shared with His friends. Jesus must have traveled the approximately twenty miles from Jericho to Bethany on Friday, arriving in Bethan just before sundown that was the beginning of the Sabbath (the day lasted from sundown to sundown), observing the Sabbath travel restrictions. Six days from the Saturday in Bethany, as the ancients counted with no zero place-value and with Saturday counting as day #1, identifies the sixth day, the day of the Passover sacrifice, as the Thursday of Jesus' last week in Jerusalem. According to the Gospel of John, and in agreement with the Synoptic Gospels of Matthew, Mark, and Luke, the Passover sacrifice the year of Jesus' Passion and resurrection was on a Thursday. The Passover sacrifice was the day before His crucifixion on Friday that the Gospels identify as the day before the Sabbath of the Holy Week of Unleavened Bread (see Mt 26:17; 27:62; 28:1; Mk 14:1, 12; 15:42; Lk 22:7, 14-16, 23:54; 24:1; Jn 12:1; 19:31 for the passages that identify the Passover as Thursday of Passion Week, the day before Jesus' crucifixion on Friday, which the Jews called the Day of Preparation for the Sabbath; see Mk 15:42 and Jn 19:31).

- Day #1: Saturday is the 9th of Nisan, *Six days before the Passover* Jesus attended a Sabbath dinner at the home of Mary, Martha, and Lazarus in Bethany (Jn 12:1) where Mary of Bethany anointed Jesus' feet = 2nd anointing (Jn 12:3; the first anointing was in Lk 7:36-38 earlier in His ministry).
- Day #2: Sunday is the 10th of Nisan, the day Jesus rode into Jerusalem (Mt 21:1-9; Mk 11:1-10; Lk 19:29-38; Jn 12:12-19) and cleansed the Temple a second time (Mt 21:12-17; the first cleansing was at the beginning of His ministry in Jn 2:13-16).

- Day #3: Monday is the 11th of Nisan. Jesus cursed the fig tree and cleansed the Temple a third time (Mk 11:12-19).
- Day #4: Tuesday is the 12th of Nisan. Jesus taught at the Temple.
- Day #5: Wednesday is the 13th of Nisan, two days before the Passover as the ancients counted. It was the last day Jesus taught at the Temple. He attended a dinner at the home of Simon the Leper in Bethany (Mt 26:2; Mk 14:1) where a woman anointed His head; it is His third anointing by a woman (#1 = Lk 7:36-38; #2 = Jn 12:3; #3 = Mt 26:6-7 and Mk 14:3-9). After supper, Judas betrayed Jesus to the chief priests (Mt 26:14-16; Mk 14:10-11).
- Day #6: Thursday is the 14th of Nisan, the day of the Passover sacrifice (Ex 12:6; Lev 23:5; Num 28:16) and six days after the dinner with Lazarus' family at Bethany (Jn 12:1).

The Law of Moses required the Passover Sacrifice to take place on the 14th of Nisan (according to the lunar calendar) and for the sacred meal of the Passover victim to take place that night, on the night of the first full moon after the spring equinox, on Nisan the 15th (Ex 12:8; Lev 23:5; Num 28:16; *Mishnah: Pesahim,* 1:1).[1] The Sabbath dinner in Bethany, therefore, was on the 9th day of the month. Jewish priest/historian Flavius Josephus (c. AD 50-100) recorded that it was the custom for the Sabbath dinner to take place at noon, the sixth-hour Jewish time (Josephus, *Life* 54).

THE ARRIVAL OF THE KING

The scepter shall not depart from Judah, nor the ruler's staff from between his feet, until he comes to whom it belongs; and to him shall be the obedience of the peoples. Binding his foal to the vine and his ass's colt to the choice vine, he washes his garments in wine and his vesture in the blood of grapes.
Genesis 49:10-11

Rejoice greatly, O daughter of Zion! Shout aloud, O daughter of Jerusalem! Lo, your king comes to you; triumphant and victorious is he, humble and riding on an ass, on a colt the foal of an ass.
Zechariah 9:9

On the day after the Saturday Sabbath dinner at Bethany, on Sunday, Nisan the 10th, five days before the Passover (as the ancients counted), Jesus entered Jerusalem through the Eastern Gate that faced the Mount of Olives. He rode into the holy city on the back of a colt of an ass, fulfilling the prophecies of Genesis 49:11 and Zechariah 9:9.

Jesus' action also recalled the historical image of King David's son, Solomon, riding into the city of Jerusalem on a mule when King David proclaimed his son, Solomon, his successor as the new King of Israel. At the time of Solomon's triumphal ride into the city of Jerusalem, the people shouted "Hosanna!" ("Save us!"), proclaiming the king's role as the anointed savior of his people (1 Kng 1:38-40; Ps 118:25-26). The Jewish crowd responded in the same way to Jesus, shouting *"Hosanna to the son of David! Blessed is he who comes in the name of the Lord! Hosanna in the highest!"* (Mt 21:9), and *"Hosanna! Blessed is he who comes in the name of the Lord, the king of Israel"* (Jn 12:13). Those in the crowd who traveled to Jerusalem from other parts of the Roman Empire to attend the pilgrim feast of Unleavened Bread that began on the 15th of Nisan who didn't know about the Galilean Rabbi asked other pilgrims, *"Who is this?"* Those in the crowd who knew about Jesus answered: *"This is the prophet Jesus from Nazareth of Galilee"* (Mt 21:10-11).

The crowd acknowledged the historical link between King Solomon's ride into Jerusalem and Jesus' entry by making the same acclamations for Jesus that their ancestors made for King Solomon. However, in their jubilation, the crowd and the disciples may have missed two other critical historical signs that were fulfilled in

Jesus' ride into Jerusalem on that particular day. He whom St. John the Baptist identified as "The Lamb of God" (Jn 1:29, 36) was riding into Jerusalem on the 10th of Nisan, the same day God commanded the selection of the victims for the first Passover sacrifice in Egypt (Ex 12:3). It was also the same day God's chosen servant Yehoshua (Joshua in English and Jesus' name in Aramaic) began the invasion of the Promised Land (Jos 4:19). Jesus is the true Passover offering whose sacrifice will liberate His people from the curse of death (1 Cor 5:7), and He is the new Joshua who, in riding into Jerusalem on the 10th of Nisan, will begin the conquest that will lead the faithful into the Promised Land of Heaven (CCC 1026). The Jewish Mishnah (c. 200 AD) records that the Jews no longer observed the practice of selecting the victim for the Passover on the 10th of Nisan in the first century AD (*Mishnah: Pesahim*, 9:5). However, Jesus kept all the commandments of the Law even in the selection of His own sacrificial offering.

Jesus was going to fulfill all the different classes of the blood sacrifices of the Sinai Covenant in His one perfect sacrifice as "the Lamb of God who takes away the sins of the world" (Jn 1:28). However, Jesus uniquely fulfilled three classes of blood sacrifice in His Passion and Resurrection:

1. He fulfilled the annual remembrance sacrifice of the Passover at the Last Supper when Jesus began His walk to the altar of the Cross.
2. In His humanity and divinity, He fulfilled the communal sacrifice of the unblemished Tamid lambs, a single sacrifice offered in a morning and afternoon liturgical service, in His Passion and sacrificial death.
3. He fulfilled the sacrifice of the single, unblemished male lamb on the Feast of Firstfruits in the climax of His Resurrection.

Jesus' first act upon entering the gates of the holy city of Jerusalem on the first day of the week, Sunday the 10th of Nisan, was to go to the Temple to attend the Tamid worship service as a faithful member of the covenant community. When Jesus entered the Temple precincts, He saw the same abuses that profaned God's holy Temple two Passovers earlier at the beginning of His ministry. Therefore, Jesus cleansed His Father's house a second time on Palm Sunday: *And Jesus entered the temple of God and drove out all who sold and bought in the temple, and he overturned the tables of the money-changers and the seats of those who sold pigeons* (Mt 21:12).

In an article entitled "Money-Changers in the Temple: The Mishnah's Explanation," Jewish scholar Jacob Neusner wrote concerning Jesus' Temple cleansing and linked it to the Tamid worship services: *The overturning of the moneychangers' tables represents an act of rejection of the most important rite of the Israelite cult, the daily whole-burnt offering, and, therefore, a statement that there is a means of atonement other than the daily whole offering, which is now null. Then what was to take the place of the daily whole-offering? It was to be the rite of the Eucharist: table for table, whole offering for whole offering.*[2]

Neusner was correct in stating that the sacrificial rite of the Eucharist replaced the communal sacrifice of the Tamid; however, he is in error in his assertion that the overturning of the money tables signaled Jesus' rejection of the Tamid liturgy at that time. Jesus assured the people that He had not come to abolish the Law but to fulfill it, and not even the smallest part of the Old Law would be invalid "until all things have taken place," referring to His Passion and Resurrection (Mt 5:17-18). Also, there was no connection between the money from the coin exchange and the sacrifice of the daily Tamid lambs. The money exchange tables were to provide acceptable coinage (without pagan images) for the covenant people to make endowments to the Temple or to purchase their individual, voluntary whole-burnt offerings, sin sacrifices, and communion sacrifices from their second tithe (Dt 14:22-26).[3]

The Temple hierarchy selected the Tamid lambs. They were a compulsory communal sacrifice purchased with the Temple tax that all covenant members paid annually: *The law requires, that out of the public expenses a lamb of the first year be killed every day, at the beginning and at the ending of the day* (*Antiquities of the Jews*, 3.10.1 [237]; also see Neh 10:32-33). Therefore, the overturning of the money tables had nothing to do with Jesus' rejection of the Tamid as the premier communal sacrifice of the covenant people, and the time for the fulfillment of the Law and the end of the Tamid had not yet come.

In His Temple cleansings, Jesus performed a prophetic sign called an *ot*, the symbolic act of a prophet. Jesus performed an *ot* in proclaiming God's cleansing of His Church in preparation for the fulfillment of the Old and the establishment of the New and everlasting covenant promised by the prophet Jeremiah (Jer 31:31-34). It was a prophetic act He would repeat the next morning (Monday) when He returned to the Temple for the morning liturgy after cursing the fig tree for its failure to bear fruit. The cursing of the fig tree was another symbolic act that condemned Israel for her failure to bear the fruit of repentance during the ministry of the Messiah (Mk 11:12-19).

After driving out the money changers, Jesus chastised the Temple authorities for using His Father's

House for profane practices, just as He had during His first Temple cleansing in the first year of His ministry (Jn 2:16). However, in the second Temple cleansing, He quoted a line from Isaiah 56:7 when He proclaimed, "*It is written, 'My house shall be called a house of prayer'*" (Mt 21:13; also see Mk 11:17 and Lk 19:46). The phrase was from a passage from the Book of Isaiah that prophesied the Gentiles coming to Yahweh's Temple as a house of prayer in the Messianic Age (Is 56:3-7). Jesus' reference to this passage suggests it was the Court of the Gentiles that the Temple authorities turned into a marketplace instead of using it as a sacred space for calling the Gentile nations to embrace the God of Israel and becoming converts/adopted sons and daughters in Yahweh's covenant family.

Jesus also referred to Yahweh's warning to the people of Jerusalem from the writings of the prophet Jeremiah. Jesus said, concerning God's holy Temple: "*but you make it a den of robbers*" (Mt 21:13; also see Mk 11:17 and Lk 19:46). In the passage from Jeremiah 7:1-15, God's prophet stood at the gate of the Temple proclaiming God's judgment against the people of Judah and the priests for profaning God's holy Temple. Jeremiah accused the covenant people of turning Yahweh's house/Temple into a "den of robbers" (Jer 7:11). Jeremiah prophesied that because of these abuses,

God would drive the covenant people out of His Temple, which would be destroyed (Jer 7:14-15).

The Babylonians fulfilled Jeremiah's prophecy in 587/6 BC by destroying Yahweh's Temple, built by King Solomon in the tenth century BC. It was a tragedy repeated by four Roman legions in the destruction of the Jerusalem Temple on the 9th of Ab in AD 70 (on the same day the Babylonians destroyed Solomon's Temple centuries earlier). Jesus alluded to both Old Testament passages during the second Temple cleansing on Sunday, and the next day, after cursing the barren fig tree, Jesus also quoted from both prophetic passages during the third Temple cleansing on Monday (Mk 11:12-19).

The Pharisees and the Temple authorities who were upset by what they considered Jesus' scandalous behavior on the first day of the week (Sunday) were probably filled with rage when Jesus repeated His Temple cleansing the next day (Monday). Not only was this Galilean rabbi claiming to be both the promised Prophet and Davidic Messiah, but He dared to judge them for failing to fulfill their duties to maintain the sanctity of the Temple. After cleansing the Temple a third time on what was Monday of His last week in Jerusalem, Jesus taught the people and healed the sick.

THE MALICE OF THE RELIGIOUS HIERARCHY

And he was teaching daily in the Temple. The chief priests and the scribes and the principal men of the people sought to destroy him; but they did not find anything they could do, for all the people hung upon his words.
Luke 19:47-48

From Sunday to Wednesday of Jesus' last week in Jerusalem, He continued teaching parables within the Temple precincts and healing the sick. He was visible for everyone to see and hear Him and to judge His perfection. Then, at the end of each day, He withdrew from the city to the east across the Kidron Valley with His disciples to spend the night on the Mount of Olives (Mt 21:17; Mk 11:11; 19; Lk 21:37-38; Jn 18:1-2). According to the Gospels, Jesus spent some of those nights with friends in the town of Bethany located on the eastern slope of the mount. He had many faithful followers in Bethany, including the families of Lazarus and Simon the (former) Leper (Mt 21:17; Mk 11:11).

When Jesus quoted twice from Isaiah 56:7 concerning the promise of salvation to the Gentiles and from Yahweh's threat in Jeremiah 7:11-15 that He would dispossess those who failed to maintain the sanctity of His Temple (Mt 21:13 and Mk 11:17), the Pharisees and

Temple authorities did not miss the implications of His warnings. As a result, they became even more determined to kill Him. Nor was it likely that they missed the fact that Jesus was comparing them to the corrupt Temple authorities condemned by Jeremiah before the destruction of Jerusalem and Solomon's Temple in 587/6 BC.

The prophetic quotations from the prophets directed at the Temple hierarchy and Jesus' double prophetic action in cleansing the Temple (on Sunday and Monday) were followed by what the religious leaders must have perceived as Jesus' most provocative act. On Wednesday, His last teaching day in Jerusalem, Jesus condemned the scribes and Pharisees, pronouncing seven curse-judgments against them in the language of a holy prophet of Yahweh delivering a covenant lawsuit against an apostate covenant people (Mt 23:13-32). Jesus' pronouncement of divine judgment must have been the final action that motivated His opposition to move forward with a plan to bring about His death.

JESUS CONCLUDES HIS PUBLIC MINISTRY AND THE RELIGIOUS AUTHORITIES SELECT HIM FOR SACRIFICE

Though he had done so many signs before them, yet they did not believe in him [...]. Nevertheless, many even of the authorities believed in him, but for fear of the Pharisees they did not confess it, lest they should be put out of the synagogue: for they loved the praise of men more than the praise of God.
John 12:37, 42-43

During Jesus' final week in Jerusalem, large numbers of people came to Him, believing that Jesus was the promised Redeemer-Messiah. There were even men among the leaders of the ecclesial community who thought Jesus was the Messiah, but they were afraid to declare their belief publicly because of the power the Pharisees had in causing their excommunicated from their local synagogues. They were more fearful of the power of the Pharisees and of losing their positions of authority within the community than they were of the power of God's divine judgment, putting human glory before God's glory.

Wednesday was the fifth day since the Saturday Sabbath dinner at Bethany (as the ancients counted), and it was the final day of Jesus' public ministry. Divine judgment was the theme of His discourse on Wednesday, the 13th of Nisan. Jesus concluded His message with a prophecy of the destruction of Jerusalem and the Temple, and with a vivid description of the Final Judgment for humanity (Mt Chapters 24-25). In His teaching on the Final/Last Judgment, Jesus said the righteous who live the law of love and mercy towards other members of the human family would go to eternal blessings, but those who persisted in seeking only selfish desires would go to everlasting punishment (Mt 25:31-45). Gone are the temporal blessings and punishments of the Old Covenant (Lev 26:3-46; Dt 28:1-68). In His kingdom, Jesus declared both the blessings and the punishments at the end of one's life are now eternal!

After His discourse on the judgment of Jerusalem, His promised Parousia (return at the end of time) and the Final Judgment (Mt Chapters 23-25), Jesus announced, "*The hour has come for the Son of Man to be glorified*" (Jn 12:23). Admitting His anxiety, Jesus told the disciples: "*I am troubled now. Yet what shall I say? 'Father, save me from this hour?' But it was for this purpose that I came to this hour. Father, glorify your name*" (Jn 12:27-28). Suddenly, those standing with Jesus heard a voice from Heaven assuring Him: "*I have glorified it, and*

I will glorify it again" (Jn 12:28b). Significantly, this is the third time God the Father publicly acknowledged God the Son. The first time was at Jesus' baptism (Mt 3:17; Mk 1:11; Lk 3:22), and the second time was at the revelation of Jesus in His glory on the Mount of Transfiguration (Mt 17:5; Mk 9:7; Lk 9:35).

When Jesus had finished all these sayings, he said to his disciples, "You know that after two days the Passover is coming, and the Son of man will be delivered up to be crucified" (Mt 26:1–2; also see Mk 14:1). Jesus concluded His teaching ministry by announcing to His disciples that He was going to be betrayed and crucified in two days (as the ancients counted from Wednesday to Thursday). At that very moment, the High Priest, Joseph Caiaphas, and the chief priests were conspiring against Him (Mt 26:3–5; Mk 14:1–2; Lk 22:1–2). With this final warning, Jesus left the city and returned to the village of Bethany on the Mount of Olives to share a dinner with the Apostles and His other friends at the home of Simon the (former) Leper (Mt 26:6–13; Mk 14:3–9).

On this last day before the Passover sacrifices, *Jesus knew that his hour had come to pass from this world to the Father. He loved his own in the world, and he loved them to the end* (Jn 13:1). On Wednesday, knowing that His hour had come, Jesus was prepared to make His "exodus" out of this world, loving those God gave Him "to the end" which was about to be fulfilled in His final "hour." The Apostle Judas Iscariot betrayed Jesus to the chief priests after the Wednesday dinner at the home of Simon (Mt 26:14-15; Mk 14:10) and set in motion the selection of Jesus as the ultimate unblemished sacrificial Lamb that all other Old Covenant animal sacrifices only prefigured.

The High Priest, Joseph Caiaphas, selected Jesus for sacrifice. It was a pronouncement by Caiaphas recorded three times in the Gospel of John (Jn 11:49-50, 51-53, and 18:14). The High Priest did not select the multiple Passover victims; each household of the covenant people chose its own lamb or goat-kid. However, the High Priest or his representative was responsible for personally inspecting and selecting the individual male Tamid lambs for the two daily worship services. In the same way that he selected the unblemished Tamid lambs for the sacrificial altar to die in atonement for the people's sins, Joseph Caiaphas chose Jesus to die as a sacrifice on the altar of the Cross.

Caiaphas defended his decision by telling the chief priests and Pharisees: *"You know nothing at all; you do not understand that it is expedient for you that one man should die for the people, and that the whole nation should not perish"* (Jn 11:49-50). The Gospel of John adds: *He did not say this of his own accord, but being high priest that year he prophesied that Jesus should die for the nation, and not for the nation only, but to gather into one the children of God who are scattered abroad. So from that day on they took counsel how to put him to death* (Jn 11:51-53).

Caiaphas argued that Jesus should die to save the nation from a revolt against their Roman overlords. He feared that the people believed Jesus was the Redeemer-Messiah who had come to liberate them from the Romans like Moses freed the children of Israel from the Egyptians. Caiaphas believed a revolt against the powerful Roman Empire could result in another destruction of Judah from which the nation might never recover. However, the Gospel of John focuses on the higher sense of Caiaphas pronouncing Jesus' death sentence in that the High Priest failed to recognize the prophetic significance of his statement concerning the necessity of Jesus' death (Jn 11:50). Jesus' death and resurrection were to bring about the promised reunification of all the lost children of Israel scattered throughout the Gentile nations of the world. In the harvest of souls into the New Covenant Church following Jesus' Resurrection, all those who believed in Him were saved from alienation from God in eternal death and granted the gift of everlasting life. Jesus' death would become the atoning blood sacrifice of the sinless Lamb of God, prophesied by John the Baptist on the banks of the Jordan River (Jn 1:29, 36), that was necessary for the salvation of the world and the fulfillment of what the Tamid only prefigured.

THE SACRIFICE OF THE PASSOVER VICTIMS WITHIN THE LITURGY OF THE AFTERNOON TAMID

And after the feast of the new moon comes the fourth festival, that of the Passover, which the Hebrews call pascha, on which the whole people offer sacrifice, beginning at noon day and continuing till evening.
Philo of Alexandria, *Special Laws II, XXVII.145*

As the ancients counted, six days after Jesus' Saturday Sabbath meal in Bethany, on Thursday the 14th of Nisan, it was the day of the Passover sacrifice (Jn 12:1). As was the custom in the first century AD, the Synoptic Gospels combine the feasts of Passover and Unleavened Bread into one eight-day celebration (Mt 26:17, Mk 14:12, and Lk 22:7). However, the Gospel of John refers to the entire eight days as "the Passover," as Jews do today (Jn 13:1). It was the day the disciples came to Jesus asking where they were to celebrate the sacred meal of the Passover victim: *Now on the first day of Unleavened Bread the disciples came to Jesus, saying,*

"Where will you have us prepare for you to eat the Passover?" (Mt 26:17). St. Mark's Gospel is more explicit in identifying the day when the disciples came to Jesus to inquire about the sacred meal of the Passover victim: *And on the first day of Unleavened Bread, when they sacrificed the Passover, his disciples said to him, "Where will you have us go and prepare for you to eat the Passover?"* (Mk 14:12, *IBGE*, vol. IV, page 140). The word "lamb" is not in the Greek text nor is the word "Passover" ever associated with the word "lamb" in the Greek translation of the Bible; it is an addition to the English translation. According to the Law, both lambs and goat-kids were the acceptable sacrifices at Passover (Ex 12:5).

The animal for the Passover sacrifice had to be an unblemished male lamb or goat-kid not younger than eight days and not older than a year (Ex 12:5; Lev 22:27). The animal had to be large enough to feed not less than ten people and not more than twenty. Concerning the hour of the Passover sacrifice and the meal of the victims, Flavius Josephus wrote: *So these high priests, upon the coming of their feast which is called the Passover, when they slay their sacrifices, from the ninth hour* [3 PM] *till the eleventh* [5 PM], *but so that a company not less than ten belong to every sacrifice (for it is not lawful for them to feast singly by themselves), and many of us are twenty in a company* (Josephus, *Wars of the Jews*, 6.9.3 [423]).

If there were more than twenty people, they formed a second group with a separate Passover victim. If the Passover victim was too small to feed a group of ten, then, in addition to the Passover sacrifice, a festival *Hagigah* offering was necessary. For the *Hagigah*, the group presented a male or female animal from the flock or the herd at the same time they offered their Passover sacrifice (*Mishnah: Pesahim*, 6:3-6:4). Every group of pilgrims also offered the communion *Hagigah* festival peace offerings for each day of the week-long Feast of Unleavened Bread. It was the way the people ate together for the entire week after the morning Tamid service in noon-day meals of joyous celebration within the walls of the city of Jerusalem.

Jesus sent the Apostles Peter and John to prepare the place where the sacred meal of the Passover was to take place after sundown on the day of the sacrifice (Lk 22:7-13, also see Mt 26:17-19, and Mk 14:12-16). When Peter and John arrived at the house, they discovered that an upper room arranged with banquet tables and couches for reclining at the meal (Mk 14:15; Lk 22:12-13a). However, Peter and John still needed to make certain necessary preparations (Mt 26:19; Mk 14:16; Lk 21:13b). They needed to ensure that there was an adequate supply of red wine for the banquet's four ritual communal cups and the individual cups of wine that the guests would consume during the meal (*Mishnah: Pesahim,* 10:1C). They needed to have stone vessels filled with enough water for the three ritual hand-washings during the night. They needed to provide the other necessary foods for the women to prepare for the meal, and they had to set up a roasting pit and a spit of pomegranate wood to roast the Passover sacrifice (*Mishnah: Pesahim,* 7:1B).

In addition to all those arrangements, Peter and John also had to personally inspect the premises to ensure that no leaven was present; leaven was a symbolic sign for sin, and their sacred meal was a gathering of a ritually holy covenant people. According to the Law, it was necessary to do a complete search of all the rooms of houses in Jerusalem before noontime and remove all leaven for the seven days of the Feast of Unleavened Bread (Ex 13:6-7; *Mishnah: Pesahim,* 1:3-1:4). They were also required to begin a fast at noon: *On the eve of Passover from just before the afternoon's daily whole offering, a person should not eat, until it gets dark* (*Mishnah: Pesahim,* 10:1A). The "afternoon's daily whole offering" is the afternoon Tamid and the "eve of Passover" refers to the Passover meal eaten on the first night of Unleavened Bread. The *Mishnah*, the writings of the Rabbis, the Gospel of John, and Jews today only refer to the entire eight days as "Passover."

The site historically identified as the Upper Room of the Last Supper is above what is believed, by both Jewish and Christian traditions, to be the location of King David's tomb in the older part of Jerusalem known as the "Citadel of Mount Zion" or "the city of David" (2 Sam 5:7-9). The house is on the eastern ridge of the city just south of the Temple Mount. In his homily on the Sunday of the Jewish feast of Pentecost (Weeks), fifty days after the Resurrection when the Holy Spirit took possession of the New Covenant Church, St. Peter stood on the street outside the Upper Room and spoke to the Jewish crowd. He told them Jesus was the fulfillment of the Messianic promises. As he gave his Gospel message, Peter mentioned King David's tomb, perhaps even gesturing to the lower floor of the building (Acts 2:29). Scripture does not identify the person who owned the house with the Upper Room. However, Acts 12:12 records that the home of the Jewess Mary of Jerusalem was where the Apostles regularly assembled after the Resurrection. Mary of Jerusalem was the mother of John-Mark, the inspired writer of the Gospel of St. Mark, and she was a kinswoman of Jesus' disciple Joseph Barnabas (Col 4:10).

All four of the Gospels and two thousand years of Christian tradition agree that the Jewish festival of the Passover and the sacrifice of the Passover victims took place on the Thursday of Jesus' last week in Jerusalem, the day before His crucifixion on Friday.

Those of the covenant community who were offering the Passover sacrifice for their family and friends gathered at the Temple with their Passover victims at noon for the afternoon Tamid worship service. The sacrificial ceremony of the Passover lambs and goat-kids began immediately after the placing of the body-parts of the afternoon Tamid lamb on the altar fire (*Mishnah: Pesahim*, 5:3).

On the day of the Passover sacrifice, it was necessary to offer the afternoon Tamid lamb an hour earlier to give enough time for the sacrifice of the many Passover victims (*Mishnah: Pesahim*, 5:1B). There was, however, an exception to the timing of the service if the day of the Passover sacrifice fell on a Friday that was "Preparation Day" for the Sabbath (Mk 15:42; Jn 19:31). In that case, the Temple priests offered the Tamid sacrifice even earlier. This gave the people enough time at the end of the worship service to prepare for the Sabbath restrictions: *If, however, the eve of Passover* [meal] *coincided with the eve of the Sabbath* [Friday], *it* [the Tamid] *was slaughtered at half after the sixth hour*

[12:30 PM] *and offered up at half after the seventh hour* [1:30 PM] (*Mishnah: Pesahim*, 5:1D).

On that Thursday, the 14th of Nisan, it was probably Peter and John who took the lamb or goat-kid to the Temple. It was not necessary for everyone to attend the sacrifice. A relative or even one's slave, if he were a Jew, could present the animal for sacrifice since Passover was not a pilgrim festival (*Mishnah: Pesahim*, 8:1-8:4). The sacrifices for the Passover usually took place from the ninth hour (3 PM) to the eleventh hour (5 PM) since the afternoon Tamid sacrifice was earlier on the Passover instead of the ninth hour (the exception was when Passover was on a Friday). The eleventh hour (5 PM) was the completion of all the Temple services (*Mishnah: Pesahim*, 5:8B). The only other change in the liturgy of the afternoon Tamid during the Passover was in the offering of the incense. The incense was usually offered immediately after placing the afternoon Tamid lamb on the altar fire followed by the concluding prayers of the worship service. However, for Passover, the incense offering was delayed and was not offered until the sacrifice of the last of the Passover victims. The offering of the community's prayers in the burning of the incense was always part of the climax of any worship service.

The groups that represented their households assembled at the Temple with their animals at noon. In fulfillment of God's command in Exodus 12:6, the different groups separated into three large divisions: *You must keep it till the fourteenth day of the month when the whole assembly of the congregation of Israel will slaughter it* (NJB):

- "whole" = division #1
- "assembly" = division #2
- "congregation" = division #3

It is a command repeated in the Mishnah: *And the whole assembly of the congregations of Israel shall slaughter it* (*Mishnah: Pesahim*, 5:5A-B).

After placing the afternoon Tamid lamb on the altar fire, the first division came forward with their animals into the Court of the Priests. As soon as they entered the courtyard, the doors were locked. The priests blew three blasts on the silver trumpets as the signal that it was time to begin the sacrifice of the lambs and goat-kids. The leader of each family/group carried a sacrificial knife with which to slit the throat of the animal while a Levite collected its blood in a golden chalice. The Levite then handed the chalice to a priest who tossed/splashed the blood against the base of the altar (2 Chr 30:16; *Mishnah: Pesahim*, 5:5-5:6). At this time, if the size of the Passover victim was not sufficient to feed the number of people who intended to eat the sacred meal in that particular group, then a free-will festival sacrifice (*Hagigah*), a male or female animal from the flock or herd, was sacrificed at the same time. Its blood was also collected and splashed against the altar (*Mishnah: Pesahim*, 6:3-6:4).

While the sacrifices were taking place, the Levitical choir sang the Hallel Psalms 113-118, also called the Egyptian psalms. Psalms 113-117 recounts the story of the Exodus liberation, while Psalm 118 gives joyous thanksgiving to God the Savior and refers to the Redeemer-Messiah as "the stone which the builders rejected" which "has become the cornerstone" (Ps 118:22). The choir repeatedly chanted the Egyptian Hallel Psalms until the completion of the sacrifice of all the animals of a division (*Mishnah: Pesahim*, 5:7).

After the first division sacrificed its victims, the priests skinned the animals, removed the fat and entrails, and washed the bodies of the animals. The entrails and fat were put in a bowl and salted before being placed on the altar fire (*Mishnah: Pesahim*, 5:10). When every group in the first division had the bodies of their animals returned to them, they left, and the second division entered the Court of the Priests to repeat the same ritual. After the sacrifice of all the animals (Passover lambs, kids, and the *Hagigah* offerings), the chief priests concluded the afternoon Tamid worship service. They poured out of the wine libation against the altar, the incensing priest burned of incense on the Altar of Incense in the Holy Place of the Sanctuary, and the priests assembled to pray the priestly blessing over the congregation: *"May Yahweh bless you and keep you. May Yahweh let his face shine on you and be gracious to you. May Yahweh show you his face and bring you peace"* (Num 6:24-26, NJB).

Flavius Josephus wrote that one year during the reign of the Roman Emperor Nero (AD 54-68) when he was serving as a chief priest in the Temple during Passover, the priests recorded the number of slain animals during the Passover sacrifice. The count was 256,500 sacrificed animals. At the end of the afternoon, the blood from the sacrificial victims splashed against the sacrificial altar reached to the ankles of the priests, and the Kidron brook where the Temple drains emptied became a river of blood (Josephus, *Wars of the Jews*, 6.9.3 [424]); *Jerusalem in the Time of Jesus*, page 44, note 33).

THE SACRED MEAL

Silence before Lord Yahweh, for the Day of Yahweh is near! Yahweh has prepared a sacrifice, he has consecrated his guests (Zephaniah 1:7; NJB).

With the competition of the liturgical celebration and sacrifice, every group took the skinned body of its Passover lamb or goat-kid and free-will *Hagigah* festival offering back into to city. The Law required them to eat the sacred meal in the "camp" of God, which was Jerusalem. They roasted the meat of the Passover victim on a pomegranate spit, exercising great care not to break any bones. The Law required the punishment of forty lashes for anyone who carelessly broke a bone of the Passover victim which made the sacrifice invalid (Ex 12:46; Num 9:12; *Mishnah: Pesahim,* 7:1B, 7:11C).

The meal had to begin after sundown, and the faithful had to complete the meal before midnight (*Mishnah: Pesahim,* 10:1A; 10:9). Sundown was the end of Nisan the 14th and the beginning of the next Jewish day, Nisan the 15th, that signaled the beginning of the celebration of the seven-day pilgrim feast of Unleavened Bread. Non-covenant members or the ritually impure could not take part in the sacred meal. It was reserved only for those in covenant with Yahweh who were circumcised (if male) and ritually clean, a condition that reflected the spiritual purity of the covenant member's circumcised/purified heart (Ex 12:43-51).

The pilgrim feast of Unleavened Bread allowed the covenant people to relive the themes of judgment and redemption that their ancestors experienced in the first Passover event. Eating the sacred meal of the Passover victim as a unified people was a sign of covenant renewal and continuation for every new generation, so it was important for children to attend. So sacred was this meal that the penalty for deliberately failing to eat the sacrifice of the Passover on the first night of the Feast of Unleavened Bread was excommunication from the covenant people (Num 9:13). However, there were exceptions made in case of illness, the death of a family member, if one was delayed because of a long journey, or if one became ritually impure. In those cases, it was possible to keep the feast a month later (Num 9:9-10; *Mishnah: Pesahim*, 9:1-9:3). There was no excuse for failing to keep the pilgrim feast of Unleavened Bread, and there was no excuse for failing to eat the sacred meal.

Jewish scholar Hayyim Schauss wrote about the connection between the festivals of Passover (Pesach) and Unleavened Bread and Jewish expectations concerning the coming of the Redeemer-Messiah at the time of Jesus' ministry in the first century AD. He wrote: *The highest point in the evolution of Pesach came in the last century of the second Temple, when the Jews suffered from the heavy oppression of the Romans. It was during this period that the Messianic hope flamed up, and in the minds of the Jews the deliverance of the future became bound up with the first redemption in Jewish history: the deliverance from Egypt. Jews had long believed that in the deliverance to come, God would show the same sort of miracles that he had performed in redeeming the Jews from Egypt. This belief gained added strength in this period of Roman occupation and oppression. Jews began to believe that the Messiah would be a second Moses and would free the Jews the self-same eve, the eve of Pesach. So Pesach became the festival of the second as well as the first redemption; in every part of the world where Jews lived, especially in Palestine Jewish hearts beat faster on the eve of Pesach, beat with the hope that this night the Jews would be freed from the bondage of Rome, just as their ancestors were released from Egyptian slavery* (*The Jewish Festivals*, pages 46–47).

Some scholars suggest that Jesus and His disciples celebrated the Last Supper a day or two earlier than the designated feast day, using a solar calendar instead of the liturgically required lunar calendar and thereby rejecting the date set by the Temple hierarchy. Other scholars suggest that no sacrificed lamb or kid was present at the meal and that the Last Supper only consisted of the bread and wine transformed into Jesus' Body and Blood.

It is unthinkable that Jesus did not celebrate this feast at its liturgically designated time and according to the obligations of the covenant. In the Sermon on the Mount, Jesus supported every aspect of Old Covenant Law saying: *Think not that I have come to abolish the law and the prophets; I have come not to abolish them but to fulfill them. For truly, I say to you, till heaven and earth pass away, not an iota, not a dot, will pass from the law until all is accomplished. Whoever then relaxes one of the least of these commandments and teaches men so, shall be called least in the kingdom of heaven; but he who does them and teaches them shall be called great in the kingdom of heaven* (Mt 5:17-19). Jesus did not accomplish His work to fulfill the Old Covenant until He pronounced the words *"It is finished"* (*fulfilled/accomplished*) from the Cross (Jn 19:30). Until that pivotal moment in salvation history, Jesus supported obedience to the Law as God intended in the commands, prohibitions, and rituals established for His people at Mount Sinai, as the "way of life" for the covenant people (Dt 30:15-20).

Jesus fully supported the authority of the ordained priesthood in fulfilling the rites and rituals of the Sinai Covenant, which certainly included appointing the dates of the designated feast days according to the lunar calendar (Num 28:11-15). His last day teaching at the Temple in Jerusalem, Jesus addressed the issue of the authority of the Temple hierarchy: *Then said Jesus to the crowds and to his disciples, "The scribes and the Pharisees sit on Moses' seat; **so practice and observe whatever they tell you**"* (Mt 23:1-3; emphasis added). Jesus would not have told the people to obey the hierarchy of the Church one day and then do the exact opposite by celebrating the Passover on a day other than what the liturgical calendar determined on the next day.

The eating of the sacrificial meal in the middle of the lunar month of Nisan at the time of the full moon was the last legitimate sacrificial meal of the Old Covenant. It was a sacred meal transformed and fulfilled in Jesus' Last Supper that became the first communion sacred "Thanksgiving" banquet of peace with God (in Hebrew *Todah*; see Lev 7:11-21) of the New Covenant faithful. It was necessary for the faithful remnant of Jews who became the restored Israel of the New Covenant to participate in this last Old Covenant ritual. They needed to comprehend its transformation and fulfillment as an authentic sacrificial meal in the offering of Christ the Lamb of God in the Eucharistic ("Thanksgiving") banquet of a New Covenant liturgy. If the Last Supper did not take place during the legitimately designated meal of the Passover victim on the first night of the Feast of Unleavened Bread, then the Jews present at the meal could not have understood Jesus' offering Himself as a continuing sacrifice and not just a symbolic gesture. The suggestion that Jesus celebrated the Last Supper on a night other than the prescribed Passover feast erodes the belief in the Real Presence of Christ in the Eucharist and the Eucharist as an actual sacrificial meal.

It is also ludicrous to suggest that unleavened bread and a communal cup of wine were the only items on the menu at the Last Supper. This theory completely contradicts the Gospel accounts. The Gospels of Matthew and Mark record that "as they were eating" Jesus took up the unleavened bread and then the red wine in which He offered Himself Body, Blood, Soul, and Divinity (Mt 26:26; Mk 14:22). The Gospel of Luke even mentions two of the four communal cups of red wine consumed in the traditional meal with Jesus statement that He would not drink wine again until He came into His Kingdom (Lk 22:17-18). It is the other cup mentioned in Luke's account (that St. Paul identifies it as the "Cup of Blessing" that was the third traditional communal cup in 1 Cor 10:16) that Jesus announces the "New Covenant in His Blood" (Lk 22:20). The Gospel of John also records that Jesus passed the "sop" (the traditional mixture of fruit folded in a piece of unleavened bread eaten before the roasted flesh of the Passover victim) to His guests after which Judas left to betray Him (Jn 13:26).

The four traditional communal cups of the sacred meal represented the four ways God promised to redeem Israel from slavery in Egypt (Ex 6:6-7):

1. The Cup of Sanctification (opened the meal)
2. The Cup of Forgiveness (probably the cup mentioned in Lk 22:17-18)
3. The Cup of Blessing/Redemption (the cup of Jesus' Blood; see 1 Cor 10:16)
4. The Cup of Consecration/Acceptance (officially sealed the covenant and closed the meal for another year)

After those assembled at the meal ate the meat of the Passover victim, they ate no other foods, and the host passed the third communal cup that signaled the beginning of the concluding rituals of the meal. For the second time, Jesus changed the ritual order of the meal; the first time was the washing of the Apostle's feet to purify them as His ministers, replacing on the three ritual hand-washings (Jn 13:5-11). He took up unleavened bread, blessed it, broke it, and gave it to them saying: *"This is my body, which is given for you. Do this in remembrance of me." And likewise the cup after supper, saying, "This cup which is poured out for you is the new covenant in my blood"* (Lk 20:19-20).

Jesus' words must have both shocked and amazed those who were present. Four points would have become immediately apparent to them:

1. Jesus dressed in the same seamless linen garment as a priestly representative of Yahweh, identifying the meal as a liturgical service (Jn 19:23).
2. He used the same words Moses used at the ratification of the Sinai Covenant when He referred to the "blood of the covenant," except He added the word "new" (Ex 24:8; Lk 22:20).
3. His words confirmed the prophecy of the prophet Jeremiah that the day would come when God would establish a new covenant to replace the Sinai Covenant (Jer 31:31; Lk 22:20).
4. Jesus was instituting a new sacred meal and the ratification of a new covenant in which He offered His Body and Blood as the means of eternal salvation.

The disciples would have realized that Jesus was fulfilling a promised He made a year earlier when He told the disciples and Jewish pilgrims traveling to Jerusalem for the feasts of Passover and Unleavened Bread (Jn 6:4) ~*"Truly, truly [Amen, amen], I say to you, unless you eat the flesh of the Son of Man and drink his blood, you have no life in you; he who eats my flesh and drinks my blood has eternal life, and I will raise him up at the last day. For my flesh is food indeed, and my blood is drink indeed. He who eats my flesh and drinks my blood abides I me, and I in him"* (Jn 6:53-56; also see verses 47-58). The disciples knew He was speaking literally and not figuratively because, when some of Jesus' disciples were shocked at His claim and walked away, He did not stop them (Jn 6:60, 66).

For Jesus' disciples, the inauguration of the New Covenant within the context of the Old Covenant Passover sacrifice and meal established the importance of the New Covenant sacred meal as the means of continued covenant union with the Messiah. Eating what Jesus identified as the sacrifice of Himself that night made His disciples one with Him and became the focus of Christian liturgical worship. On the night of the Last Supper, Jesus became the true paschal victim. He instituted the first sacred communion meal of the New Covenant Todah ("Thanksgiving") as His disciples took part in the ratification ceremony and sacred meal of the everlasting Kingdom in the Divine Presence of God the Son just as their ancestors inaugurated the Sinai Covenant in a sacred meal in the presence of God on Mount Sinai (cf. Ex 24:9-11). Later, Christians would apply the Greek word to replace the Hebrew word Todah to this meal, signifying communion with Christ, *Eucharistia.*

The faithful across Jerusalem concluded the Passover sacred meal by midnight, and they burned the bones and any remaining parts of the Passover victim before sunrise (*Mishnah: Pesahim,* 10:9). After the concluding hymn, Jesus and the Apostles left the Upper Room. Passing through the city's Eastern Gate, they crossed the Kidron Valley Bridge by the light of the full moon. Jesus did not offer the 4th Cup, the Cup of Consecration/Acceptance, that concluded the meal and sealed the Sinai Covenant for another year. None of the accounts of the Last Supper, mention the 4th Cup, and Jesus swore an oath between the second and third communal cups that He would not consume wine again until He came into His Kingdom (Lk 22:17; Mt 26:29; Mk 14:25).

Jesus led them to a garden on the Mount of Olives (Jn 18:1-2). As they approached the olive grove of Gethsemane, the olive trees must have shut out much of the light of the full moon, casting the garden into darkness. Despite the lateness of the hour, Jesus gathered His Apostles around Him as He asked them to stay and pray with Him in His "hour of darkness." The "hour" of His Passion would begin at the same hour as the beginning of the preparations for the morning liturgy of the Tamid sacrifice.

CHAPTER SUMMARY POINTS: THE LAST JOURNEY TO JERUSALEM

1. Jesus rode into the holy city of Jerusalem on Sunday, the 10th of Nisan. He came in fulfillment of the prophecy of the prophet Zechariah as the people proclaimed Him the King of Israel (Lk 19:38; Jn 12:13). This momentous event occurred on the same day of the month of Nisan (Abib) in the Exodus Passover when God commanded the people to select their Passover victims (Ex 12:3). It was also the day the priests chose the Tamid lambs for the liturgical service that would embrace the Passover sacrifices.

2. The triumphal ride into Jerusalem on the 10th of Nisan signified that Jesus is both the promised Davidic Messiah and the chosen sinless victim of the divine Passover that would cause eternal death to "pass over" those who are safe under the sign of the blood of the Lamb (Ex 12:13, 23).

3. Jesus cleansed the Temple a second time on Sunday, the 10th and a third time on Monday the 11th of

Nisan. In Scripture, a repetition of three of anything signifies the coming of an important event in salvation history. The third Temple cleansing was the final preparation of the Old Covenant Church for the completion of Jesus' teaching ministry and the coming of His Passion.

4. The High Priest, Joseph Caiaphas, made the decision that Jesus had to die.

It was Caiaphas in his role as God's priestly representative who chose Jesus as the unblemished victim for sacrifice upon the altar of the Cross, just as the High Priest had the final approval for the selection of the Tamid lambs.

5. According to the four Gospels, the Passover sacrifice on the last week of Jesus' life took place on a Thursday.

6. The Passover sacrifice took place within the liturgical service of the afternoon Tamid. The sacrifices began after the offering of the Tamid lamb on the altar fire and concluded before the end of the Tamid worship service in the burning of the incense and priestly blessing.

7. Jesus became the true paschal victim as He offered His Body and Blood in a sacred meal to those assembled

in the Upper Room on the first night of Unleavened Bread. He instituted the New Covenant Todah ("Thanksgiving" communion meal) in the first sacred meal we designate by the word, Eucharist (from "Thanksgiving" in Greek). Jesus repeated the words of Moses at Sinai, identifying "the blood of the covenant" in the cup of wine that became His Blood (Ex 24:8). His disciples took part in the ratification ceremony and sacred meal of the New Covenant and everlasting Kingdom in the Divine Presence of God the Son, recalling the ratification and sacred meal in the Divine Presence of Yahweh at Mt. Sinai (Ex 24:9-11).

Endnotes: The Last Journey to Jerusalem

1. Today Jews do not observe the Passover sacrifice on the 14th of Nisan since there is no longer a Temple in Jerusalem or a sacrificial altar where the Passover sacrifices had to take place. Using a lunar calendar, today Jews celebrate the Passover from the 15th to 21st of Nisan in Israel and a day longer in the Diaspora (*The Jewish Book of Why*, vol. I, page 185). Like the Gospel of John and the Mishnah, modern Jews only refer to the week-long feast as the "Passover." The Catholic Church sets the "appointed time" for Holy Week and Easter in much the same way as the priestly hierarchy of the Sinai Covenant set the time for the Passover and Unleavened Bread. They establish Easter as the first Sunday after the first full moon after the spring equinox. Holy Thursday is always the night of the month's full moon.

2. Jacob Neusner, "Money-Changers in the Temple: The Mishnah's Explanation," *New Testament Studies* 35 (1989):287-290, as cited by Brant Pitre, "Jesus, the New Temple and the New Priesthood," *Letter and Spirit*, vol. IV, page 67.
3. Also, see *Mishnah: Maaser* Sheni, 1:3-1:4 *and Jerusalem in the Time of Jesus*, pages 48-49.

CHAPTER VIII THE ALTAR OF THE CROSS

"But all this has taken place that the scriptures of the prophets might be fulfilled."
Matthew 26:56

THE CRISIS IN THE GARDEN

The Gospels of Matthew and Mark identify the plot of land on the Mount of Olives where Jesus led His disciples as Gethsemane. It is an Aramaic name meaning "oil press," suggesting the location of a grove of olive trees with a near-by press (Mt 26:36; Mk 14:32). The Gospel of John, however, identifies the place to which Jesus led His disciples as a garden (Jn 18:1). It was in a garden that the first man, Adam, failed the first test of covenant obedience in his sin of rejecting God's sovereignty over his life by eating the fruit of the forbidden tree (Gen 2:16; 3:6). Adam's disobedience left him disgraced in the loss of God's divine, sanctifying grace and introduced sin into the world. The result was the contamination of sin that affected all creation and every generation of our first parent's descendants. Now Jesus, the second Adam, began to undo the damage wrought by the first Adam in a covenant ordeal in which He had to decide if He was willing to submit Himself to the will of God the Father for His life, no matter what the cost (CCC 359).

In His supreme act of obedience, Jesus was going to fulfill the promise of Genesis 3:15, to defeat the work of the serpent by destroying the power of Satan over man and creation (Gen 3:1-4; Rev 12:9). As St. John wrote: *The reason the Son of God appeared was to destroy the works of the devil* (1 Jn 3:8b). And in destroying the power of Satan, Jesus was going to fulfill the Old Covenant with the gift of sanctifying grace through a new and eternal covenant: *He abolishes the first in order to establish the second. And by that, we have been sanctified through the offering of the body of Jesus Christ once for all* (Heb 10:9-10).

In His anguish over what He knew was going to be the human cost of His obedience and submission, Jesus knelt and prayed in the garden at Gethsemane as His sweat fell to the ground like drops of blood (Lk 22:44). Twice He returned to the three Apostles who He asked to keep watch with Him and found them asleep (Mt

26:37-46; Mk 14:32-42). In His agony, Jesus prayed, *"Father, if it be possible, let this cup pass from me; nevertheless, not as I will, but as thou wilt,"* referring to His suffering (Mt 26:39). And then, in Jesus' prayer of submission to the will of the Father, He said, *"My Father, if this cannot pass unless I drink it, thy will be done"* (Mt 26:42). After praying three times, Jesus roused His Apostles saying: *"Behold, the hour is at hand, and the Son of Man is betrayed into the hands of sinners"* (Mt 26:45). At that moment Judas Iscariot appeared in the garden, leading men from the Temple guard and a detachment of Roman soldiers to arrest Jesus (Mt 26:47-50; Mk 14:43-46; Lk 22:47-48; Jn 18:3-9).

Coming forward, Jesus took command by demanding to know who they wanted. The crowd of armed men answered that they sought Jesus of Nazareth. Jesus responded, *"Ego eimi," "I AM."*[1] When Jesus spoke "I AM," indicating the Divine Name, either the power of His words or His opponent's fear of Him caused the men, both Jews and Gentiles, to fall back onto the ground (Jn 18:5-6). For a second time, Jesus asked them who they wanted, and when they repeated "Jesus the Nazarene," He again responded using the Divine Name and saying, *"I told you that I AM"* (Jn 18:8 IBGE, vol. IV, page 307). When a servant of the High Priest Caiaphas reached out to grab Jesus' arm, Peter swung his sword, cutting off the man's right ear. Jesus rebuked Peter saying: *Put your sword into its sheath; shall I not drink the cup which the Father has given me?* (Jn 18:11).

In Scripture, "drinking wine" is one of the reoccurring symbolic images of the Old Testament prophets (see Appendix III). The joy of drinking good wine symbolizes covenant union with Yahweh and the promise of the future Messianic banquet (e.g., Ps 23:5; Is 25:6; 62:9; Zech 9:15-16). But imagery of "the cup" can also refer to judgment for sin associated with drinking "the cup of suffering" or the "cup of God's wrath" that the wicked deserve for their sins (e.g. Is 51:17; 63:2-3; Jer 25:15-31; Joel 4:13). In the same way that every Tamid lamb accepted his "cup" of judgment before his sacrifice for the atonement and sanctification of the covenant people (*Mishnah: Tamid*, 3:4B), Jesus was prepared to accept "the cup of suffering" and "the cup of God's wrath." He stated His willingness in His prayer to the Father to receive "the cup" to free humanity and all creation from the burden of sin and death. Then, in a final demonstration of His power and authority, Jesus healed the wounded man's ear, giving the crowd a miracle and revealing His true nature—He is the "I AM" who revealed Himself to the Patriarchs and spoke to Moses at the burning bush (Lk 22:51). And still, the guards, soldiers, and the disgraced Judas Iscariot were blinded by the darkness of their sins and did not believe in Him.

THE LAMB OF GOD JUDGED WORTHY OF SACRIFICE

Not in every place, my brethren, are the daily sacrifices [the Tamid] offered or the free will offerings, or the sin offerings and trespass offerings, but only in Jerusalem; and there also the offering is not made in every place but before the shrine, at the altar, and the offering [the Tamid lamb] is first inspected by the High Priest ...
Pope St. Clement, 1 Clement, 41:2

The guards bound Jesus and took Him to the house of the former high priest, Annas, the father-in-law of the current High Priest, Joseph Caiaphas. The Romans no longer allowed the High Priest to serve for life as was previously the tradition of the covenant people (*Jerusalem in the Time of Jesus*, page 148; *Mishnah: Nazir*, 7.1). Annas was forced to give up the role of Yahweh's anointed High Priest in AD 16 (*Antiquities of the Jews*, 18.2.2 [34-35]), but he still wielded the authority of that priestly office. Then too, perhaps taking Jesus to Annas was the plan to give Caiaphas enough time to convene an illicit assembly of the Sanhedrin (the Jewish high court) and to prepare the false witnesses to testify against Jesus. After questioning Jesus, Annas sent Him to Caiaphas (Jn 18:24).

The guards led Jesus to the palace of the High Priest, there the chief priests, the elders, and the scribes of the Sanhedrin were assembled to pass judgment on the Son of God (Mk 14:53). In this hastily convened trial, members of the council questioned Jesus and brought forward false witnesses to speak against Him (Mt 26:59-61). As the reigning High Priest, Joseph Caiaphas was there as the president of the Sanhedrin, but he also took up the role of prosecutor and chief judge. The most dramatic moment of the trial came when Caiaphas stood up and addressing Jesus demanded: *Have you no answer to make? What is it that these men testify against you* (Mt 27:62; Mk 14:60)? When Jesus remained silent, Caiaphas bound Him by an oath in the name of God to tell them if He is the Messiah (Mt 26:63). This time Jesus answered, speaking the Divine Name again and invoking the words of both King David and the Prophet Daniel: *Jesus said, "I am, and you will see the Son of Man sitting at the right hand of Power, and coming with the clouds of heaven"* (Mk 14:62).

Jesus' use of the Divine Name in His "I AM" declaration and His claim to Daniel's vision of the glorified "Son of Man" Messiah from Daniel 7:13-14, coupled with David's prophecy of a priestly Messiah in

Psalms 110:1 was all Caiaphas needed to condemn Jesus for the capital crime of blasphemy. According to the Law: *He who blasphemes is liable only when he will have fully pronounced the Divine Name;* if there was evidence that the offense of blasphemy occurred, then *the judges stand on their feet and tear their clothing, and never sew them back up* (*Mishnah: Sanhedrin,* 7:5E). The penalty for blaspheming the Divine Name was death (Lev 24:16). After Jesus' statement, Caiaphas immediately tore his robes (Mt 26:65; Mk 14:63). The tearing of the judges' garments and the prohibition against repairing them symbolized that the offender had broken with the covenant in such a way that restoration of his membership in the covenant family was impossible (*Mishnah: Sanhedrin,* 7:1). Addressing the court, Caiaphas said: *"Why do we still need witnesses? You have heard his blasphemy. What is your decision?"* (Mk 14:63-64).

As these events were transpiring, below in the courtyard St. Peter was facing his own ordeal. Servants in the High Priest's household recognized him as one of Jesus' followers; it was a claim Peter denied twice as those in the courtyard heard the "cockcrow." When Peter denied the Christ a third time, he heard the "cockcrow" a second time in fulfillment of what Jesus told Peter earlier in the evening: *And Jesus said to him,*

"Truly, I say to you, this very night, before the cock crows twice, you will deny me three times" (Mk 14:30, 72). Like Jesus, Peter also experienced condemnation; his lack of trust in Christ in his crisis of expectation condemned him. The two "cockcrows" heard by those assembled in the courtyard were the trumpet signals of the guards of the night watches from the Temple and the Roman Antonia fortress. The time was 3 AM.

THE TAMID AND THE PASSION OF THE CHRIST

The Passion of Christ reveals the significance of the Tamid sacrifice in God's plan for the salvation of humanity. At the trumpet signal of the "cockcrow," the priests in the Temple were rising to take their ritual baths before dressing in their priestly robes and preparing for the morning sacrifice of the Tamid lamb (*Mishnah: Tamid,* 1:2; *Mishnah: Yoma,* 1:8). When they were ready, the priests presented themselves for the first drawing of lots to determine who was to clean the sacrificial altar in the Temple's inner courtyard and prepare it for the morning sacrifice. After the trumpet signal of the "cockcrow," the guards placed Jesus in the dungeon of Caiaphas' palace where they beat and ridiculed Him, preparing the victim for His sacrifice (Mk 14:65).

The Sanhedrin did not have the political power to condemn Jesus to death. In the Roman provinces, only the Roman governing authority had control over life and death (Jn 18:31). But the Jewish leaders were also using the excuse that the prerogative of capital punishment belonged to Roman justice to avoid executing Jesus themselves. It wasn't to their advantage to have Jesus become a martyr to the people. It was to their advantage to have Jesus condemned by the pagan Roman authority and discredited as a common criminal. They wanted Him disgraced by being "hung on a tree" in the Roman custom of crucifixion.

Jesus' crucifixion fulfilled the Law's covenant curse in Deuteronomy 21:22-23: *And if a man has committed a crime punishable by death and he is put to death, and you hang him on a tree, his body shall not remain all night upon the tree, but you shall bury him the same day; for a hanged man is accursed by God.* The Jewish religious authorities did not comprehend that in demanding a form of execution that was abhorrent to the Jewish sense of justice that they were fulfilling the prophecies Jesus made of His crucifixion and God's plan for the salvation of humanity (e.g., Mt 20:18-19). On His last day teaching in Jerusalem, Jesus told the crowd: *"Now is the judgment of this world, now shall the ruler of this world be cast out; and I, when I am lifted up from the earth, will draw all men to myself." He said this to show by what death he was to die* (Jn 12:31–33; also see 1 Pt 2:24 and Gal 3:13 quoting from Dt 21:23).

At dawn, the Sanhedrin condemned Jesus to death (Lk 22:66, 71). At dawn, a Levite stationed on the pinnacle of the Temple shouted "Barkai!"— "Morning has arrived!" It was the signal that the ritual for the morning Tamid sacrifice could begin. A priest led the unblemished male Tamid lamb from its enclosure into the courtyard of the Priests and tied it near the sacrificial altar.

After condemning Jesus, the members of the Sanhedrin led Him to the courtyard of the residence of the Roman governor: *When morning came, all the chief priests and the elders of the people took counsel against Jesus to put him to death; and they bound him and led him away and delivered him to Pilate the governor* (Mt 27:1–2). Caiaphas did not accompany the other chief priests charged with taking Jesus to the Roman governor, Pontus Pilate. As the reigning High Priest, he had to return to the Temple to prepare for the day's Sacred Assembly for the Feast of Unleavened Bread and Tamid liturgical service over which he was required to officiate (Lev 23:5–8; Num 28:17–18).

Pontius Pilate was the fifth governor of Judea-Samaria, and he was the second-longest holder of that office, governing from AD 26-36. Pilate always traveled from his official residence in Caesarea Maritima to Jerusalem to maintain order during the holy days of the pilgrim feasts when Jews from across the Roman world converged on their Holy City. According to the Gospels, it was now the morning of the 15th of Nisan and the first morning of the seven-day Feast of Unleavened Bread (the feast that began at sundown twelve hours earlier). It was also the sixth day of the week, Friday, which is called "Preparation Day" in the Gospels, meaning the day to prepare for the Jewish Sabbath that began at sundown (Mk 15:42; Jn 19:31).

The Roman governor established his residence at Herod's palace when he visited Jerusalem. Jewish theologian Philo of Alexandria called Herod's palace "the house of the procurators" when they were in Jerusalem (*Legatio ad Gaium,* 306). Wherever the man who represented the power and authority of the Roman Empire resided, it was where a court of Roman justice convened (Jeremias, *Jerusalem in the Time of Jesus Christ,* page 48).

When the members of the Sanhedrin and the crowd of Jews accompanying them arrived at the Jerusalem residence of the governor, it was necessary for Pontius

Pilate to come out into the courtyard to meet them, since the Jews refused to enter the building. Jews could become ritually defiled by entering a Gentile dwelling, but to remain in the open area of a courtyard was not subject to the Law regarding the defilement of ritual purity (*Mishnah: Ohalot*, 18:7B; 18:10). Jewish historian Flavius Josephus noted that Pilate's judgment chair was on an open-air platform on the east side of the palace (*Jewish Wars*, 2.301).

If the Jews became defiled, they could not attend the required Sacred Assembly that began with the Tamid worship service at the Temple that morning at 9 AM (the third-hour Jewish time). Nor could they present or eat their *Hagigah* communion offerings they were to consume in groups that day: *They themselves did not enter the Praetorium, so that they might not be defiled, but might eat the Passover* (Jn 18:28b). This verse concerns eating the *Hagigah* festival communion meal on the first day of Passover week and could NOT be referring to the meal of the Passover victim that occurred the night before. If a member of the covenant became ritually defiled by contact with a Gentile, that person only had to take a ritual bath and be declared cleansed by sundown that marked the end of the day. The Passover sacred meal on the first night of Unleavened Bread didn't take place until after sunset; therefore, if someone became ritually unclean in the morning, there was more than enough time to become purified before it was time for the meal. In John's Gospel, he only refers to the holy eight days of Passover and Unleavened Bread as "Passover." Therefore, one cannot interpret the reference to "eat the Passover" in John 18:28b as referring to the Passover sacrifice; it can only refer to eating the *Hagigah* festival communion meal at noon on the first daytime liturgy of the week of Passover/Unleavened Bread.

In the first century AD as well as today, the term "Passover" referred to the entire eight days of Passover and Unleavened Bread from the 14th to the 21st of Nisan. According to the Law, the faithful presented the required festival *Hagigah* communion offerings at the morning liturgical service: *On the first day, there shall be a holy convocation; you shall do no laborious work, but offer an offering by fire* (Num 28:18-19a).[2] The Nisan 14th *Hagigah*, presented in addition to the Passover sacrifice, was entirely voluntary. However, on the 15th of Nisan, at the daytime Sacred Assembly during the Tamid liturgy, the *Hagigah* was a compulsory sacrifice. If a covenant member neglected this obligation, the *Hagigah* became a required peace offering for each of the following days of the feast (1.6; 2 Chr 30:22; *Mishnah: Hagigah*, 1:6A). It is ironic that the religious leaders, who so outrageously violated every aspect of their own moral and civil law in their treatment of Jesus, was now concerned about the state of their religious purity.[3]

Accommodating the Jews' religious observances, Pilate came out into the courtyard. He immediately challenged the Jewish delegation on their reason for bringing Jesus to him for trial by asking why they didn't try Him themselves. Their answer was straightforward; they wanted Jesus to be executed (Jn 18:29-31). Governor Pilate then took Jesus into the Praetorium to question him privately. In the exchange that followed, Pilate became convinced of Jesus' innocence.

At the Temple, the High Priest inspected the morning Tamid lamb one final time. Finding the victim to be ritually perfect, he announced, "I find no fault" and condemned the lamb to death. At the Praetorium, Pilate returned with Jesus to the courtyard to address Jesus' accusers. He pronounced that he found "no fault" [*aitia*] in the man (Jn 18:38 IBGE, vol. IV, page 310, the Greek word *aitia* can mean "case, crime, cause, or fault;" see Thayer's Greek-English Lexicon, page 18).).

When the Jewish authorities again insisted on Jesus' execution, Pilate attempted to free himself from the obligation to condemn an innocent man, having perceived that *it was out of envy that the chief priests had handed him over*, and having been warned by his wife who had a dream about "the righteous man" (Mt 27:18,

19; Mk 15:10). Pilate brought up a jurisdictional technicality and insisted that, as a Galilean, Jesus should be sent to Herod Antipas, tetrarch of the Galilee, who was in Jerusalem for the pilgrim feast. When Jesus refused to answer Herod's questions or to provide a miracle, Antipas grew bored and returned Jesus to Pilate (Lk 23:6–11). If both Pilate and Herod Antipas were staying at the Herodian palace, which most scholars agree was the case, then, Jesus could have been passed back and forth between the courts of these men relatively quickly.

Pilate attempted to defuse the demand for Jesus' death by having Him beaten (Jn 19:1), and again Pilate announced that he did not find Jesus guilty of any crime (Jn 19:4). But when the chief priests and guards saw Jesus they cried out *"Crucify him, crucify him"* (Jn 19:6), to which Pilate taunted them by saying that they should take Jesus and crucify Him themselves, stating for a third time that he found "no fault" in Jesus (see Jn 18:38; 19:4 and 6). Nevertheless, the chief priests and elders continued to demand Jesus' death, telling Pilate that according to their law Jesus deserved to die for claiming to be the Son of God (Jn 19:7). Unnerved by their threat and their claim that Jesus was a rival to Caesar's sovereignty by claiming to be the Son of God, Pilate talked to Jesus privately a second time. Again,

Jesus took charge, telling Pilate: *You have no power over me at all if it had not been given you from above; that is why the one who handed me over to you has the greater guilt* (Jn 18:11b), referring to Caiaphas and the members of the Sanhedrin.

Then Jesus' adversaries leveraged their demand with a threat, telling Pilate: *"If you release this man, you are not Caesar's friend; everyone who makes himself a king sets himself against Caesar"* (Jn 19:12). They were referring to the Jewish crowd hailing Jesus as "the King of Israel" when He entered Jerusalem on Palm Sunday (Lk 19:38; Jn 12:13). In this statement, the religious leaders accused Jesus of attempting to usurp the sovereignty of Roman Emperor Tiberius Caesar, a man who was the acknowledged "son of a god" as the adopted step-son of the deified former emperor, Augustus Caesar, and ruled as King of Judah (*A History of Rome*, page 340–350).

With this claim, the men who opposed Jesus repeated the sin that resulted in Adam's fall from grace. Adam's disobedience in his covenant ordeal in the Garden of Eden wasn't merely an illegal fruit harvest from the Master Gardener's forbidden Tree of the Knowledge of Good and Evil. The greater sin of Adam and Eve resulted from the action of attempting to usurp the power and authority of God in the desire to decide for themselves what was good and what was evil, becoming, as Satan suggested, like gods themselves (Gen 3:5). Now, the descendants of the man Adam claimed that God the Son had no sovereign authority over them, and all power belonged to the man Tiberius Caesar, the son of a false god.

It is ironic that the High Priest, Joseph Caiaphas, as God's covenant representative to the people, had pronounced Jesus' death sentence. In essence, Caiaphas selected Jesus as a sacrifice for the sake of the people; a pronouncement recorded three times in John 11:50, 51, and 18:14. It is also ironic that a pagan Roman Gentile pronounced Jesus' fitness as the unblemished sacrifice by telling the Jewish crowd three times: *I find no crime [fault] in this man* (Lk 23:4, 14, 22; and Jn 18:38; 19:4 and 6). That there was "no fault" was the same pronouncement of perfection made over the Tamid lamb that morning in preparation for the Temple liturgy and the offering of the Tamid lamb in sacrifice.

When the crowd rejected Pilate's assessment of Jesus' innocence a third time, the Roman governor taunted them again. Pilate referred to the acclamations the Jewish crowd showered upon Jesus as He rode into the city of Jerusalem when the people hailed Him as the Messiah and Davidic King (Mt 21:9; Mk 11:9-10; Lk 19:38). Pilate asked them: *"Shall I crucify your king?"* The response of the chief priests was: *"We have no king but Caesar"* (Jn 19:14-15). Speaking these words sealed the Old Covenant hierarchy's final rejection of their Messiah, shattering the bond of the covenant by rejecting Yahweh's kingship over His people and acknowledging the ultimate sovereignty of a pagan king (Dt 17:15).

St. Matthew's Gospel records the climax of the trial when Pilate, attempting to separate himself from the injustice of Jesus' execution, washed his hands in a symbolic act, signifying Jesus' blood was not on his conscience and saying, *"I am innocent of this righteous man's blood; see to it yourselves"* (Mt 27:24). In response, the Jews in the crowd took upon themselves the responsibility for Christ's death by calling out a self-curse, saying, *"His blood be on us and on our children!"* (Mt 27:25). But Jesus did not come to die as a curse upon His people. He came to turn the curse-judgments of covenant disobedience (Lev 26:14-45; Dt 28:15-68) into the promises of an eternal blessing. He offered His righteous blood for them, for their children, and for the forgiveness of all sinners. In His sacrificial death on the altar of the Cross, Jesus turned the self-curse of the crowd into the world-wide blessing promised to Abraham and his descendants (Gen 12:3; 22:18; 26:4;

28:14; Gal 3:8, 29)—the blessing of universal and eternal salvation.

St. John's Gospel records that the drama of Jesus' trial before Pilate was *on the day of Preparation of the Passover, it was about the sixth hour* (19:14). "The Passover" refers to the eight days of Passover and Unleavened Bread, and the "sixth hour" has to be a reference to Roman time which would make the "hour" of the trial between 6-7 AM in agreement with the other Gospels and not Jewish time which would have been noon (Mt 27:1-2; Mk 15:1; Lk 22:66; 23:1). It could not have been noon Jewish time because the Gospel of Mark records that Jesus' crucifixion was at the third hour or 9 AM (Mk 15:25). And all the Synoptic Gospels record that <u>after</u> Jesus was hanging on the Cross for a length of time, it turned dark from "the sixth hour to the ninth hour" Jewish time, or from noon to 3 PM (Mt 27:43; Mk 15:33; Lk 23:44). "Preparation Day" referred to in John 19:14 has to be a reference to the day before the Sabbath. According to St. Mark's Gospel, the trial and Jesus' crucifixion was on Friday, the day before the Saturday Sabbath: *And when the evening had come, since it was the day of Preparation, that is, the day before the Sabbath* (Mk 15:42 also see Jn 19:31). Jesus suffered His crucifixion on the sixth day of the week, the day before the Jewish Sabbath that was a special Sabbath in the holy week of

Passover/Unleavened Bread, which John's Gospel only refers to as "the Passover," *for that Sabbath was a high day* (Jn 19:31).

We keep Roman time, beginning the day and counting hours from midnight (Pliny the Elder, *Natural History 2.79.188*). If Jesus was with Pilate at about the 6th-hour Roman time, John's account agrees with the Synoptic Gospels. According to many early Church Fathers, St. John wrote his Gospel years after the events of the Crucifixion from the city of Ephesus in the Roman province of Asia Minor where he was the bishop of a mostly Roman congregation. The 1st-century AD geographer Strabo identifies Ephesus as the second most important city in the Roman Empire after Rome (Strabo, *Geography,* vol. 1-7, 14.1.24, Cambridge: Loeb Classical Library, Harvard University Press). Writing for a mostly Gentile audience, why would John use Jewish time?

The Gospel of John also uses Roman place names, identifying the Sea of Galilee only by its Roman name, the Sea of Tiberias (c.f., 6:1, 23 and 21:1), a designation not found in any other Gospel. St. John also explains Hebrew/Aramaic terms like "rabbi" and "Golgotha" to his Gentile Christian audience (e.g., Jn 1:38; 19:17). And in another time reference, the Gospel of John records that Andrew and another man "spent the day" with

Jesus beginning at the 10th hour (Jn 1:39). If this was Jewish time, the 10th hour is 4 in the afternoon with the day ending at sundown which was 6 PM (the ancients observed 12 seasonal hours from dawn to dusk), and they could not have claimed they spent "the day" with Jesus. But if John were using Roman time, the 10th hour is 10 in the morning, and they would have spent the entire day with Jesus until sundown. St. Augustine (AD 354-430), Bishop of Hippo, stated, "If we are perplexed by any apparent contradiction in Scripture, it is not allowable to say, the author of this book is mistaken; but either the manuscript is faulty, or the translation is wrong, or you have not understood."

THE SACRIFICE OF THE LAMB OF GOD

We have our own altar from which those who serve the Tent have no right to eat. The bodies of the animals whose blood is taken into the sanctuary by the high priest for the rite of expiation are burnt outside the camp, and so Jesus too suffered outside the gate to sanctify the people with his own blood.

Hebrews 13:10-11

(referring to the sacrifices on the Day of Atonement, the only day of the year when the High Priest entered the Holy of Holies; see Lev 16:11-19, 27)

... in Jesus, God participates in time. Through this participation, He operates in time in the form of love. His love purifies men; through purification [and not otherwise] men are identified and united with Him.
Joseph Ratzinger, Pope Emeritus Benedict XVI

Forced to carry the despised instrument of His crucifixion, Jesus made His way from Pilate's judgment seat to the designated site of Roman execution. He staggered through a tangle of jeering and profane humanity, intermixed with a few of His tearful followers and His beloved and ever-faithful mother. He carried His Cross to a place outside the gates of Jerusalem called Golgotha, an old quarry and gravesite on a lower slope of Mount Moriah. Jesus, the beloved Son of God, was going to be offered in sacrifice just as Isaac, the beloved son of Abraham, was offered in sacrifice on the same mountain (Gen 22:2; Mt 3:17). In Abraham's test of covenant obedience, God provided a substitute sacrifice (Gen 22:11-13). But this time, it was Jesus who was the substitute sacrifice that *Yahweh yireh*, "Yahweh will provide," the words Abraham used just before God spared his son by providing the sacrifice of a ram (Gen 22:2, 8, 13-14). The executioners offered Jesus as a subsidiary sacrifice in place of a sinful humanity outside the gates of Jerusalem like the communal sin sacrifice on the Feast of Atonement when the destruction of the sacrificial victim's life, in atonement for the people's sins, took place outside the gates of the city (Lev 16:27; c.f., Heb 10:11-12; 13:11-12).

Like the Tamid lamb that received a drink before its sacrifice at the Temple altar that same morning, the Roman soldiers offered Jesus a drink before they nailed Him on the altar of the Cross (*Mishnah: Tamid,* 3:4B). It was the practice of the soldiers performing the executions to offer the condemned man wine mixed with a narcotic to dull the pain (prepared by the women of Jerusalem) before nailing and tying the limbs of the crucifixion victim to the beams of wood. Tasting the drink, Jesus refused the rest of it (Mt 27:34). At the Last Supper, Jesus vowed not to drink wine again until He came into His kingdom (Lk 22:18), but He tasted the wine in an action that mirrored the preparations for the sacrifice of the Tamid lamb in the Temple courtyard.

According to St. Mark's Gospel, Jesus was crucified at the third hour (9 AM) outside the walls of Jerusalem (Mk 15:25). After they crucified Him, the four Roman soldiers took His garments and divided them into four shares. However, they cast lots for His expensive seamless linen tunic (Jn 19:23-24a). The Gospel of John records that their action was a fulfillment of prophecy from Psalm 22:19: *They divided my garments among them, and for my vesture they cast lots.* Jesus' seamless linen tunic was the garment of a chief priest. A priest could only wear the seamless priestly garment when performing his duties in the Temple, and he had to wear ordinary clothes when not in service (Ez 44:17-19). That Jesus wore the priestly seamless linen tunic to both the Last Supper and His crucifixion identifies both events as liturgical.

At the same time that Jesus' crucifixion was taking place outside the gates of Jerusalem, the gates of the Temple were opening for the morning liturgical service just as the sacrifice of the unblemished male Tamid lamb took place at the Temple altar of Burnt Offerings. Throughout the morning worship service, the altar fire consumed the entire body of the Tamid lamb. Later, priests would deposit its ashes outside the gates of Jerusalem (Lev 6:8b-11/6:1-4; *Mishnah: Tamid,* 1:2-2:5). The life of Jesus of Nazareth, the sinless Lamb of God, was consumed on the altar of the Cross, and like the ashes of the other whole-burnt offerings including the Tamid lambs, His remains were also left outside the holy city (Jn 20:41).

All faithful and religiously observant people were attending the morning worship service of the Tamid at the Temple. It was the first day of the Feast of Unleavened Bread that began at sundown the night before, and it was the first of two required Sacred Assemblies of the covenant people on the first and last day of the feast: *And on the fifteenth day of this month is a feast; seven days shall unleavened bread be eaten. On the first day, there shall be a holy convocation [...] On the eighth day, you shall have a solemn assembly: you shall do no laborious work [...] You shall offer these besides the burnt offering of the morning* [the morning Tamid lamb], *which is for a continual burnt offering ['olat ha-Tamid]* (Num 28:17-35). It was perfect timing on the part of the elders and chief priests. They counted on Jesus' followers either being in hiding in fear for their lives or attending the Temple worship service and Sacred Assembly.

It was a lengthy liturgical service; in addition to the morning Tamid, there were eleven separate communal animal sacrifices for the Feast of Unleavened Bread as well as the people's *Hagigah* festival offerings that groups of the faithful intended to eat in the holy city that day (Num 28:17-25). The religious Jews who were Jesus' followers and believed He was the Messiah were attending the Temple services did not discover the crucifixion their beloved Lord until long after the darkness that began at noon (and lifted at 3 PM) and the conclusion of the afternoon Temple services at 5 PM when it was too late to intervene.

The Roman governor, Pontus Pilate, took one last action that showed his contempt for the Temple hierarchy who forced him to condemn Jesus of

Nazareth. Despite the protests of the chief priests, Pilate insisted that the plaque naming the crime of the convicted criminal in Jesus' case should read in three languages, Latin, Greek, and Hebrew (or Aramaic): *Jesus of Nazareth, King of the Jews* (Jn 19:19-22). The Roman historian Suetonius mentions it was a common practice to publicly display the criminal's crime on a board called a *titulus* (*Caligula*, 32). Ironically, the plaque truthfully proclaimed not Jesus' crime but His true identity.

Suspended from the Cross, the first words Jesus spoke recalled Isaiah's prophecy of the suffering Messiah: *because he poured out his soul to death, and was numbered with the transgressors; yet he bore the sin of many, and made intercession for the transgressors* (Is 53:12b; underlining added). Jesus offered words of intercession for His enemies and executioners: *"Father, forgive them, for they know not what they do"* (Lk 23:34). The Son of God judged the sins of those responsible for His unjust condemnation and execution to be forgivable.

The Synoptic Gospels record that total darkness, like that of a solar eclipse, began at the sixth-hour Jewish time (noon our time) and lasted until about the ninth hour Jewish time which is 3 PM (Mt 27:45; Mk 15:33; Lk 23:44). The day of Jesus' execution on the 15th of Nisan according to the lunar calendar was during the full moon cycle. A solar eclipse during a full moon cycle is impossible according to the laws of nature since, during a full moon, the earth is between the moon and the sun. This event was a miracle not associated with any natural cause, and it was a phenomenon noted by Roman historians.[4]

At the Temple, in preparation for the afternoon liturgical service, noon was when a priest led the second male Tamid lamb out to the altar for its last inspection by the High Priest. Suddenly, darkness engulfed the entire Temple complex. However, even this event could not stop the ritual of the *'olat ha-Tamid.* By the light of the altar fire, Caiaphas judged the Tamid lamb worthy of sacrifice by declaring the victim without "fault" after which the afternoon Tamid lamb received a final drink (*Mishnah: Tamid,* 4:1G). It may have been at this point that Jesus, the Lamb of God, was offered a second drink (see Lk 23:36-38 where Jesus received the offer of another drink as He hung on the Cross but before His final the final drink in Jn 19:28-29).

The plunging of the world into darkness must have caused panic at the Temple just as it must have frightened those Jews and Gentiles who were attending the crucifixion of the three men on the hill called Golgotha outside the city gates (Mk 15:27). The Temple worship service continued with the congregation unaware of the events taking place on Golgotha. The afternoon service would not conclude until the final priestly benediction at about 5 PM, the eleventh-hour Jewish time.

At about the ninth-hour Jewish time (3 PM), Jesus said: "*I thirst.*" St. John writes that Jesus' words fulfilled Scriptural prophecy (Jn 19:28). A Roman soldier dipped a hyssop branch in some sour red wine and extended it on a stick up to Jesus' mouth (Mt 27:48; Lk 23:36; Jn 19:29). A hyssop branch was used to splash the blood of the Passover victims in the sign of a cross over the doors of the Israelites in the first Passover event in Egypt from the threshold to the lintel to the two doorposts (Ex 12:22). Hyssop was also used to sprinkle the blood of the sacrifice on the people and the altar in the covenant ratification ceremony at Mount Sinai (Heb 9:19). And hyssop dipped in the holy water mixed with the ashes of the sin sacrifice of an unblemished red heifer purified the covenant people when they became ritually defiled by death (Num 19:19, 17-22).

12 Seasonal Daylight Hours
Divisions in the Litergy of the Tamid Worship Service
Compared to Christ's Crucifixion

"...since the priests ...did still twice each day, in the morning and about the ninth hour, offer their sacrifice on the altar" Josephus, Antiquities of the Jews 14.4.3 [65]

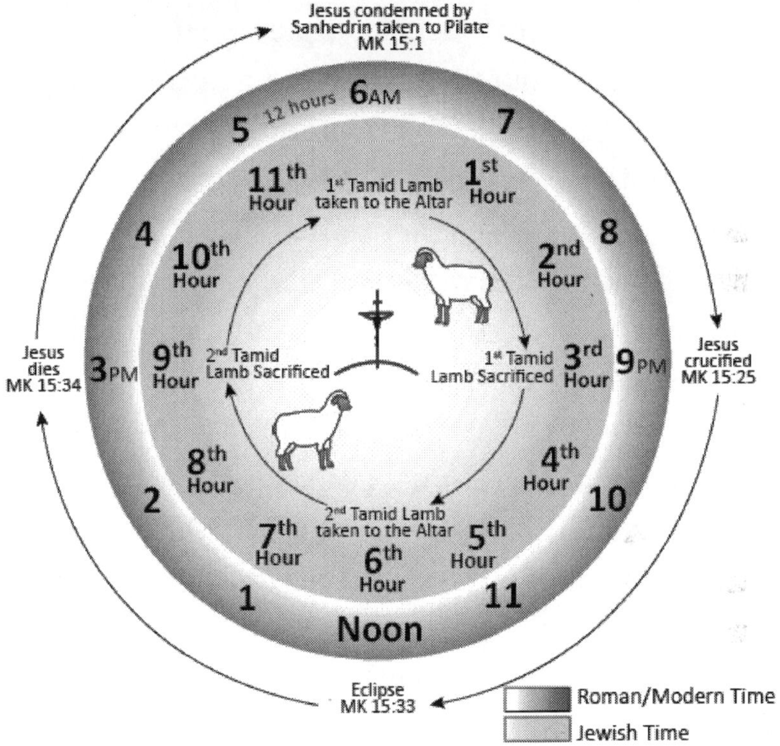

This critical moment in salvation history approached its climax when Jesus said, *"I thirst,"* and the Roman soldier offered the Lamb of God His last drink before His sacrificial death. The wine Jesus accepted was the final symbolic moment in the ratification ceremony of the New Covenant people of God—a covenant which was prophesied to cleanse humanity from the contamination of sin that leads to eternal death (Jer 31:31, 34). Jesus completed His sworn oath at the Last Supper not to drink wine again until He came into His kingdom in His acceptance of this last drink of wine from the Cross (Mt 26:29; Mk 14:25; Lk 22:17-18). It was "the cup" Jesus mentioned in His petition to the Father in the garden of Gethsemane (Mt 26:39, 42; Mk 14:36; Lk 22:42) and the cup of God's wrath that Jesus drank on behalf of a sinful humanity (Is 51:17, 22; Jer 25:15). But it was also the Cup of Acceptance/Consecration, the cup that marked the acceptance of God's covenant with His people in the sacred meal of the Passover victim—the fourth ritual cup He didn't take at the Last Supper. It was the cup that sealed a New and Everlasting Covenant of Christ's eternal Kingdom (Jer 32:40; 50:5; 1 Pt 1:11).

As Jesus drank the wine, He cried out the last two of His seven statements from the Cross: *"It is finished/fulfilled!"* (Jn 19:30) and *"Father into Your hands I commit my Spirit!"* (Mt 27:50; Mk 15:36; Lk 23:46).[5] As Jesus promised, He fulfilled the Old Covenant, paid the debt of humanity's sin, and ratified the New Covenant in His blood—the "blood of the covenant." Jesus Christ is the end and the fulfillment of the Old Covenant Law in two ways:

1. Jesus fulfills the purpose and goal of the Old Covenant Law. He stated in Matthew 5:17, *"I have not come to abolish the Law but to fulfill it."* He does this by perfectly exemplifying God's desires for humans created in His image; no other man except the Jesus Christ could perfectly keep the Law without sinning.

2. Jesus is also the termination of the Old Covenant Law because, without Him, the Old Law was powerless to offer the gifts of the Holy Spirit and eternal salvation (CCC 1963, 1966). Taking His last breath, He then breathed out His Spirit upon the world (Jn 19:30).

The old Law prefigured Christ. The sacrificial system was a temporary measure of salvation meant to instruct and prepare humanity for the coming of the Messiah (Heb 10:1-4). Christ was the reason for animal sacrifice and the ritual purity laws—the Law pointed to Christ who fulfilled it. Only through Jesus Christ will humanity receive the gift of eternal salvation and the indwelling of the Holy Spirit (CCC 601-04, 729, 1287).

According to the Gospel of Mark, and in agreement with the other Synoptic Gospels, Jesus suffered on the Cross from the third to the ninth hours (9 AM to 3 PM). As the ancients counted, He suffered for six hours and then gave up His life at the beginning of the seventh hour. Six is the number of human beings, created on the sixth day of Creation, and seven is the number of fulfillment and completion. Jesus came to fulfill, just as He said in His last statement from the Cross in St. John's Gospel (Jn 19:30). At the beginning of His seventh hour on the Cross, Jesus willingly gave up His life, breathing out His Spirit upon the earth and all of humanity.

At the Temple, despite the darkness, the second Tamid lamb was slain (*Mishnah: Tamid,* 3:4B) at the ninth hour (3 PM); it was the same time Jesus gave us His life as a sacrifice for all humanity (Mt 27:46, 50; Mk 15:34, 36; Lk 23:44, 46). A priest splashed and poured out the lamb's atoning and sanctifying blood against the altar as a Roman soldier pierced Jesus side and blood and water poured out of His chest (Jn 19:34). In the Temple, other priests had just entered the Holy Place in the Sanctuary to attend to the Menorah lampstand and cleanse the golden incense altar. At that moment, the earth shook and groaned as Jesus' sacrifice tore creation from the power of Satan. And to the shock and horror of the priests ministering in the Holy Place, the curtain that was as thick as a man's hand that covered the entrance to the Holy of Holies was torn in half from top to bottom (Mt 27:51; Mk 15:38; Lk 23:45b).

The curtain that covered the entrance to the Holy of Holies in the Temple was a continual reminder to the covenant people of the separation from God imposed by their covenant failure in the sin of the Golden Calf (Ex 33:3-4). The curtain was ripped apart from top to bottom, removing the barrier between God and humanity by God's acceptance of the Son's sacrifice. Jesus took the burden of humanity's covenant failure in Eden upon Himself, and He opened the way into the presence of God for all men and women in every age and generation. The renting of the curtain symbolized the gates of Heaven torn open, ready to receive the first fruits of the harvest of souls into God's heavenly storehouse (Mk 1:9-10; 1 Pt 3:18-22; Rev 4:1; CCC 536 and 1026).

At this climactic moment in salvation history, when Jesus, "the Lamb of God," poured out His life as He hung on the altar of the Cross, it is significant that the liturgical ritual and sacrificial deaths of the morning and afternoon Tamid lambs marked the beginning and end of Christ's Passion. See the chart on the Tamid and Christ's crucifixion. The coming together of the single sacrifice of the two unblemished Tamid lambs with the New Covenant sacrifice of the sinless Jesus, "the Lamb of God who takes away the sins of the world" (Jn 1:29), establishes the centuries of the "standing/continual" Tamid sacrifice as a foreshadowing of the Passion of the Redeemer-Messiah.

The Tamid was the single sacrifice of two perfect male lambs. It was the premier sacrifice of the Sinai Covenant offered perpetually in atonement for the sins and sanctification of the covenant people and all humanity. Prefiguring the Passion of the Christ, the morning Tamid lamb symbolized Jesus' human nature, and the afternoon Tamid lamb symbolized His divinity. The two natures of Christ offered in one sacrifice. The offering of each lamb included unleavened bread and a red wine libation, prefiguring the Eucharistic banquet of the New Covenant. In the New Covenant sacred meal of "Thanksgiving," the bread and wine become the sacrificed Lamb—the Body and Blood, Soul and Divinity of the Savior of humanity in a New Covenant sacred meal that, through the healing power of Christ's blood, forgives sins and sanctifies the people of the Triune God (Mt 26:28; CCC 1393-95).

Jesus suffered and died on a Friday, the sixth day of the week, the day when God created humankind in the first Creation event (Gen 1:26-31). On the Cross from 9 in the morning until 3 in the afternoon, Jesus suffered for seven hours (as the ancients counted); it was one hour for each day of the old creation that had become contaminated by sin and death through the fall of the first Adam. He also suffered one hour for each of the seven covenants of God previously made in anticipation of the final, eternal Covenant in Christ Jesus (see Appendix I). In the hour of fulfillment, in the seventh hour, Jesus the second Adam gave up His life for His Bride, the Church, and for the salvation of humanity.

After Jesus gave up His life and breathed out His Spirit, there were only a few hours left before the Jewish day came to an end at sundown. At sundown, the Great Sabbath of the holy, seven-day celebration of Unleavened Bread began. Today the Jews, except for the Karaites and Samaritans, celebrate the "Great Sabbath" either before or after the Passover "holy week." However, before the Resurrection of the Christ, the "Great Sabbath" fell within the seven days of Unleavened Bread. It was a religious requirement that all activities must cease with the coming of the Sabbath (Ex 20:8-11). Therefore, the Jewish authorities required the hastening of the deaths of the crucifixion victims so their bodies could be removed and buried before sundown. *Since it was the day of Preparation, in order to prevent the bodies from remaining on the cross on the Sabbath (for that Sabbath was a high day), the Jews asked Pilate that their legs might be broken, and that they might be taken away* (Jn 19:31). The Roman soldiers broke the legs of the two men crucified on either side of Jesus. When one of the soldiers approached Jesus, he did not break

Jesus' legs; instead, he thrust a spear into His side, *and at once there came out blood and water* (19:34).

The inspired writer of the Gospel of John who, according to Christian tradition and the testimony of the early Church Fathers like Bishop St. Irenaeus (m. AD 200/202, *Against Heresies, 3.1.1*) was the Apostle John Zebedee, testified that he was an eyewitness to these events (Jn 20:35; 21:24-25). St. John recorded that everything took place to fulfill the words of Sacred Scripture. Then he quoted two passages: *"Not a bone of him shall be broken." And again another scripture says, "They shall look on him whom they have pierced"* (Jn 19:36-37). The first Scripture reference fulfilled the command that none of the bones of the Passover victim were to be broken (Ex 12:46; *Mishnah: Pesahim,* 7:11C), identifying Jesus as the sacrificial victim of the last Passover, which the first Passover prefigured. The second reference fulfilled the oracle of the 6th-century BC prophet Zechariah when the people of Jerusalem grieved over the death of the Jesus, the Davidic Messiah, whose side the Roman soldier pierced. Zechariah wrote: *And I will pour out on the house of David and the inhabitants of Jerusalem a spirit of compassion and supplication, so that, when they look on him whom they have pierced, they shall mourn for him, as one mourns for an only child, and weep bitterly over him, as one weeps over a firstborn* (Zec 12:10, underlining added for emphasis).

On the altar of the Cross, Jesus' arms were extended to embrace the world. From His chest, pierced by the Roman lance, flowed out water and blood (Jn 19:34). As St. John wrote years later in his letter to the universal Church: *There are three witnesses, the Spirit, the water and the blood; and these three agree* (1 Jn 5:8). St. John meant that the three testimonies converged with the blood and water from Jesus' side, joining the Spirit to the mission of the Son who gave His life for the salvation of the world. The water and the blood that flowed from Jesus' side are the witnesses of the Sacraments of Baptism and the Eucharist (CCC 1225).

Baptism infuses new life in transforming the sons and daughters of Adam into the sons and daughters of God, re-born through the regenerative power of water and the Holy Spirit (Jn 3:3-6). It is a spiritual rebirth that restores Christians to the relationship of divine sonship/daughtership lost in the Fall of Adam and Eve (Jn 3:3, 5; Rom 6:1-4; 8:14-17; Gal 3:27; 4:5-7; Col 2:11-13). The Eucharist is a sacramental meal of covenant continuation that has the power to purify and nourish the reborn children of God on their journey through earthly life to the promised land of Heaven (Jn 3:3, 5-8; 6:53-58). At that moment, as the blood and water flowed from Jesus' side, the eternal blessing for which God created the first humans in the Garden of Eden were again available to humanity through Jesus' perfect sacrifice: *He was in the world, and the world was made through him, yet the world knew him not. He came to his own home, and his own people received him not. But to all who received him, who believed in his name, he gave power to become children of God; who were born, not of blood nor of the will of the flesh nor of the will of man, but of God* (Jn 1:10–13).

By the power of His sacrificial death, Jesus, the author of the first creation (Jn 1:1–5; Col 1:15–18), redeemed both creation and humanity (the masterpiece of the first creation). Jesus brought about a New Covenant for a new creation (Rev 21:5) and established as the new Eden the universal Kingdom of Jesus Christ, the Church, where humanity and God commune as a united family. St. John wrote: *And from his fullness have we all received, grace upon grace. For the law was given to Moses; grace and truth came through Jesus Christ. No one has ever seen God; the only Son, who is in the bosom of the Father, he has made him known* (Jn 1:16–17).

God established the New Covenant, like the seven previous old covenants, by oath swearing, a blood sacrifice, and a sacred meal. These are the three elements that also promised covenant continuation for every succeeding generation:

- **Jesus' sworn oath:** He vowed not to eat the sacred meal again until it was fulfilled in the kingdom of God (Lk 22:16), and not to drink wine again until He came into His Kingdom (Mt 26:29; Mk 14:25; Lk 22:18).
- **The blood sacrifice:** Jesus offered His blood sacrifice in the cup of His blood that He passed at the Last Supper and which was made present on the altar of the Cross (Lk 22:20Eph 5:2; Heb 10:12).
- **The sacred meal:** The New Covenant sacred meal was inaugurated at the Last Supper and carried forward in the New Covenant Todah of the Eucharist. The sacred meal of the Eucharist is, like the first corporate covenant ratification ceremony on Mount Sinai, a moment suspended in time when the faithful consume a communal meal in the presence of God. It is a meal of bread and wine that becomes Jesus' Body and Blood and promises covenant continuation throughout the generations (Ex 24:9-11; Mt 26:26-28; Mk 14:22-24; Lk 22:19-20; 1 Cor 11:23-27).

The perfect sacrifice of Jesus Christ fulfills the old Sinai Covenant and its premier atoning and sanctifying sacrifice, the *'olat ha-Tamid.* In its place is the New Covenant, with its worldwide blessing promised to the Patriarchs, the eternal kingdom promised to David and the prophets, and the atoning and sanctifying sacrifice of "the Lamb of God who takes away the sins of the world," all foreshadowed in the Tamid. It is established now and forever in the eternal Kingdom of God the Son.

CHAPTER SUMMARY POINTS: THE ALTAR OF THE CROSS

1. Like the first Adam, Jesus, the second Adam faced a covenant ordeal in a garden that changed the destiny of humanity.

2. Jesus agonized over His decision, but in the end, in obedience to the will of the Father, He accepted His cup of suffering and God's cup of wrath. The cup of God's wrath was a judgment Israel deserved for covenant disobedience and the world deserved for sins against humanity.

3. Satan attempted again to usurp and destroy God's plan for humanity, but even during His arrest, trials, and crucifixion, Jesus was in charge of His destiny.

4. Jesus submitted to His arrest and unjust trials. First, He was condemned by many of His countrymen and women for claiming to be the Son of God, and He was condemned by the anointed High Priest who chose Jesus to die for the sake of the people. Then, the Gentile Roman governor, who knew He was innocent and pronounced Him "without fault," condemned Jesus to death. Later, in the morning Temple liturgy, the High Priest chose the Tamid lamb to die to atone for the people's sins and pronounced it "without fault." The Tamid was an unblemished victim like Jesus that the Jewish High Priest selected for sacrifice and a Roman pagan declared "without fault."

5. Most of Jesus' Apostles and disciples abandoned Him and faced their own covenant ordeals in a crisis of failed expectations and imperfect faith in their inability to trust God's plan.

6. On Friday, the 15th of Nisan, AD 30, Roman soldiers nailed Jesus to the Cross at about 9 AM when the Temple gates opened for the sacrifice of the first Tamid lamb. Most of His friends and followers were either in hiding in fear or were attending the required

Sacred Assembly at the Temple. Only His mother, the Apostle John Zebedee, and a faithful remnant of His woman disciples accompanied Him to the site of His crucifixion.

7. Jesus suffered on the Cross for six full hours and gave up His life at the beginning of the seventh hour (as the ancients counted). He suffered for each day of the old creation and for each of the seven covenants God had previously made with individuals and the children of Israel as a covenant nation. The second Tamid lamb received a drink before its sacrifice at about the ninth hour Jewish time (3 PM). After requesting and accepting a drink of wine, symbolizing the "cup of God's wrath," the divine judgment deserved by sinful humanity, and the Cup of Consecration/Acceptance of the New Covenant, Jesus breathed His last and exhaled His Spirit out upon the earth at about the ninth hour Jewish time (3 PM). Jesus' one perfect sacrifice of His life, offered as fully man and fully God on the altar of the Cross, fulfilled all the necessary blood sacrifices of the Old Covenant. It also uniquely fulfilled the Tamid sacrifice, opening the way into the presence of God for all baptized New Covenant believers.

8. Oath swearing, blood sacrifice, and the sacred meal continue as the principal elements of covenant

formation and continuation in the New Covenant of the everlasting Kingdom of Jesus Christ.

Endnotes: The Altar of the Cross

1. The Divine Name is rendered "YHWH" in the Old Testament. Based on etymology and context, most scholars agree that YHWH is an archaic form of the verb "to be" (hwh in Hebrew, pronounced "hawah") and should be translated "I AM who I AM" or "I will be who I will be." Or, for those scholars who believe the verb is in the causative imperfect masculine singular form, "He causes to be; brings into existence; He brings to pass, He creates" (Propp, Studies in Exodus, page 72-73). The use of the Greek Ego Ami by Jesus also supports the "I AM" translation.
2. See *Mishnah: Hagigah*, 1:3 and 1:5. The reference to the offering of the festival Hagigah on the first day of the Feast of Unleavened Bread in the Hagigah tractate of the Mishnah only uses only the term "Passover" even though the passages concern the communion sacrifices during Sacred Assembly on the first day of the festival of Unleavened Bread (*Mishnah: Hagigah*, 3:1 III). *Mishnah: Pesahim*, 4:4 refers to the "nights of the Passover" plural when eating the "meat of the Passover," referring to the Hagigah communion offerings consumed during the entire week.
3. The only exception to becoming ritually cleansed by sundown after contamination was if one came into contact with a dead body, a defilement requiring a seven-day purification process (Num 19:11-22). The

Jews would not have come into contact with a dead body in Pilate's private residence. They could, however, come into contact with a lesser defilement through the ritually unclean practices of Gentiles from which they could receive ritual cleansing at sundown (Lev 22:6-7) but not in time for the morning Sacred Assembly and eating the hagigah in a communal meal that day.

4. A full solar eclipse occurs when the new moon passes between the earth and the sun with the moon blocking the sun's light on that portion of the earth in the shadow of the moon, as the moon's disk fully covers the sun for several minutes. During a full moon cycle, however, the full moon is on the opposite side of the earth with the earth between the sun and the moon and with the moon reflecting the sun's light (Goldsmith, The Astronomers, page 294). Therefore, according to the rules of physics, it is impossible for a solar eclipse during a full moon cycle. There is no explanation for this phenomenon during Jesus' crucifixion much less for an eclipse that lasted for hours instead of minutes, as it was on the 15th of Nisan in AD 30 from noon until 3 PM. Julius Africanus quoted a Roman scholar named Phlegon who wrote a history in which he commented on the rare phenomenon of a solar eclipse during a full moon cycle at the time of Christ's crucifixion: During the time of Tiberius Caesar an eclipse of the sun occurred during the full moon (Julius Africanus, *Chronography*, 18.1 quoting from *Phlegon's Chronicles*). The third century AD Christian scholar and apologist, Origen, also referenced Phlegon's comments on the event (*Celsum*, 2.14, 33, 59) as did the sixth-century writer Philopon (*De.opif.mund.* II, 21).

5. Jesus' seven last statements from the Cross (*Interlinear Bible Greek-English*, vol. IV): 1. "Father, forgive them, they know not what they do" (Lk 23:34); 2. "Amen I say to you, today you will be with me in Paradise" (Lk 23:42); 3. "Woman, behold, your son"... "Behold, your mother" (Jn 19:26–27); 4. "My God, my God, why have you forsaken me?" (Mt 27:46; Mk 15:34); 5. "I thirst" (Jn 19:28); 6. "It has been finished/fulfilled [tetelestai]" (Jn 19:30); 7. "Father, into your hands, I commit my Spirit" (Lk 23:46).

CHAPTER IX
THE RESURRECTED MESSIAH

For from the rising of the sun to its setting my name is great among the nations, and in every place incense is offered to my name, and a pure offering; for my name is great among the nations, says the LORD of hosts.
Malachi 1:11

Now the point of what we are saying is this: we have such a high priest, one who is seated at the right hand of the throne of the Majesty in heaven, a minister in the sanctuary and the true tent which is set up not by man but by the Lord. For every high priest is appointed to offer gifts and sacrifices; hence it is necessary for this priest also to have something to offer.
Hebrews 8:1-3

JESUS DESCENDS TO THE REALM OF THE DEAD

Before sundown on Friday, the 15th of Nisan, Jesus' disciples laid His lifeless body in a newly hewn tomb outside the walls of Jerusalem (Mt 27:59-60; Mk 15:42-46; Lk 23:50-54). The disciples did not have enough time to prepare His body before the beginning of the Sabbath at sundown. They left Him wrapped in a burial shroud, with a rolled cloth tied around His head and chin in the custom of Jewish burial preparation (Jn 19:38-42; 20:6-7).[1]

Since He was fully human as well as fully divine, Jesus' spirit descended into *Sheol* (*Hades* in Greek), the destination after the death of all men and women since the Fall of Adam.[2] In the depths of *Sheol*, the souls of the dead awaited their liberation by the promised Redeemer. Some souls were waiting in the torment of purifying judgment, and others were waiting in the company of the righteous (Lk 16:19-31; CCC 633).[3] Jesus' atoning sacrifice justified the dead in *Sheol* who accepted His Gospel of salvation, and He led those redeemed souls out of *Sheol* and through the gates of Heaven (1 Pt 3:18, 4:6). For the first time in salvation history, redeemed humanity entered into the "promised land" of Heaven (CCC 1026).

Jesus liberated the dead on Friday, and He rested in the tomb on the Old Covenant Sabbath (Saturday). He rested from His work of salvation as God rested from His work on the seventh day of the first Creation (Gen 2:2-3). On the significant third day (as the ancients counted) since His death, on the first day of the week (our Sunday), Jesus arose from the dead, leaving behind His valuable grave clothes as proof of His Resurrection (Mt 28:1, 6; Mk 16:2, 5-6; Lk 24:1, 5-6; Jn 20:1, 6-9). Jesus' atoning sacrifice and the defeat of death made His bodily Resurrection possible and brought about a new creation in the glorified Redeemer-Messiah.

In His Resurrection on the first day of the week, which was also the eighth consecutive day (the day after the seventh day Old Covenant Sabbath), Jesus healed both humanity and creation of the corrupting power of Satan. Rising on the eighth day, He established the New Covenant Lord's Day on the first day of the new creation, which had also been the first day of the first Creation event in Genesis 1:1. The Catechism acclaims the beginning of the Messianic Era on the eighth day: *But for us, a new day has dawned: the day of Christ's Resurrection. The seventh day completes the first creation. The eighth day begins the new creation. Thus, the work of creation culminates in the greater work of redemption. The first creation finds its meaning and its summit in the new creation in Christ, the splendor of which surpasses that of the first creation* (CCC 349; prayer after the first reading of the Easter Vigil; also see CCC 2174).

The Gospel of Matthew records that in Jerusalem, some of the spirits of the righteous dead also rose up and came out of their tombs on Resurrection Sunday (Mt 27:52-53). The appearance of these long-dead saints was evidence that Jesus was truly raised from death and not only resuscitated. His rising from the dead was a supernatural event intended to impact all humanity, the living and the dead (see 1 Pt 3:18-20 and 4:6). In His resurrection victory, Jesus established a renewed creation in which humanity was no longer bound in slavery to sin and death. Through Jesus' new "exodus liberation," humankind received the promised gift of entering into God's eternal "rest" in the heavenly Kingdom.

In the free-will acceptance of that gift, humanity also received the promise of rebirth through a baptism of water and the Spirit in which every baptized person was no longer a child in the family of Adam but a child in the family of God (Jn 3:3, 5; Rom 6:1-6; 8:14-17). As co-heirs with Christ, the New Covenant children of God inherited the promises made to the Patriarchs and repeated by the prophets that included the world-wide blessing of an eternal kingdom destined to have moral and spiritual authority over all nations and their peoples. The promises of the seven previous old covenants were united to the eternal blessings of the everlasting New Covenant that promised forgiveness of sins, eternal life in the "Promised Land" of Heaven, and the blessing of a resurrected body at the end of time (Jn 11:25-26; 1 Cor 15:20-25; 1 Thes 4:14-17; see the Chart of "Yahweh's Eight Covenants).

According to the Sinai Covenant's liturgical calendar, the day of Jesus' Resurrection was the day on which God commanded the covenant community to celebrate the annual remembrance Feast of Firstfruits (*Yom HaBikkurim*). In Yahweh's words to Moses at Mount Sinai concerning the liturgical calendar and the seven holy remembrance festivals, He gave instructions for keeping the Passover sacrifice on the 14th of Abib/Nisan and the feast of Unleavened Bread beginning on the 15th and lasting for seven days (as the ancients counted) until the 21st (Lev 23:5-8). However, there was another feast within those two, encompassing one entire week and a day or eight days. Yahweh commanded Moses: *"Speak to the Israelites and say: 'When you enter the country which I am giving you and reap the harvest there, you will bring the priest the first sheaf of your harvest, and he will present it to Yahweh with the gesture of offering, for you to be acceptable. The priest will make this offering* ***on the day after the Sabbath****, and on the same day as you make this offering, you will offer Yahweh an unblemished lamb one year old as a burnt offering'"* (Lev 23:9–12 NJB; emphasis added). The grain offering and the sacrifice of a single lamb on the Feast of Firstfruits were on the first day of the week during the holy week of Unleavened Bread, on our Sunday.

JESUS IS THE FIRST FRUITS OF THE RESURRECTION OF THE DEAD

But in fact Christ has been raised from the dead, the first fruits of those who have fallen asleep. For as by a man came death, by a man has come also the resurrection of the dead. For as in Adam all die, so also in Christ shall all be made alive. But each in his own order: Christ the first fruits, then at his coming those who belong to Christ.
1 Corinthians 15:20–23

God commanded at Sinai that the Feast of Firstfruits must fall on the day after the Sabbath (our Saturday), on the first day of the week that we call Sunday. At that time, the Feast of Firstfruits fell within the eight holy days of the celebrations of the feasts of Passover and Unleavened Bread. The days of the week for those feasts (on Nisan the 14th to the 21st) changed every year, but the covenant people were to celebrate Firstfruits on the first day of the week within those eight days. The required communal sacrifice for Firstfruits was the whole-burnt offering of a single, unblemished male lamb, unleavened wheat flour mixed with oil and formed into a small cake as a grain offering, and a red wine libation. In addition to the lamb sacrifice, grain offering, and wine libation, the covenant community was to offer Yahweh the first fruits of the spring barley harvest (Lev 23:11-14).

In the blessing of new life celebrated in the harvest after the death of winter, the covenant people commemorated the miracle of crossing over from death to renewed life. In the early springtime of the first Passover event, the first generation of the children of Israel passed through the waters of the Red Sea, leaving behind their old lives and emerging as a newly created free people. In crossing the miraculously parted waters in the Exodus out of Egypt, the Israelites escaped the bonds of slavery and rejoiced in their baptism of rebirth as the "first fruits" of a holy nation (Ex 14:15-31; Jer 2:2-3; 1 Cor 10:1-3). A symbol of their new life was the offering of the first cutting of the spring grain in the land God promised to the Patriarchs.

The people offered Yahweh the first of the barley harvest as part of the Temple worship service after the sacrifice of the morning Tamid lamb and in conjunction with, but separate from, the continuing communal offerings of the Feast of Unleavened Bread. The Law designated the observance of this feast within a feast a perpetual (*tamid* as an adverb) statute for all generations of the covenant people wherever they lived. *And you shall eat neither bread nor grain parched or fresh until this same day, until you have brought the offering of your God: it is a statute forever [tamid] throughout your generations in all your dwellings* (Lev 23:13-14). On the designated day of the Feast of Firstfruits, Jesus arose from His grave. The feast prefigured Jesus as the "first fruits" of the Resurrection of the dead when He became the first of the great harvest of souls escaping the bonds of death and given the power to enter into God's eternal storehouse in Heaven (1 Cor 15:20-23).

At Mount Sinai, God commanded the covenant people not to begin the annual celebration of the Feast of Firstfruits until they took possession of the Promised Land (Lev 23:10). It is significant that the sacrifice for the Feast of Firstfruits was not part of the multiple sacrifices for the seven-day observance of the Feast of Unleavened Bread and was a separate observance with its unique sacrificial offerings. It is also significant that the festival of Firstfruits determined the date of the next feast in the liturgical calendar, the pilgrim Feast of Weeks (*Hag HaShavuot* in Hebrew, Lev 23:15-21; Num

28:26–31; Dt 16:10–12, 16). It was known as the Feast of Harvest, *Hag HaKatzir,* (Ex 23:16) and later, among Greek-speaking Jews in the first century AD, as "Pentecost" (Tob 2:1; Acts 2:1).

The Greek word *penetkoste* means "fiftieth day" and refers to the timing of the festival fifty days after Firstfruits (as the ancients counted). From the Feast of Firstfruits, seven weeks were counted, with the Feast of Pentecost observed at the end of the seventh week on the fiftieth day (Lev 23:15–23). The festival celebrated the first fruits of the wheat harvest and commemorated Israel's rendezvous with Yahweh at Mount Sinai fifty days after leaving Egypt (Ex 19:6). The Jews viewed Pentecost as a covenant renewal ceremony (*Jubilees* 6:17–21), and the Babylonian Talmud (c. AD 250) also identified the feast with the "day the Torah was given" to Israel (*Babylonian Talmud: Pes.*, 68b). The celebration of the feasts of Firstfruits and Pentecost always fell on the first day of the week (our Sunday) within the Tamid liturgical service with specific communal sacrifices and the offering of the first fruits of the barley harvest and fifty days later the wheat harvest at God's altar. Accompanying the offerings was a formal profession of faith by the offeror, recounting the history God's redemption of Israel from slavery in Egypt and the giving of the Promised Land (Num 28:31; Dt 26:1-10; *Antiquities of the Jews*, 13.8.4 [252]).

The Feast of Firstfruits, on the first day after the Sabbath of the holy week of Unleavened Bread, and the Feast of Weeks/Pentecost, fifty days later, also on a Sunday, fulfilled two New Covenant miracles:

1. The Resurrection of the divine Messiah, Jesus of Nazareth (Mt 28:1-8), who was the
2. "first fruits of the resurrected dead, and
3. The birth of the New Covenant Church in the Upper Room on Mount Zion in Jerusalem, the "first fruits" of the New Covenant people of God (Acts 2:1-4).

Significantly, it was part of God's divine plan that these were the only two feasts in the Old Covenant annual liturgical calendar that did not have a specific date assigned to them according to the commands God gave Moses (Lev Chapter 23).[4] The New Covenant remembrances of the miracles of Jesus' Resurrection and the coming of the Holy Spirit to the Church on the Feast of Pentecost continue to be observed on Sundays, according to two thousand years of Christian tradition.

On Resurrection Sunday, Jesus repeated His earlier command by giving the ministers of His Church the powers to bind and loose in matters of sin and forgiveness (Mt 16:16; 18:18 and repeated in Jn 20:22-

23). Jesus taught the New Covenant community for forty days after His Resurrection: *To them he presented himself alive after his passion by many proofs, appearing to them during forty days, and speaking of the kingdom of God* (Acts 1:3). The resurrected Savior told them: *"everything written about me in the law of Moses and the prophets and the psalms must be fulfilled." Then he opened their minds to understand the scriptures* (Lk 24:44-47). Jesus instructed His followers to teach future generations how He fulfilled everything promised and prophesied in the (Old Testament) Scriptures.

At the end of the forty days since His Resurrection, Jesus had a meeting with His faithful disciples. He told them to stay in Jerusalem, to remain in prayer, and to be prepared to be baptized with the Holy Spirit (Acts 1:4-5). Then, taking them to the Mount of Olives, located about a half a mile to the east of the city, He reminded them again of His promise and told them their destiny was to be His witnesses as they carried the Gospel message of salvation from Jerusalem, Samaria, and the ends of the earth (Acts 1:6-8).

As the Apostles and disciples watched Jesus, they saw the same vision as the 6th-century BC prophet Daniel when he saw *one like a Son of man* coming on the clouds of Heaven *to the Ancient of Days* and being *presented before him* (Dan 7:13). They saw the vision fulfilled before their eyes as Jesus ascended in a white cloud into the heavenly Sanctuary to be received by God the Father (Acts 1:9). Like the unblemished Tamid lamb burning on the Temple altar whose essence rose up to Heaven to be accepted by God in the smoky white cloud of the *Olah*, Jesus, the unblemished Lamb of God that all other lambs of sacrifice prefigured, ascended to God the Father in His heavenly Temple. There Jesus took His place as both the Davidic King of the Kingdom of God and the High Priest of the heavenly Sanctuary (Lk 1:32-33; Heb 8:1-2). And, as Daniel saw in his vision, *to him was given dominion and glory and kingdom, that all peoples, nations, and languages should serve him, his dominion is an everlasting dominion, which shall not pass away and his kingdom one that shall not be destroyed* (Dan 7:14; also see Ps 110:1-4; Mt 22:41-45; Heb 5:5-6; 8:1b-3).

Obeying Jesus' command to stay in Jerusalem and to continue in prayer until the coming of the Holy Spirit, the disciples returned to the Upper Room and prayed together for nine days in the presence of the Virgin Mary (Acts 1:4-5, 12-14).[5] On the fiftieth day since Jesus' Resurrection, it was the Jewish pilgrim feast of Weeks/Pentecost (Dt 16:16; 2 Chr 8:13; Acts 2:1). Jews from across the Roman world came to Jerusalem to celebrate the feast that commemorated God's fiery Theophany on Mount Sinai when He took the children of Israel as His holy priestly nation (Ex 19:6, 16-19). They came to attend the Sacred Assembly, to offer the required communal sacrifices within the liturgy of the morning Tamid, and to offer the first fruits of the holy land's wheat harvest at the Temple (Num 28:26-31).

On that Sunday, the promised Paraclete (Advocate), God the Holy Spirit, descended from Heaven to take possession of the faithful remnant of the old Israel. They were a community of one hundred and twenty New Covenant people of God, praying with the Virgin Mary in the Upper Room on Mount Zion in old part of Jerusalem that was also called "the city of David" (Jn 14:15-16, 26; 15:26; Acts 1:13-15; 2:1-3). It was fitting that the Virgin Mary, who was a key figure at the beginning of God's great plan, experiencing the indwelling of God the Holy Spirit at the Incarnation, was present to witness the indwelling of the Holy Spirit as He took possession of Her Son's Kingdom of the Church (Lk 1:35). It was a baptism of holy fire that transformed Jesus' disciples into the priestly nation of the spiritually restored Israel promised by the prophets (Jer 31:31-34; Ez 36:24-27). They became the "first fruits" of the New Covenant people, receiving the first spiritual fruits of the Holy Spirit and becoming the first community of the universal Church of the everlasting Kingdom (Acts 2:1-4).

At 9 AM that morning, the people of Jerusalem and all visiting pilgrims were on their way to the Temple to celebrate the Feast of Pentecost within the liturgy of the morning Tamid worship service (Num 28:26, 31). Those passing by the house witnessed the spiritual ecstasy of Jesus' Apostles and disciples as they poured out of the Upper Room into the street, declaring Jesus' Gospel of salvation in all the languages and dialects of the Jewish pilgrims who had traveled to Jerusalem from across the Roman Empire (Acts 2:5-11). God planned that the Resurrection of God the Son and the coming of the Paraclete were to be precisely at these two appointed times in salvation history: on the Old Covenant harvest feasts of Firstfruits and Pentecost. Not only were the feasts of Passover, Unleavened Bread, Firstfruits and Pentecost fulfilled in the First Advent of the Messiah, but Jesus fulfilled all the sacred feasts and all the different classes of bloody and unbloody sacrifices in His one perfect sacrifice. St. Paul wrote to the Jewish Christians at Colossus: *Then never let anyone criticize you for what you eat or drink, or about the observance of Annual Festivals, New Moons or Sabbaths. These are only a shadow of what was coming: the reality is the body of Christ* (Col 2:16).[6]

It is significant that the Feast of Firstfruits was the only communal blood sacrifice of the Sinai Covenant, other than the morning and afternoon Tamid and the additional Sabbath holocaust, that required the sacrificial offering of a single, unblemished male lamb (Ex 29:38-39; Lev 22:27; 23:12; Num 28:3-4, 9-10). All the other sacrifices either required multiple male lambs (festival communal burnt offerings) or lambs and kids (Passover), or adult rams or ewes, or goats, or cattle. It is also significant that the daily Tamid sacrifice of the morning and afternoon and the sacrifice of the single male lamb on the Feast of Firstfruits were the only single lamb sacrifices designated as "tamid," meaning "standing" as in continual or perpetual sacrifices (the Sabbath lambs were not).

According to God's command, the sacrifices of both the daily morning and afternoon Tamid and the annual Firstfruits lamb must include the offerings of unleavened bread and red wine (Ex 29:38-42; Lev 23:12-14; Num 28:3).[7] The Firstfruits lamb sacrifice, in addition to the twice-daily Tamid lambs, uniquely prefigured the Passion of the Christ, His Resurrection, and the Eucharistic offering of the unleavened bread and the red wine that became the resurrected Lamb on New Covenant altars. It is the Eucharist that becomes the "perpetual" (*tamid*) feast of the New Covenant Church that Jesus offered at the Last Supper, and which the covenant people must observe until Christ's Second Advent at the end of time as we know it.

The Feast of Firstfruits foreshadowed God's plan that the Christ should be resurrected on the Feast of Firstfruits, on a Sunday within the seven-day pilgrim feast of Unleavened Bread. And the Feast of Pentecost foreshadowed that the birth of the New Covenant Church should fall on a Sunday on the Feast of Pentecost, which commemorated the fiery Theophany at Mount Sinai and Israel's election as God's holy covenant community and the Church of the Old Covenant. On the pilgrim feast of Pentecost in AD 30, faithful Jews and God-fearing Gentiles from across the Roman world were present in Jerusalem for the miracle of the birth of the New Covenant Church. The men and women who gathered in obedience to Yahweh's command to appear before His altar on the pilgrim Feast of Pentecost had the opportunity to hear of the redeeming work of Jesus Christ preached in their national dialects from the mouths of Jesus' Apostles and disciples.

Speaking in the universal language of the Gospel of salvation, the second great Pentecost's divine visitation was a reversal of the dismemberment of the universal family of humanity and the confusion of tongues in the event of the Tower of Babel (cf., Gen 11:1-9 and Acts 2:5-

12). Men and women from across the Roman world heard the Gospel of Jesus Christ preached in their diverse languages, and they carried the message of salvation back to their homelands. It was also a reversal of the loss of the 3,000 souls in the Exodus rebellion of the Golden Calf as, in response to Peter's homily, 3,000 of the Old Covenant people became converts to the New Covenant in Christ Jesus (Ex 32:28 and Acts 2:41).

The identification of these feasts and the events associated with them in the Resurrection of the Messiah and the coming of the divine Paraclete (God the Holy Spirit) is what determined for Christians that the first day of the week, Sunday, became the day of worship for the New Covenant people of the Messiah's Kingdom. It was the celebration of the new creation which they called "the Lord's Day" (Jn 20:19; Acts 20:7; Rev 1:10).[8] That the observance of the Feast of Firstfruits was to be *tamid,* literally "standing" as in continual, meant it was to be a perpetual observance for all time (Lev 23:14). The life of the Church fulfills this divine command as she relives the event of the Resurrection of the Messiah and His gift of salvation on every Easter Sunday, every Pentecost Sunday, and every Sunday celebration of the Mass. Today, in the New Covenant celebration of the first fruits of Christ's Resurrection, we count fifty days from Easter Sunday to Pentecost Sunday, just as the ancients counted, with the first day counting as day #1 in the sequence.

CHAPTER SUMMARY POINTS: THE RESURRECTION OF THE MESSIAH

1. Immediately after His death, Jesus descended into *Sheol* to preach His Gospel of salvation to the dead. He redeemed all repentant and purified souls and led them into Heaven. Three days after his death (as the ancients counted), Jesus rose from the dead on the first day of the week (Sunday), the day after the Jewish Sabbath on the Feast of Firstfruits.

2. Jesus' death and resurrection fulfilled all the God-ordained rituals of blood sacrifices under the Old Covenant and also the annual holy feast days, especially the first three festivals that fell within the eight-day period that included Passover, Unleavened Bread, and Firstfruits:

- He was the Passover victim who offered Himself in sacrifice for the liberation of humanity from death and sin.
- He was the sacrifice without sin consumed in a sacred meal as prefigured in eating the

Passover victims on the first night of the Feast of Unleavened Bread.

- He was the first fruits of the harvest of souls into God's storehouse as He led the souls of those redeemed by His sacrifice across the barrier of death into the "Promised Land" of Heaven.
- He fulfilled and brought to completion salvation history's repeated theme of covenant and blood, judgment and redemption. He completed the two-fold purpose that the blood of sacrifice had in God's plan for humanity: blood was the chief agent in covenant-making, and blood was the necessary agent in expiation/atonement for sins.

3. Jesus Christ provided a path into Heaven; a way that had remained closed since the Fall of Adam (CCC 536, 1026). Now, because of Jesus' self-sacrifice, the gates of Heaven were open to receive the great harvest of souls. The blessings and promises of the New Covenant both fulfill and surpass those of the Old (Heb 8:6):

- The promise of God's "rest": Jesus is the "first fruits" of the harvest of souls, and His disciples also receive the "first fruits" of the Spirit of God, granted to them at the miracle of the second "great Pentecost" (Acts 1:3-4; the first great Pentecost was the Theophany at Mt. Sinai). The prophets promised that one day God would pour out His Spirit upon all humanity (Num 11:25-30; Is 2:2; 32:15; Ez 39:29 Jl 3:1-5; Acts 2:17-21). God fulfilled that promise on the Jewish Feast of Weeks/Pentecost on a Sunday in AD 30, and it continues for all Christians in the Sacraments of Baptism and Confirmation (Acts 2:1, 38-39; Eph 1:13).

- The promise of the eternal Kingdom: Jesus is the "stone" that shattered and absorbed the previous world kingdoms that dominated the people of God (Dan 2:34). His Church is the fifth and everlasting Kingdom (Dan 2:35; 44-45).

- The promise of eternal life: Entrance into the Kingdom of God is now the hope of all New Covenant believers. The Church is Christ's Kingdom of Heaven on earth. Mother Church is both the guide and the portal that leads to the promise of entrance into Christ's heavenly Kingdom. His promise belongs to those who remain faithful to the will of God (Jas 2:5; Heb 10:26, 35, 39). Jesus assures those who persevere in faithfulness to the end of their lives will wear the crown of eternal life (Jas 1:12; 1 Jn 2:25; Rev 2:10).

- The promises made to the Patriarchs and the Prophets: Jesus fulfills the promises of a worldwide blessing, forgiveness of sins, and restored fellowship with God (Gen 22:17-18; Jer 31:31-34; Ez 37:26-28; Lk 24:44; Acts 13:38-39; 26:18; Gal 3:24-29; Eph 1:7-10; Col 1:13-14; 1 Jn 1:9; 2:12).

- The promise of the restored Zion (the new Israel of the Universal Church): *And he will come to Zion as Redeemer, to those in Jacob who turn from transgression, says the LORD. "And as for me, this is my covenant with them," says the LORD [Yahweh]: "my spirit which is upon you, and my words which I have put in your mouth, shall not depart out of your mouth, or out of the mouth of your children, or out of the mouth of your children's children, says the LORD, from this time forth and forevermore"* (Is 59:20-21).

Endnotes: The Resurrection of the Messiah

1. It was the custom not to wash the bodies of Jews who died a violent death because it was necessary to preserve the blood with the body. It was customary for a cloth to be rolled and then tied under the chin and around the head to hold the dead person's jaw in place. Sts. John and Peter saw a headcloth rolled and set to one side in Jesus' empty tomb, apparently in the same loop shape (Jn 20:6). It was the same type of cloth used in Lazarus' burial (Jn 11:44). See *The Blood and the Shroud*, pages 54-55; *The Anchor Study Bible: The Gospel According to John*, pages 986-987.
2. The gates of Heaven were closed after the Fall of Adam and not opened until the coming of the Messiah (CCC 536, 1026). After His death, Jesus descended into *Sheol/Hades*, the abode of the dead, and not into the hell of the damned (CCC 631-633). The hell of the damned, which Jesus called Gehenna (Mt 5:22, 29, 30; 10:28; 18:9; 23:15; 23:33; Mk 9:43, 45, 47; Lk 12:5; CCC 1034), was not the destination of the wicked until Heaven's gates opened, and both blessings and punishments became eternal (Wis 3:1-12; Lk 16:19-23; Mt 25:45-46). Jesus' references to *Sheol* in the New Testament use the Greek word for the netherworld, *Hades* (Mt 11:23; 16:18; Lk 10:15; 16:23). The same designation appears in Acts (2:27, 31) and in Revelation (1:18; 6:8; 20:13, 14). *Sheol/Hades* will remain until the Final Judgment. At that time, death and *Hades* are no longer necessary and destroyed in the eternal Hell/the Lake of Fire (Rev 20:14).

3. See the Apostles' Creed that states: "He descended into hell [Hades]." The Catholic Catechism defines the difference between the Hell of the damned and Hades that is the abode of the dead in CCC 633.
4. The Church still reckons the date for Pentecost by counting 50 days from Easter Sunday as the ancients counted with no zero place-value and by counting Easter Sunday as day #1 of the 50 days.
5. A novena is nine days of communal or private prayer for a special occasion or specific intention. The disciples prayed communally with Virgin Mary in the Upper Room for nine days before the coming of the Holy Spirit on the tenth day; this is the origin of the novena tradition (etymology = Latin *novem*, meaning "nine").
6. The Karaites and Samaritans are the only Jews who continue to observe Firstfruits as a feast within the seven-day celebration of Unleavened Bread. They also celebrate the Feast of Pentecost fifty days later (as the ancients counted) with both festivals falling on the first day of the week, Sunday (*A History of The Jewish People in the Time Jesus*, page 37; *The Second Jewish Book of Why*, page 38). The Temple hierarchy altered the dates sometime after Jesus' Resurrection. Josephus, a former Temple priest, recorded his recollection of the celebration of Pentecost on the first day of the week. His testimony means that Firstfruits also had to fall on the first day of the week (a Sunday) fifty days earlier. Josephus wrote: *And truly he did not speak falsely in saying so; for the festival, which we call Pentecost, did then fall out to be <u>the next day to the Sabbath</u>* (*Antiquities of the Jews* 13.9.3 [252]; emphasis added).
7. The two lambs for the Sabbath day sacrifice, offered in addition to the Tamid (Num 28:9-10), are not designated as

"tamid" = standing/perpetual sacrifices. The Passover victims could be lambs or goat kids: *It must be an animal without blemish, a male one year old; you may choose it either from the sheep or from the goats* (Ex 12:5 NJB).

8. Also see Mt 28:1–8; Mk 16:1–8; and Lk 24:1–10.

CHAPTER X THE STANDING LAMB AND ETERNAL HIGH PRIEST

After this I looked, and lo, in heaven an open door! ... And between the throne and the four living creatures and among the elders, I saw a Lamb standing, as though it had been slain....

Revelation 4:1; 5:6

Now the point in what we are saying is this: we have such a high priest, one who is seated at the right hand of the throne of the Majesty in heaven, a minister in the sanctuary and the true tent which is set up not by man but by the Lord. For every high priest is appointed to offer gifts and sacrifices; hence it is necessary for this priest also to have something to offer.

Hebrews 8:1–3

THE SACRIFICE OF JESUS PREFIGURED IN THE TAMID

God planned to prefigure the sacrifice of Jesus Christ in:

- the blood sacrifice of the Passover lambs and goat-kids
- the sacred meal of the Passover victim on the first night of Unleavened Bread
- the single sacrifice of the two Tamid lambs offered daily for the atonement and sanctification of the covenant people

God planned to prefigure the Resurrection of Jesus and the descent of God the Holy Spirit in:

- the sacrificial offering of the single, unblemished, male lamb on the Feast of Firstfruits
- the commemoration of the birth of the nation of Israel as God's holy people (the Old Covenant Church) at Mount Sinai on the Feast of Weeks/Pentecost

The death of the first Passover lambs and goat kids provided divine protection for the children of Israel as death "passed over" them on the night of terror that was the first Passover in Egypt. That event prefigured

Jesus' offering of Himself as God's divine paschal sacrifice: He who protects God's people from the terror of eternal death (1 Cor 5:7b). On the first night of the tenth plague in Egypt, under the protection of the sign of the cross formed by the blood of the Passover victim painted across the doorways of Israelite houses, the people of God ate a sacred meal of the sacrificed victims. This event prefigured Jesus offering the New Covenant people of God His Body and Blood in a sacred meal on the first night of Unleavened Bread in AD 30. It was an event that marked the beginning of His walk to the Cross, and it was the Cross that became the sign under which God offered humanity Christ's gift of redemption and salvation.

Jesus suffered His Passion and crucifixion at the times associated with the offering and sacrifice of the morning Tamid lamb. He suffered on the Cross and died at the times associated with the offering and sacrifice of the afternoon Tamid lamb. The Tamid prefigured Christ's Passion and death on the altar of the Cross as the single unblemished sacrifice of the One who was fully God and fully man (single sacrifice of the two lambs of the Tamid). But the single sacrifice of the Tamid on the altar together with unleavened bread and wine also prefigured the sacrifice of the Eucharistic banquet in the offering of unleavened bread and wine that becomes the unblemished *Lamb of God who takes away the sins of the world* on the altar of the Eucharistic table in the Catholic Mass.

However, the New Covenant *Todah* ("Thanksgiving") communion sacrifice of the Eucharist, the sacred meal of the New Covenant Church, is not offered annually like the Passover sacrifice. Instead, the Eucharistic sacrifice, like the Tamid sacrifice, is a "standing" sacrifice that is offered perpetually on altars from one end of the Kingdom of Heaven on earth to the other through the on-going sacrifice of the Resurrected and glorified Christ. It is the same sacrificial offering from the altar of the Cross in AD 30 made present on the altars of His priestly people when His priestly representative pronounces Jesus' words of consecration from the Last Supper over the bread and wine that are supernaturally transformed into His Body and Blood.

In fulfillment of the Scriptures, the Resurrection of the Christ from the dead was on the Feast of Firstfruits, a feast that commemorated God's gift of new life to the Israelites living as a free people in the Promised Land. In the victory of His Resurrection, Jesus fulfilled Ezekiel's messianic prophecy of the Anointed Prince destined to provide all of the required sacrifices, gifts, and festival offerings for Israel/the Church: *The Prince must make himself responsible for providing the burnt offerings, the oblation and the libations for feasts, New Moons, Sabbaths and all the solemn festivals of the House of Israel. He must provide the sacrifice for sin, the oblation, the burnt offerings and the communion sacrifices to make expiation for the House of Israel* (Ez 45:17, NJB).

As the Anointed Prince, Jesus became responsible for providing all sacrifices in His one perfect sacrifice, just as Ezekiel prophesied and St. Paul confirmed (Col 2:16-17). Jesus, the Davidic Prince who ascended to Heaven take His rightful place as the King of Kings and the High Priest of the new covenantal order, offered His one perfect sacrifice on the altar of the Cross. But the offering to God of that one perfect sacrifice of God the Son has not ended because the struggle against sin and the continuing process of humanity's journey to salvation has not ended. As in the command for the "standing," perpetual Tamid, Jesus' one sacrificial offering of redemption and sanctification is perpetually ongoing.

The Prophet Daniel wrote that the sacrifice of the Tamid in the Jerusalem Temple was to remain a perpetual sacrifice, continually burning on the altar fire until the time of the Davidic Messiah (Dan 12:5-13). The Tamid sacrifice offered for the atonement and sanctification of humanity in the Jerusalem Temple ended just before the destruction of the Jerusalem in AD 70, forty years after Jesus' Resurrection and Ascension. Its continuation was no longer necessary since it fulfilled its role in salvation history by prefiguring Jesus' Passion and death.

But there is a mystery, revealed to St. John, in which the Tamid is still present, continuous, and relevant. In the Book of Revelation, many years after Jesus' Ascension, St. John saw Jesus Christ in His role as both the High Priest of the New Covenant, wearing priestly robes like the Jewish high priest on the Feast of Atonement, and as the unblemished sacrificial Lamb of God. In his first vision, John identified the glorified Christ as the one who addressed him: *Then I turned to see the voice that was speaking to me, and on turning I saw seven golden lampstands, and in the midst of the lampstands one like a son of man, clothed with a long robe and with a golden girdle round his breast [...]. When I saw him, I fell at his feet as though dead. But he laid his right hand upon me, saying, "Fear not, I am the first and the last, and the living one; I died, and behold I am alive for evermore, and I have the keys of Death and Hades"* (Rev 1:12-13, 17-18).[1] It was after this first vision that St. John was drawn up into the heavenly Sanctuary: *After this, I looked, and lo, in heaven an open door* (Rev 4:1)![2]

What John was privileged to witnesses in the Book of Revelation was the Divine Liturgy of the heavenly Sanctuary. St. John saw the seven flaming lampstands that surround the Presence of God on His heavenly throne, and he saw priestly elders wearing crowns that symbolize their ministerial authority. They were dressed in white liturgical garments and kneeling in worship (Rev 4:4; 5:8). He saw the heavenly altar (Rev 6:9), and He heard the angelic hymn of praise to the Triune God: "Holy, Holy, Holy" (Rev 4: 8) and the heavenly congregation singing "Alleluia," or "Hallelujah" in Hebrew, which means "Praise God Yahweh" (Rev 19:1). He also heard the hymns of praise for the Lamb of God who has triumphed, sung by a congregation of angels and saints "from every nation, race, tribe, and language" (Rev 7:9). In witnessing the heavenly liturgy, St. John also saw angels who held trumpets and another angel with a censer filled with incense offering the prayers of the saints (Rev 8:2, 3-4), all of which must have looked very familiar to him from his years worshiping during the Tamid liturgy at the Jerusalem Temple. But the center of the liturgical celebration was "the Lamb" in His place of honor before the throne of God.

St. John described his vision of the glorified Messiah when the elders announced that the "Lion of the tribe of Judah," the "root of David" has triumphed: *And between the throne and the four living creatures and among the elders, I saw a* ***Lamb standing,*** *as though it had been slain* (Rev 5:6; emphasis added). The Greek words used for Christ the Lamb in Revelation 5:6 are *Arnion Hestekos*, literally *"Lamb Standing"* (Chilton, *Days of Vengeance*, page 595).[3] St. John's "standing" Lamb of sacrifice is an odd way to express Christ's presence in the heavenly Sanctuary. Slain lambs don't stand. But if John is using Greek to express a Hebrew concept, then what he is describing is Jesus as the eternal Tamid, the "standing" Lamb that the Old Covenant daily "standing" sacrifice (the literal meaning of the word *tamid* to describe something continual) prefigured. However, St. John's use of the archaic Greek word *arnion* for lamb in the Book of Revelation is both peculiar and significant.

Jesus is called "the Lamb" in Revelation just as He is called "the Lamb" in the Gospel of St. John (Jn 1:29, 36). However, the Greek word in Revelation 5:6 is not the same word for "lamb/*arnion*" that appears in other New Testament passages where Jesus is called the "lamb/*amnos*." In the New Testament, the use of the Greek word *amnos* is limited to John's Gospel (Jn 1:29; 35), to Acts where St. Luke quotes the Septuagint Old Testament passage from Isaiah 53:7-8 (Acts 8:32), and to St. Peter's letter to the universal Church in 1 Peter 1:19. Significantly, *amnos* is the same Greek word for lamb used in the instructions for the sacrifice of the Tamid in the Septuagint Old Testament Greek translation (Ex 29:38-41) and all other references to the lambs of sacrifice, including the single male lamb offered on the Feast of Firstfruits.

When St. John the Baptist publicly announced to the crowds of Jews that Jesus was the "Lamb of God" (Jn 1: 29, 36), he used the same Greek word for lamb (*amnos*) as the word from the Greek Septuagint Old Testament passages that required the sacrifice of the Tamid lamb. He did not use the designation for the Passover sacrifice which was a male animal from the flock (a lamb or a goat-kid). In his Gospel, St. John uses this particular Greek word for lamb (*amnos*) to illustrate that Jesus was the necessary, unblemished blood sacrifice for the forgiveness of sins. John the Baptist's dramatic statement, identifying Jesus as "the Lamb of God," must have evoked for the Jews the image of the daily Tamid, the first and most important blood sacrifice in the sacrificial system around which every day revolved in the liturgy the Old Covenant people of God.

While all the animal sacrifices of the Old Covenant prefigured Jesus' one sacrifice, in St. John's description of Jesus offering His perfect sacrifice before the throne of God in the book of Revelation, Jesus is uniquely identified as the unblemished "Lamb Standing," in Greek the *Arnion Hestekos* (*Offerings, Sacrifice, and Worship in the Old Testament,* page 57; CCC 614, 1330). Bible scholars have asked, if St. John is the inspired writer of the fourth Gospel and the Book of Revelation, then what is the reason he used the word *arnion* for the Christ the "Lamb" in Revelation as opposed to the Greek word *amnos* for Jesus the "Lamb of God" in John 1:29 and 36? The Greek word *amnos* is the common word used for lamb in the Greek New Testament texts and the Old Testament Greek translation of the Septuagint. In contrast, the word *arnion* (which scholars identify as an archaic term for "lamb") appears once in the Gospel of John where it refers to the faithful New Covenant people of God when Jesus commanded St. Peter to *Feed my lambs* (*arnion*) in John 21:15. It also appears an amazing twenty-nine times in the Book of Revelation where *arnion* is the only term used to identify Jesus as "the Lamb."

The connection between the unusual and archaic form of the Greek word *arnion*

for "lamb" in John 21:15 used for believers in Jesus Christ, and its use in the Book of Revelation for Jesus Himself, may be connected to St. John's interpretation of Jesus' resurrected and glorified state. In His glorification, Jesus is no longer the *Amnos* (Lamb) but is now the glorified *Arnion* (Lamb) of God who is One with the *arnion* of His Church (Jn 21:15; 1 Cor 12:27). But there may also be a more profound connection to the Greek words in Revelation 5:6 which identify Jesus as the *Arnion Hestekos*, the "Lamb Standing as though it had been slain," since this "Lamb Standing" takes center stage in the Divine Liturgy of the heavenly Sanctuary. The key to the mystery is the lamb who took center stage in the Old Covenant Temple liturgy, the "standing" lamb of the *'olat ha-Tamid.*

Unlike the Hebrew word for "standing," which like our English word has the double meaning of "standing" as in "upright" and standing as in "continual" or "perpetual," the Greek word *hestekos* only means "standing" in the literal sense. Bible scholar Philip Carrington suggests that St. John is writing in Greek but is thinking in Hebrew, using the Greek word *hestekos* = "standing" as in upright since there was no Greek equivalent for *tamid* which means both "standing" and "continual." He suggests St. John is using *hestekos* as "a rough Greek translation of the Hebrew word *tamid* as it refers to the twice daily communal burnt offering in the Temple" (*Days of Vengeance*, page 171-172).[4]

Since there was no Greek word to adequately convey the Hebrew meaning of this unique daily offering,

Carrington proposes that the Greek words *Arnion Hestekos* became the technical term of the Jewish Temple hierarchy for the Tamid lamb of the daily sacrifice. And, therefore, it was the term used in the catechesis of Greek-speaking Gentiles who sought instruction in understanding the obligations of the Sinai Covenant. (*Days of Vengeance,* page 171-172). The only other time the complete term *Arnion Hestekos* appears is in Revelation 14:1 when St. John sees the *Arnion Hestekos* as Christ the King on Mount Zion: *Then I looked, and lo, on Mount Zion stood the Lamb [Arnion Hestekos], and with him a hundred and forty-four thousand who had his name and his Father's name written on their foreheads* ([...] = literal Greek translation, IBGE, vol. IV, page 682). It is a vision that is the fulfillment of Psalms 2:6 ~ *I myself have anointed my king on Zion my holy mountain.*

As St. John watched the "Lamb Standing" (*Arnion Hestekos*) in the heavenly Sanctuary, he heard the prayers and praise of the saints. Prayer and praise are part of liturgical worship, but prayer and praise cannot replace the sacrifice; only the anointed priest can offer the sacrifice in the earthly Temple and in the heavenly Temple. As St. John turned toward the throne, he saw that the priest and the sacrifice were one and the same when the "Lamb Standing" (*Arnion Hestekos*) stepped forward to receive a scroll from the hand of God (Rev

5:5-10). At the same moment, the heavenly worshipers sang: *You are worthy to take the scroll and to break its seals, because you were sacrificed, and with your blood you bought people for God of every race, language, people and nation and made them a line of kings and priests for God, to rule the world* (Rev 5:9-10, NJB). Like all previous Old Covenant high priests, in His role as the Divine High Priest, Jesus has a sacrifice that He must offer: *Now the point in what we are saying is this: we have such a high priest, one who is seated at the right hand of the throne of the Majesty in heaven, a minister in the sanctuary and a true tent which is set up not by man but by the Lord. For every high priest is appointed to offer gifts and sacrifices;* ***hence it is necessary for this priest also to have something to offer*** (Heb 8:1-3; emphasis added). The sacrifice that Jesus offers is the continual/perpetual (tamid) sacrifice of Himself.

In the afternoon liturgy of worship, the gates to the Jerusalem Temple opened at the ninth hour (3 PM), the precise moment of the sacrifice of the afternoon Tamid lamb. When Jesus died on the altar of the Cross at 3 PM, the ninth hour Jewish time (Mt 27:46, 50; Mk 15:34-37), the curtain covering the Holy of Holies that symbolized the separation of sinful humanity from the presence of the holy God was torn open (Mt 27:51; Mk 15:38; Lk 23:45-46), and as the earth shook and rocks split apart, the gates of Heaven were wrenched asunder (Mt 27:51).

In St. John's vision of the heavenly Sanctuary in the Book of Revelation, it is significant that the gates/doors of Heaven stood open (Rev 4:1). The doors to Heaven were open because the Lamb prepared the way. The Lamb of God who was slain but is now the "Lamb Standing" before the throne of God is He who is the perpetual sacrifice offered for the salvation of the world who made a way for the souls of the faithful to enter into the presence of God.

Jesus Christ is the true Tamid of the heavenly Sanctuary that the earthly Tamid and the earthly Temple only prefigured. As previously mentioned, Christ's Passion unfolded in the same time frame as the Tamid:

- At dawn, when the first Tamid lamb was brought out to the altar, Jesus was condemned (Mt 27:1).
- At 9 AM (third-hour Jewish time) when the first Tamid lamb was sacrificed, Jesus was sacrificed (Mk 15:25-6).
- At noon (sixth-hour Jewish time) when the second Tamid lamb was led out to the altar, darkness engulfed the earth until 3 PM (Mt 27:45; Mk 15:33; Lk 23:44).
- At 3 PM (ninth hour Jewish time) as the second Tamid lamb was sacrificed, Jesus died

on the altar of the Cross (Mt 27:46, 50; Mk 15:34, 37; Lk 23:44, 46).

At the same moment that Jesus willingly gave up His life, the veil that covered the Holy of Holies in the Temple was torn from the top to the bottom as the gates of Heaven were thrown opened to receive the righteous dead (Mt 27:51-52; Lk 23:45). In the Old Covenant, the Tamid was the symbol of God's continuous, daily presence with Israel; in the New Covenant, it is Jesus the Lamb who is the Emmanuel, the "God with us" perpetually to the end of time (Is 7:14; Mt 28:20).

God's relationship with humanity in both the Old and New Testaments are bound up in the themes of faith, hope, and love: faith in God's promises, hope in the fulfillment of His promises, and the love of God which must instill in His covenant people the motivation to remain faithful and hopeful. The exercise of these virtues rests upon the promises God made to the Patriarchs, the covenantal promises, and the promises made to the New Covenant faithful, establishing the continuity of the promise of salvation throughout the history of humanity. Just as God revealed Himself in a very personal and intimate way to Adam and Eve in Eden, He intimately reveals Himself to humanity in Jesus Christ. On our faith journey to salvation, God commands us to continue in Christ's presence as He stands as the sacrificed Lamb at the heavenly altar and continuously reveals Himself to us in the sacred meal of the Eucharist. At the Last Supper when Jesus offered the "first fruits" of the New Covenant faithful His Body and Blood, He commanded "**Do this**" (Lk 22:19; 1 Cor 11:25); He didn't say "Do whatever you feel is right."

THE REAL PRESENCE OF CHRIST IN THE SACRED MEAL OF THE EUCHARIST

In the earthly liturgy we take part in a foretaste of that heavenly liturgy which is celebrated in the holy city of Jerusalem toward which we journey as pilgrims, where Christ is sitting at the right hand of God, a minister of the holies and of the true tabernacle
(cf. Rev. 21:2; Col. 3:1; Heb. 8:2) Sacrosanctum Concilium, 8.

Reason teaches that we should condemn this present world with our whole souls and offer to God the daily sacrifice of his Body and Blood. For the Eucharistic sacrifice, which in mystery renews for us the death of the Son of God, saves our souls from everlasting damnation. When we participate at Mass, we should also sacrifice ourselves to almighty God with heartfelt contrition. For when we celebrate the mystery of our Lord's passion, we ought to imitate it. If we also offer ourselves to him in sacrifice, then the Eucharist shall truly be a sacrifice to God for us.
Pope St. Gregory the Great, c. 540 – 604

In his vision of the heavenly liturgy, St. John saw Jesus as the *Arnion Hestekos*, the "Lamb Standing," the perpetual (*tamid*) sacrifice of the New Covenant people of God. Jesus, the Tamid sacrifice of the New Covenant, is also the High Priest of the new covenantal order, continually offering the unbloody sacrifice of Himself before the throne of God on behalf of all peoples of the earth (Heb 8:1-3; Rev 5:9-14). According to Rabbinic tradition, the Tamid and all the other sacrifices of the Sinai Covenant would end at the time the Davidic Redeemer-Messiah came to fulfill the covenant promises. At that time, the Rabbis taught, only the *Todah* (in Hebrew "Thanksgiving" and translated as *Eucharistia* in the Greek Old Testament texts) communion sacrifice that expressed the people's renewed peace with Yahweh and their gratitude to Him was to continue as the single sacrifice in the liturgy of the people of God (*The JPS Torah Commentary: Leviticus*, page 43).[5] Jesus, the Davidic Messiah, transformed the Sinai Covenant's Tamid into His one perpetual sacrifice. Therefore, it was necessary that what had become a counterfeit Tamid after Jesus' Ascension should end, as it did in AD 70.

Jesus stands before the throne of God in Heaven, inviting all the faithful in His earthly kingdom to come and taste His perpetual (*tamid*) sacrifice. It is this sacrifice that is made present in the "Thanksgiving" of the New Covenant *Todah* that Catholics call the Eucharist, offered to the faithful on New Covenant altars where God renews His peace with His faithful and where His people receive Him with thanksgiving (Lev 7:11-15). It is in the on-going sacrifice experienced in the Eucharist of the New Covenant *Todah* whereby Christ is really and substantially present.

In the sacrifice of the Mass, our sacred meal is the offering of Jesus' sacrifice on the Cross that is made present before us just as that reality was made present to His disciples at the Last Supper. Heavenly and earthly liturgy join together as we "raise our hearts to Heaven," and Christ's earthly ministers repeat His words at the Last Supper when He first offered Himself in the sacred meal of His glorified Flesh and Blood. We are united not only with the faithful of the universal (catholic) Church on earth but also with the saints in Heaven as we stand at the foot of the Cross with the Virgin Mary, seeking the intercession of Christ, our divine Advocate and High Priest (1 Cor 11:23-26; CCC 1326; 1370; 1383). In the Eucharistic banquet, the tamid/standing sacrifice of Jesus Christ is supernaturally transformed into a sacred meal through the miracle of transubstantiation (Latin *trans*-, "so as to change" = *substantia*, "substance"). The substance of bread and wine change into the substance of Christ's Body and Blood through the intercession of a validly ordained priest standing in *Persona Christi* (in the Person of Christ) during the consecration so that only the accidents of bread and wine remain. The Eucharist becomes the "Thanksgiving" communion offering of the New Covenant people of God consumed continually, day and night, by the faithful across the face of the earth.

In His single sacrifice, Jesus made expiation for the people of every age, and He established the New Covenant people of redeemed Israel in His Kingdom of Heaven on earth, the Universal (Catholic) Church of Christ the King (Heb 9:25-28; CCC 877). As the second Moses who freed His people from sin and death on the Passover festival of redemption, Jesus Christ, the unblemished victim selected before the creation of the world (1 Pt 18-20) and the eternal Tamid Lamb, made the atoning sacrifice for the sin and sanctification of His people individually and collectively.

The Eucharistic banquet is also the sacred meal of eternal life promised by Jesus in the Bread of Life Discourse when He said, *"he who eats my flesh and drinks my blood has eternal life, and I will raise him up at the last day. For my flesh is food indeed, and my blood is drink indeed. He who eats my flesh and drinks my blood abides in me, and I in him"* (Jn 6:54-56). After this declaration, many of the disciples who followed Jesus turned away from Him because they could not accept that He was linking the promise of eternal life to His blood sacrifice by literally eating His Flesh and drinking His Blood (Jn 6:66). The Law prohibited eating raw flesh or drinking blood since the time of the redemption of Noah's family and afterward, repeated the prohibition seven times (Gen 9:4; Lev 3:17; 7:26; 17:10-12, 14; 19:26; Dt 12:16). The violation of the restriction required the excommunication of the offender from the covenant community (Lev 7:27; 17:10, 14). Jesus did not stop those disciples who were offended by His words from leaving because He meant what He said. However, He was speaking of His glorified flesh and not His human flesh that gives life (Jn 6:63). It was after these statements in the Bread of Life Discourse that Scripture records the first prophecy of Judas' betrayal (Jn 6:70-71). Judas stayed, but he did not believe.

Men and women have the freedom to make the same mistakes today. They can either reject Jesus' gift of eternal life in consuming the perpetual sacrifice of His Body and Blood by walking away, or they can stay, not believing in the supernatural power of the Eucharist, and thereby eat and drink, as St. Paul wrote, "to one's condemnation." St. Paul severely warned the Christians of Corinth that only the faithful in a state of grace could eat the sacred meal of the Body and Blood of Jesus Christ. Before partaking of the life of Christ in the Eucharist, the believer must make an examination of conscience, receive forgiveness for their sins, and believe in the Real Presence of Christ in the Eucharist: *For as often as you eat this bread and drink the cup, you proclaim the Lord's death until he comes. Whoever, therefore, eats the bread or drinks the cup of the Lord in an unworthy manner will be guilty of profaning the body and blood of the Lord. Let a man examine himself and so eat of the bread and drink of the cup.* <u>*For anyone who eats and drinks without discerning the body eats and drinks judgment upon himself*</u> (1 Cor 11:26-29; emphasis added; also see CCC 1374-81).

Believing in the invisible Presence of Christ in the Eucharist requires the same belief in the invisible Presence of God required of the Old Covenant faithful. It took faith for them to believe God was present to accept their sacrifice of the Tamid that expiated their collective sins and sanctified them as God's holy people. It took faith to believe that the Mercy-seat of the Ark of the Covenant became an altar of sacrifice and dispenser of divine grace on the Feast of Atonement, the Old Covenant feast of communal repentance and expiation (Lev. 16:1-34; 23:26-32; Num 29:7-11). On that occasion, God did not come only in the form of the visible rising cloud of the *Olah* on the sacrificial altar in the Temple courtyard. He also came invisibly in a manner not seen in the natural world, which required the obedient faith of His people to believe in His Divine Presence among them.

God reveals Himself to us in the same manner in the celebration of the Mass. Christ comes to us from the Mercy-seat of the Cross in the sacrifice of the Eucharist as He offers Himself sacramentally in atonement for the sins of the world upon the altar of every Catholic Church. He comes to His covenant people as He manifests Himself through the power of God the Holy Spirit, becoming present in what only appears to be bread and wine. At that moment, God requires the faith of His people, just as in ancient times when the invisible miracle of atonement required the faith of covenant believers.

While it is true that Jesus' sacrifice on the altar of the Cross fulfilled all the sacrifices of the Old Covenant sacrificial system, in a unique way the Tamid prefigured His Passion while the meal of the Last Supper on the first night of the Feast of Unleavened Bread prefigured the Eucharistic banquet. The Last Supper/Unleavened Bread Feast became the *Todah* of the Resurrected Christ while the perpetual Tamid, which uniquely foreshadowed Christ's Passion and death, became the continual offering of the Christ the Lamb before the throne of God.[6]

The celebration of the "Thanksgiving" communion sacred meal of the Eucharist stands at the center of the Church's life and expresses its deepest mystery in the Mass of the Roman Catholic Church. The Mass is a worship celebration that is a foretaste of the heavenly reality. The liturgy of the Mass is a pattern of the heavenly liturgy witnessed by St. John in the book of Revelation with prayers, hymns of praise, readings from the Book (scroll), the offering of incense, the priest standing before the altar, and most importantly, the sacrifice (e.g., Rev 4:8; 5:5-14; 8:3-4).

The Roman Catholic Church has always taught that the celebration of the Holy Eucharist is a true sacrifice to God. In their writings, the disciples of the Apostles, the Apostolic Bishops who are the Fathers of the Church, testified to this truth. When the belief in the Real Presence of Christ in the Eucharist came under attack by Protestants in the 16th century, the Council of Trent reaffirmed the teaching of the Eucharist as a true sacrifice. The Council proclaimed that the sacrifice of Christ at Calvary and the sacrifice of the Eucharist are one single sacrifice with the "substance" of Christ being the same but with the "manner" of the offering of

Christ being different: *The victim is one and the same ... who then offered himself on the cross; only the manner of offering is different ... In this divine sacrifice which is celebrated in the Mass, the same Christ who offered himself once in a bloody manner on the altar of the cross is contained and is offered in an unbloody manner* (Council of Trent [1562] DS 1743).

The requirement for taking part in the sacred meal of the Passover victim that became the Last Supper and the first Eucharistic meal for Jesus' faithful disciples didn't mean they had to be present at the Temple earlier that day for the ritual sacrifice of the lambs and kids (*Mishnah: Pesahim*, 8:1-2). However, it was a covenant obligation for the Old Covenant faithful to be present for the sacred meal of the sacrificial victim. God applied the atonement of the sacrifice to those who ate the meal, and their participation became a vow of covenant obedience and continuation. For Christians, it is at the Eucharistic Banquet that the faithful become present at Christ's sacrifice on the altar of the Cross and receive the miracle of His sacrifice applied to their lives.

In the New Covenant, as in the Old, the faithful demonstrate their devotion to God by obeying His command to be present at the sacred meal that marks covenant commitment and continuation (CCC 2042). However, the difference is that our sacred meal is also a participation in the life of Jesus Christ. Faithful Christians must keep their covenantal appointed time with God in the same way Adam and Eve kept their appointed liturgical hour in Eden (Gen 3:8). It is a rendezvous with God in which time is suspended, as Pope Benedict XVI explained in his homily during the Solemnity of the Feast of Corpus Christi on June 11, 2009: *With the Eucharist*, the Pope explained, *heaven comes down to earth, God's tomorrow descends into the present moment and time is, as it were, embraced by divine eternity.*

THE NEW COVENANT TAMID LAMB

I am coming to gather every nation and every language.
They will come to witness my glory. I shall give them a sign
and send some of their survivors to the nations.
Isaiah 66:18–19

When Israel rendezvoused with God at Mount Sinai, on the fiftieth day after crossing the Red Sea (Sea of Reeds), Yahweh called the children of Israel to become a kingdom of priests serving the King of Heaven (Ex 19:6). However, years after taking possession of the Promised Land, the people came to prefer the authority of earthly kings over the guidance of God's representatives, their anointed priests (1 Sam 8:4–5). It was a choice that expressed their resistance to God's kingship and their lack of trust in His providential care.

At the rebirth of the new Israel on Mount Zion, on the day of the second great Pentecost in AD 30 (fifty days after Christ's Resurrection), the New Covenant faithful were again called to divine service. They were supernaturally empowered to serve the Most Holy Trinity as a kingdom of priests, with some men set apart to serve as Christ's ordained representatives in the ministerial priesthood (1 Pt 2:9–10). Those called to serve in the ministerial priesthood sit on earthly thrones in the earthly Sanctuary, leading the faithful in liturgical worship just as the twenty-four elder-priests of Heaven sit on thrones and lead the heavenly liturgy (Rev 4:10; 5:8–10). Through the sacrifice of the Eucharist, Christ's Kingdom on Earth unites to the Divine Liturgy of the "Lamb Standing" in the Sanctuary in Heaven.

The old covenants established in blood sacrifice were how God governed, guided, trained, and preserved the fallen human family of Adam. The New Covenant in Christ is God's plan for re-establishing, through the blood sacrifice of God the Son, the blood tie of unity in God's eternal family. The central unifying theme of salvation history is God calling men and women to fulfill the destiny for which He created them. Through the sacrifice of the Son, God has opened the way to infusing human beings with His own divine life, giving all peoples the means of fulfilling the destiny for which God created them—eternal unity with the Most Holy Trinity (2 Pt 1:4).

In the first creation event, God breathed life into Adam. In the new creation event, the Resurrected Savior, as a foretaste of the coming of the Paraclete, breathed out His Spirit upon the earth in death and then breathed His Spirit upon the Apostles in the Upper Room the day of His Resurrection (Lk 23:46; Jn 19:20:22). The New Covenant is God's master plan for fathering His eternal family through the blood sacrifice of the Son and the infusion of new life through the Holy Spirit. With the breath of the Spirit, the same divine wind that hovered over the earth in the first creation and infused the first man with life (Gen 1:2; 2:7), gives new birth to believers through the supernatural power of Christian Baptism. With Christ we die to sin and death, which was our inheritance from the human family of Adam, and we are raised, through the regenerative power of God the Holy Spirit, to new life as sons and daughters in the family of God and co-heirs with Jesus Christ (Rom 8:14-17; CCC 1265-70).

The first generation of Israelites journeyed forty years in the wilderness before a new generation obediently embraced the obligations of the Sinai Covenant and took possession of the Promised Land. God, in His mercy, gave the last generation of the Sinai Covenant forty years after Jesus' Ascension to let go of what was good in the Old Covenant to fully grasp the greater and eternal blessings in the New (CCC 1963-64). In AD 66, the province of Judea revolted against the Roman Empire. Rome responded by sending four legions of Roman soldiers to descend in a fury upon Judea, Samaria, and the Galilee like a voracious plague of locusts. During the Passover/Feast of Unleavened Bread in AD 70, when Jerusalem was overflowing with pilgrims, the Romans laid siege to the holy city. The Jewish priest/historian Flavius Josephus was an eyewitness to the horrific events that became the end of the world for the people of the Sinai Covenant.

The holy city suffered under the Roman siege for three and a half months. The Tamid sacrifice ended on Tammuz 17th, and the city fell to the Romans about three and a half weeks later on the 9th of Ab (*The Jewish Wars*, 6.2. [94]). On the same day that the Babylonian army destroyed the Temple of Solomon centuries earlier in 587/6 BC, the Romans burned Jerusalem and the Second Temple to the ground. As Jesus prophesied, not one stone of the Temple was left standing (Mt 24:1-2). The Roman soldiers poured water over the fire-scorched

Temple stones to break them apart so they could collect the gold that melted into the cracks from the gold fence around the roof of the Sanctuary.

The Old Covenant daily Tamid liturgy and all blood sacrifices ended in 70 AD. But the true Tamid continues as an offering for the atonement and sanctification of the faithful disciples of Christ. Jesus makes the offering of Himself in the heavenly Sanctuary where the "Lamb Standing" is made present daily in the sacred meal of the Eucharist on the altars of every Catholic Church in every generation of the New Covenant people of God across the face of the earth.

THE NEW COVENANT PEOPLE OF GOD

The Church is an earthly heaven. The souls of Christians are called together to assemble with the prophets, apostles, and hierarchs in order to recline with Abraham, Isaac, and Jacob at the mystical banquet of the Kingdom of Christ. Thereby having come into the unity of faith and communion of the Spirit through the dispensation of the One who died for us and is sitting at the right hand of the Father, we are no longer on earth but standing by the royal Throne of God in heaven, where Christ is, just as He Himself says: "Righteous Father, sanctify in Your name those whom You gave me, so that where I am, they may be with Me."

St. Germanus, Bishop of Paris (d. 576)

On the altar of the Cross, on a tree which became a symbol of the curse for covenant disobedience extending back to the time of Adam, Jesus, the obedient firstborn Son of "the Woman," Mary of Nazareth, and the only begotten Son of God, defeated Satan, the prince of this world. He claimed Satan's former kingdom for His own and elevated the Cross as the New Covenant sign of the Tree of Life of the restored Eden (Dt 21:22-23; Gal 3:13). In the Sanctuaries of Jesus' earthly Kingdom, the faithful experience the union of Heaven and earth in a liturgical celebration of the resurrected and glorified Savior and Redeemer, the "Lamb Standing," as the High Priest and sinless victim before the throne of God. Jesus the Messiah, in defeating Satan, became the Anointed Prince of this world and the King of the universal Kingdom that the prophet Daniel promised was destined to shatter and absorb all previous kingdoms (Dan 2:44; 7:13-14).

In St. John's final vision of the heavenly liturgy in the Book of Revelation, he received a message of assurance to carry to the world: *And he who sat on the throne said, "Behold, I make all things new." Also, he said, "Write this, for these words are trustworthy and true." And he said to me, "It is done! I am the Alpha and the Omega, the beginning and the end. To the thirsty I will give water without price from the fountain of the water of life. He who conquers shall have this heritage, and I will be his God, and he shall be my son"* (Rev 21:5-7).

As the New Covenant faithful and the priestly people of the Triune God, we continue the bond of our covenant relationship with our Lord through oath swearing, blood sacrifice, and the continuation of our covenant through the communal eating of a sacred meal. We eat the "Living Manna" from Heaven that is the Body and Blood, the Soul and Divinity of the *Arnion Hestekos*, the "Lamb Standing," who was completely consumed on the altar of the Cross and yet continues to nourish the faithful on their journey to salvation. We are invited to drink deeply from the well of life in the sacred cup of the Blood of the Lamb in our Eucharistic banquet, and we swear our oath of continuing fidelity to the covenant through our participation in the seven Sacraments instituted by Christ.[7]

EPILOGUE: THE WEDDING FEAST OF THE LAMB AND HIS BRIDE

Alleluia! The reign of the Lord our God Almighty has begun, let us be glad and joyful and give glory to God, because this is the time for the marriage of the Lamb.
Revelation 19:6b-7

The worship of the resurrected, glorified Christ in the sacrificial meal of the Eucharist is the celebration of all the citizens of God's Kingdom, on earth and in Heaven. It is a sacred meal that looks back in time to the Last Supper and Jesus' sacrifice in AD 30, and forward in time to the union of God's Kingdom in the heavenly banquet at the end of time (Rev 19-21). Jesus, our High Priest, stands before the throne of God as the perpetual Tamid Lamb; and His worship in the earthly sanctuaries of our churches reflects both the heavenly Divine Liturgy and the Liturgy of Old Covenant Temple worship. The New Covenant people of God are the inheritors of the promises made to the Patriarchs in the Abrahamic Covenant and Israel in the Sinai Covenant. They are also the inheritors of the rites of Divine Liturgy that Moses and St. John witnessed in the Sacred Assembly of the heavenly Sanctuary.

The worship service of the Catholic Mass divides into three parts, reflecting the Jerusalem Temple's (and desert Tabernacle's) division of the inner courtyard, the Holy Place and the Holy of Holies. Like the liturgical service of the Tamid, the Lamb victim is slain, and the faithful enter through the open doors into the "courtyard" in the Introductory Rites of the Mass. Like worship in the Jerusalem Temple, worship in the Catholic Mass is an exhilarating assault upon the senses. There is the sound of the priestly prayers, the congregation singing the Sanctus (the Holy, Holy, Holy that the angels singing in the heavenly Sanctuary; see Rev 4:8 and Is 6:3), the other hymns of praise, and the reading of the words of God in Sacred Scripture. There is the smell of incense, the feel of the pews, kneelers, hymnals, and missals. And there is the sight of priests in colorful liturgical vestments and the members of the congregation gathered for worship. But the focus of the worshippers is the Sanctuary where the glow of candles signals the presence of God. In the center of the sacred space is the altar, representing the empty tomb, the table of the Last Supper, and the altar of sacrifice.

From the Courtyard of the Introductory Rites, Christ's priestly people proceed to the Holy Place in the Liturgy of the Word, singing "Alleluia" in honor of the Gospel of salvation. Then, in the Liturgy of the Eucharist, the presiding priest and the priestly people enter the Holy Place of the worship service. Chosen members of the priesthood of believers carry the gifts of the people forward to the altar. The presiding priest ritually purifies his hands before taking up the unleavened bread and wine that will become the Body and Blood of the Lamb. The faithful prepare to enter into the holiest moment of the liturgy, singing the

Messianic acclamation *Hosanna!* ("Save us"; see Mt 21:9; Mk 11:9; Jn 12:13).

Then the members of the assembly, united as the Bride of Christ, begin the bridal procession to welcome the embrace of the Bridegroom. The congregation symbolically enters the Holy of Holies of the Mass into the Real Presence of God the Son in the intimate celebration of the communion *Todah* ("Thanksgiving") in the earthly Eucharistic wedding supper of the Lamb that looks forward to the final banquet at the end of time (Rev 19:6–9). At that moment, in the suspension of earthly time, believers are united to the life of the sacrificial victim who offered Himself in atonement for the sins of humanity on the altar of the Cross outside the walls of Jerusalem in AD 30. Christ, the Bridegroom, is present and gives Himself to His Bride, the Church, in a sacred meal of covenant continuation where heavenly and earthly liturgies join in a mystical unity with the Triune God.

For our part, the personal sacrifice God desires from us is that we offer up to Him our repentant and purified selves (Rom 12:1); it is the same personal sacrifice He asked Old Covenant believers to make (Ps 51:16–17/18–19). However, in the New Covenant, He calls us to unite the sacrifice of our lives to the Living sacrifice of Jesus the Lamb (Rom 12:1; 1 Pt 2:5) as we "lift up" our circumcised hearts to Heaven. Pope St. Gregory the Great (c. 590 – 604) advised the faithful: *Reason teaches that we should condemn this present world with our whole souls and offer to God the daily sacrifice of his Body and Blood. For the Eucharistic sacrifice, which in mystery renews for us the death of the Son of God, saves our souls from everlasting damnation. When we participate at Mass, we should also sacrifice ourselves to almighty God with heartfelt contrition. For when we celebrate the mystery of our Lord's passion, we ought to imitate it. If we also offer ourselves to him in sacrifice, then the Eucharist shall truly be a sacrifice to God for us.*

It is the blood sacrifice of Jesus of Nazareth, the righteous son of Adam and the only begotten Son of God, that allows humanity freedom from the stain of sin and death and to become reconciled to God (Rom 6:22-23). As our heavenly High Priest and unblemished Lamb of the New Covenant sacrifice, Jesus purifies our sins and sanctifies our souls as we make our journey through the wilderness of this life to the Promised Land of Heaven: *but he holds his priesthood permanently because he continues forever. Consequently, he is able for all time to save those who draw near to God through him, since he always lives to make intercession for them* (Heb 7:24-25).

The Temple Tamid ended on the 17th of Tamuz (Panemus) in AD 70, but Jesus is the true and eternal

Tamid Lamb that every Old Covenant Tamid sacrifice prefigured. He is the Son of God who died on the altar of the Cross and perpetually offers Himself as the *Arnion Hestekos*—the "Lamb Standing" in the heavenly Sanctuary (Rev 5:6). He ended the requirement for communal and individual blood sacrifices by continually offering Himself as the unbloody sacrifice of the New Covenant communion *Todah*/Eucharistic sacrifice. His sacrifice is the same sacrifice offered on the Cross 2,000 years ago forever present in time before the throne of God in the heavenly Sanctuary and the earthly liturgy of His covenant people in the sacrifice of the Mass. Jesus, the true Tamid comes to His people on the Eucharistic table, offering Himself for the salvation of humankind until the end of time when, as the Conquering Lamb, He will return to claim His Bride, the Church.

CHAPTER SUMMARY POINTS: THE STANDING LAMB AND ETERNAL HIGH PRIEST

1. Jesus is the rightful Davidic heir, the eternal High Priest of God's Sanctuary in Heaven, and the "Standing

Lamb,"*Arnion Hestekos,* who is the true Tamid of the heavenly Temple, offered once and for all time in a bloody sacrifice on the altar of the Cross.

2. In His role as both the eternal High Priest of the New Covenant and the unblemished Lamb of sacrifice, Jesus offers Himself continually (*tamid*) in an unbloody sacrifice before the throne of God and upon every altar in the Catholic Mass for the salvation of all humanity.

3. The sacrifice of the Mass is the joining of the earthly and heavenly liturgies in the on-going sacrifice and sacred meal of covenant obedience and continuation. It is the wedding supper of the eternal Tamid Lamb and His Bride, the Church.

Endnotes: The Standing Lamb and Eternal High Priest

1. St. John saw the same vision as the 6th century BC prophet Daniel (compare Dan 10:5 with Rev 1:13). Jesus' liturgical garment in Revelation is similar to the liturgical garment the High Priest wore when he entered the Holy of Holies on the Feast of Atonement (Lev 16:4).

2. The Greek word for "door" in this passage is *thura,* meaning "a portal or entrance; door, gate." It is the same Greek word Jesus used when He said: *I am the door of the sheep ... I am the door; if any one enters by me, he will be saved* (Jn 10:7, 9). Jesus used the word *thura* ten times: Lk 11:7; 13:25 (twice); Jn 10:1, 2, 7, 9; Rev 3:8, 20 (twice). See *Strong's # 2374; Thayer's Greek-English Lexicon of the New Testament,* page 293.

3. The term *Arnion Hestekos* appears in Rev 5:6 and again in Rev 14:1. The literal Greek reads: *And I saw, and behold, in midst of the throne and of the four living creatures, and amidst the elders, Lamb Standing [Arnion Hestekos] as having been slain* (Rev 5:6 IBGE, page 665); *And I saw, and behold, Lamb Standing [Arnion Hestekos] on the mount Zion...* (Rev. 14:1 IBGE, vol. IV, page 682).

4. Quote from Philip Carrington, *The Meaning of Revelation* (London, SPCK, 1931), page 119. It was not uncommon for both Jews and Christians to adapt Greek words to specialized Hebrew terms.

5. Also see *Feast of Faith*, Joseph Ratzinger (Pope Emeritus Benedict XVI), pages 57-58.

6. Cardinal Ratzinger (Pope Emeritus Benedict XVI) quotes the rabbinic dictum cited by H. Gese in *Zur Biblischen Theologie*, page 122: *In the coming (Messianic) time, all sacrifices will cease except the toda sacrifice. This will never cease in all eternity. All (religious) song will cease too, but the songs of toda will never cease in all eternity* (Ratzinger, *Feast of Faith*, pages 58).

7. The word "sacrament" is from the Latin word *sacramentum*, meaning "oath," "solemn obligation" (*Modern Catholic Dictionary*, "sacrament," page 380). See CCC 1114; 1129; 1210.

BIBLIOGRAPHY

1. *A History of Israel*, John Bright, Westminster John Knox Press, 2000.
2. *A History of Rome*, M. Cary and H. H. Scullard, Palgrave, 1988.
3. *A History of the Ancient Near East ca 3000 – 323 BC*, Marc Van De Mieroop, Blackwell Publishing, 2004.
4. *A History of the Jewish People in the Time of Jesus Christ*, volumes I – VI, Emil Schurer, Hendrickson Publishers, 2008.
5. *A Passover Haggadah, Ellie Wiesel*, Simon & Schuster, Inc., 1993.
6. *A Practical Commentary on Holy Scripture*, Bishop Frederick Justus Knecht, Tan Books and Publishers, Inc., 1923.
7. *A Rabbi Talks With Jesus*, Jacob Neusner, McGill-Queen's University Press, 2000.
8. *Ancient Christian Writers: Diary of a Pilgrimage*, translated and annotated by George E. Gingras, Newman Press, 1970.
9. *Ancient Israel*, edited by Hershel Shanks, Biblical Archaeology Society, Washington D.C., 1999.
10. *Augustus to Constantine: The Rise and Triumph of Christianity in the Roman World*, Robert M. Grant, Westminster John Knox Press, 2004.
11. *Bible Dictionary*, Paul Achtemeir, general editor, Harper Collins, 1996 edition.
12. *Bethlehem to Patmos*, Paul Barnett, Paternoster Press, 1989.
13. *Calendar: Humanity's Epic Struggle to Determine a True and Accurate Year*, David Ewing Duncan, Avon Books, Inc., 1998.

14. *Caesar and Christ,* Will Durant, Simon & Schuster Inc., 1944, republished by MPF Books, 1971.

15. *Catechism of the Catholic Church*, Libreria Editrice Vaticana, 1997.

16. *Catholicism and Fundamentalism*, Karl Keating, Ignatius Press, 1988.

17. *Christ in the Passover,* Ceil and Moishe Rosen, Moody Press, Chicago 1978.

18. *Christianity and the Roman Empire,* Ralph Martin Novak, Trinity Press International, 2001.

19. *Church History,* Fr. John Laux, Tan Books and Publishers, Inc., Rockford, Illinois, 1930 (republished edition 1989).

20. *Dictionary of the Bible*, John L. McKenzie, S.J., Simon and Schuster, 1995.

21. *Feast of Faith,* Joseph Cardinal Ratzinger, Ignatius Press, San Francisco, 1986.

22. *Jerusalem in the Time of Jesus,* Joachim Jeremias, Fortress Press, Philadelphia, 1968.

23. *Jesus of Nazareth,* Joseph Ratzinger (Pope Benedict XVI), Doubleday, 2007.

24. *Jesus of Nazareth*, Joseph Ratzinger (Pope Benedict XVI), vol. II, Ignatius Press, 2011.

25. *Jewish Literacy,* Rabbi Joseph Telushkin, William Morrow and Company, Inc., 2001 edition.

26. *Judaism and the Interpretation of Scripture,* Jacob Neusner, Hendrickson Publishers, 2004.

27. *Letter and Spirit*, vol. IV, St. Paul Center for Biblical Theology, 2008.

28. *Leviticus,* Robert I. Vasholz, Mentor: Christian Focus Publications, 2007.

29. *Many Religions—One Covenant,* Joseph Cardinal Ratzinger, Ignatius Press, San Francisco, 1999.

30. *Mapping Time: The Calendar and its History,* E. G. Richards, Oxford University Press, 1998; reprinted 2005.

31. *Mesopotamia and the Bible,* edited by Mark W. Chavalas and K. Lawson Younger, Jr., Baker Academic, 2002.

32. *Nicene and Post-Nicene Fathers, Second Series,* vol. 1, Church History, Eusebius, Hendrickson Publishers, 1995.

33. *Offerings, Sacrifices and Worship in the Old Testament*, J. H. Kurtz, Hendrickson Publishers, 1998.

34. *Sinai & Zion: An entry into the Jewish Bible,* Jon D. Levenson, Harper San Francisco, 1985.

35. *Sketches of Jewish Social Life,* Alfred Edersheim, Hendrickson Publishers, 1994.

36. *Strong's Exhaustive Concordance of the Bible,* James Strong, Thomas Nelson Publishers, 1994 edition.

37. *Thayer's Greek-English Lexicon of the New Testament,* Joseph H. Thayer, Hendrickson Publishers, 2007.

38. *The Age of Faith,* Will Durant, Simon & Schuster Inc., 1950, republished by MPF Books, 1971.

39. *The Anchor Bible Dictionary,* volumes 1-6, Doubleday, 1992 edition.

40. *The Anchor Bible: The Book of Daniel,* Louis F. Hartman and Alexander A. Di Lella, Doubleday, 1978.

41. *The Anchor Bible: The Gospel According to Luke,* vol. I-II, Joseph Fitzmyer, Doubleday & Company, Inc., New York, 1985.

42. *The Anchor Bible: The Gospel According to John,* vol. I-II, Raymond Brown, Doubleday & Company, Inc., New York, 1966.

43. *The Ancient Synagogue: The First Thousand Years,* Lee I. Levine, Yale University Press, 2005.

44. *The Brown-Driver-Briggs Hebrew and English Lexicon,* E. Brown, S. Driver, and C. Griggs, Hendrickson Publishers, 2000.

45. *The Days of Vengeance*, David Chilton, Dominion Press, 1990 edition.

46. *The Feasts of the Lord,* Kevin Howard and Marvin Rosenthal, Thomas Nelson, Inc., Nashville, 1997.

47. *The History of the Jewish People in the Time of Jesus Christ,* vol. 1-5, Emil Schurer, Hendrickson Publishers, 2008 edition.

48. *The Holy Bible:* Revised Standard Version Catholic Edition, Ignatius Press, 1966.

49. *The Interlinear Bible, vol. I-IV,* Jay P. Green, Sr., General Editor and Translator, Hendrickson Publishers, 2005.

50. *The Jewish Book of Why,* volumes I and II, Alfred J. Kolatch, Johathan David Publishers, Inc. 1981 revised 1995.

51. *The Jewish Festivals from Their Beginnings to Our Own Day,* Hayyim Schauss, Union of American Hebrew Congregations, New York, 1938.

52. *The Jewish Study Bible,* editors Adele Berlin and Marc Zvi Brettler, The Jewish Publication Society, Oxford University Press, 1999 edition.

53. *The New American Bible,* Oxford University Press, 1986.

54. *The New Jerusalem Bible,* Doubleday, 1985.

55. *The New Jewish Wedding,* Anita Diamant, Simon & Schuster, Inc., N.Y., 1985, 2001.

56. *The JPS Guide to Jewish* Traditions, Ronald L. Eisenberg, The Jewish Publication Society, Philadelphia, 2004.

57. *The JPS Torah Commentary: Exodus,* The Jewish Publication Society, 1991.

58. *The JPS Torah Commentary: Leviticus,* Baruch A. Levine, Jewish Publication Society, 1998.

59. *The JPS Torah Commentary: Numbers,* Jacob Milgrom, Jewish Publication Society, 1990.

60. *The Landmark Herodotus: The Histories,* editor: Robert B. Strassler, Pantheon Books, New York, 2007.

61. *The Mishnah*, editor Jacob Neusner, Yale University Press, 1988.

62. *The Navarre Bible: Pentateuch,* Faculty of Theology, Navarre University, Four Courts Press, 1999.

63. *The Navarre Bible: Major Prophets,* Faculty of Theology, Navarre University, Four Courts Press, 1999.

64. *The Pentateuch as Narrative,* John Sailhamer, Zondervan Publishing, 1992.

65. *The Second Jewish Book of Why,* Alfred J. Kolatch, Johathan David Publishers, Inc. 1985.

66. *The Septuagint with Apocrypha*, translator Sir Lancelot Brenton, Hendrickson Publishers, 1999.

67. *The Sixteen Documents of Vatican II,* Pauline Books, 1999.

68. *The Temple and the Church's Mission*, G. K. Beale, InterVarsity Press, 2004.

69. *The Temple: Its Ministry and Services,* Alfred Edersheim, Hendrickson, 1994 edition.

70. *The Temple Haggadah, Israel Ariel,* The Temple Institute, Carta- Cana, Jerusalem, 1996.

71. *The Temple of Jerusalem,* Simon Goldhill, Harvard University Press, 2005.

72. *The Works of Josephus,* translated by William Whiston, Hendrickson Publishers, 1987.

73. *The Works of Philo of Alexandria,* translated by C. D. Yonge, Hendrickson Publishers, 1997.

APPENDIX

Appendix I: Yahweh's Eight Covenants

But Yahweh's faithful love for those who fear Him is from eternity and forever; and His saving justice to their children's children; as long as they keep His covenant, and carefully obey his precepts. Psalm 103:17-18

COVENANT	SIGN	SCRIPTURE
1. Adam -fertity -dominion over the earth	Tree of Life	Genesis 1:28-30; Genesis 2:15-17; Hosea 6:7 can be translated *they have broken their covenant like Adam*
2. Noah and the earth -The earth will never be destroyed by flood waters again (water will become a sign of salvation)	Rainbow	Genesis 6:18; 9:9-17; Sirach 44:17-18.
3. Abraham (continues with Isaac, Jacob & descendants) -Land, nation (descendants) & worldwide blessing	Circumcision on the 8th day	Genesis 12:3; 15:1-18; 17: 1-27; 18:18 & 22:13-18; 26:3-5; 28:10-14; Exodus 2:24; Psalm 105:8-11; Sirach 44:19-20

Yahweh's Eight Covenants (continued)

COVENANT	SIGN	SCRIPTURE
4. Moses & Israel -Sinai Covenant: Ordained priesthood, liturgy & covenant Law	Tabernacle & Sabbath obligation (sacred time and space)	Exodus 19-24; 31:13, 17; 34:10, 27-28; Deuteronomy 5:2-3; 29:12.
5. Aaron & Sons -Perpetual ministerial priesthood of the Levites	Salt	Exodus 40:15; Leviticus 2:13; Numbers 18:19; Jeremiah 33:21; Sirach 45:7.
6. Phinehas -Perpetual priesthood in a Covenant of Peace (prefigures Christ)	Seamless robe & miter	Numbers 25:11-15; Sirach 45:24.
7. David & descendants -Dynasty and throne forever	Throne/ Temple	2 Samuel 7:11-17; 23:5; 2 Chronicles 31:5; Sirach 45:25.
8. New Covenant in Christ Jesus. He is the fulfillment of all the covenantal promises.	The Cross (the true "Tree of Life") & the Eucharist	Isaiah 55:3; Jeremiah 31:31-34; Matthew 26:28; Mark 14:24; Luke 22:20; 1 Corinthians 11:25; Hebrews 12:24.

Appendix II: Offerings and Sacrifices

The Classifications of Offerings and Sacrifices			
Types of offerings	Tribute Offering/ Vassal payment	Sanctuary endowments	Alter sacrifices
	(compulsory)	(voluntary)	(voluntary and compulsory)
Scripture reference	Ex 13:11–16; Lev 27:26–33; Num 3:45–48; 18:21, 25–29	Ex 25:1–2; 35:4–5, 29; 36:3; Ezra 7:16; 8:28–30	Lev chapters 1–7; 16; 23;
Reason	Owed for services rendered by God to His people	To support God's Sanctuary	Liturgical service and covenant continuation
Gifts and Offeror	First fruits of animals, sons, and harvests presented to God by individuals	Any gift for use in the Sanctuary presented by the people	Offerings to God made by individuals or presented by the priests for the whole community
Purpose	For the maintenance of the ministerial priesthood	Used by the priests for the Sanctuary and liturgical services	1. To provide for communal and personal expiation of sins 2. To reestablish communion with God through a sacred meal
Who received	Priests and Levites	Priests on behalf of the Sanctuary	God or shared with God in a sacred meal

The Classifications of Offerings and Sacrifices

Types of offerings	Tribute Offering/ Vassal payment	Sanctuary endowments	Alter sacrifices
Categories	A. first produce of the harvest 1. Grains 2. Fruits B. first-born animals 1. clean 2. unclean C. first-born sons redeemed by a redemption tax	Bloodless offerings 1. grain 2. olive oil 3. wine 4. money 5. anything of value	Bleeding sacrifices from 5 kinds of animals (cattle, sheep, goats, turtledoves, pigeons): 1. Whole-burnt offerings: Compulsory = Tamid, Sabbath, New Moon & Feast days Voluntary = individual offerings 2. Sin sacrifices: Compulsory = communal Voluntary = individual; in both priests eat a sacred meal 3. Reparation sacrifices: Voluntary = individual; priests eat a sacred meal 4. Communion sacrifices: Voluntary = 3 kinds (thank, vow & free-will); offeror & members of community eat a sacred meal Bloodless offerings: a. five classes of wheat flour/unleavened bread offerings b. wine c. incense d. olive oil e. salt

Appendix III: THE SYMBOLIC IMAGES OF THE OLD TESTAMENT PROPHETS

Each of the images consist of four parts:

Part I: Yahweh and his people enter into a covenant relationship. Yahweh will bind His people to Himself in the blessings of security and prosperity in return for obedience to the covenant commands.

Part II: The covenant people ignore the Laws of the Covenant; they rebel by going their own way.

Part III: God sends His holy prophets to call His people back to Him. When the people fail to repent, the prophet calls down a Covenant Lawsuit which results in Covenant curses—temporal punishments meant to bring about repentance and restoration

Part IV: In response to repentance, Yahweh reaches out to restore and to take His people back into the covenant relationship.

THE SYMBOLIC IMAGES OF THE OLD TESTAMENT PROPHETS

Image Groups	Part I Covenant relationship	Part II Rebellion	Part III Redemptive Judgment	Part IV Restoration Fulfilled in Jesus
Covenant Marriage	Israel Bride of Yahweh	Unfaithful adulteress/harlot	Humiliated, abused & abandoned by lovers	The Bride restored to her Bridegroom
Examples in Scripture	Isaiah 61:10-11; Jeremiah 2:2; Ezekiel 16:4-14	Isaiah 1:21 Jeremiah 3:6-8; 13:22-23, 26; 23:10; Ezekiel 16:15-34; 23:1-12; Hosea 4:10-14	Jeremiah 3:1b-2; Ezekiel 16:23-61; 23:35-49; Amos 4:7-8; 4:30-31; Hosea 2:4-15	Promised: Isaiah 54:6-8; Hosea 2:16-25 Fulfilled: John 3:28-29; 2 Corinthians 11:2; Ephesians 5:25-27; Revelation 19:7-9; 21:2;9; 22:17
Vineyard or Fig tree	Well-tended vineyard/fruitful fig tree	Vines grow wild/failure to produce fruit	Weeds overgrow vineyard/ ruin and destruction	Vines are replanted/ fruitfulness restored
Examples in Scripture	Isaiah 5:1-4; Jeremiah 24:4-7; Ezekiel 19:10-11	Jeremiah 2:21 Hosea 2:14; Micah 7:1-4; Joel 1:11-12; 7:1-4	Isaiah 5:3-6; Jeremiah 8:13; Ezekiel 19:12-14; Nahum 3:12-15	Promise: Hosea 14:2-9; Fulfilled: John 15:1-2, 4-6

THE SYMBOLIC IMAGES OF THE OLD TESTAMENT PROPHETS (Continued)

Image Groups	**Part I** **Covenant relationship**	**Part II** **Rebellion**	**Part III** **Redemptive Judgment**	**Part IV** **Restoration Fulfilled in Jesus**
Animals	Domesticated animals are obedient to the yoke	They run away and become wild	They are ravaged by wild beasts or birds of prey	Animals rescued by their Master
Examples in Scripture	Isaiah 40:10-11; 65:25; Ezekiel 34:15-16; Micah 4:13	Isaiah 50:6; 53:6 Jeremiah 5:5d-6; 8:6b-7; 23:1-2; Ezekiel 19:1-9	Isaiah 50:7; Jeremiah 8:15-17; 50:6-7; Hosea 8:1-14; 13:6-8	Promise: Ezekiel 34; Fulfilled: Matthew 11:28-30; John 1:29, 36; 10:1-18; Hebrews 3:20; Revelation 5:6, 13; 7:9-17; 14:1-10; 19:2-9; 21:9-23; 22:1-3
Drinking Wine	The joy of drinking good wine	Becoming drunk	Drinking the "cup of God's wrath"	Rejoicing in the best "new wine" at the Master's table (Messianic banquet)
Examples in Scripture	Psalm 23:5; Isaiah 25:6; 62:9; Jeremiah 40:12	Isaiah 5:11-12; 28:1; Jeremiah 8:13; 48:26; 51:7; Joel 1:5	Joel 4:13; Isaiah 51:17; 63:2-3; Jeremiah 13:12-14; 25:15-31; 48:26	Promised: Zechariah 9:15-17; Fulfilled: Luke 22:19-20; 1 Corinthians 11:23-32 and Revelation 19:7-9

Appendix IV: Israel's Liturgical and Civil Calendar

Seven annual feasts are God-ordained feasts (Ex 12:1-28; 43-51; 13:1-10; Lev 23:5-44; Num 28:16-29:39) including three pilgrim feasts – Passover, Unleavened Bread, and Tabernacles. The Feasts of Unleavened Bread and Tabernacles fell respectively near the spring and fall equinoxes.

*Hanukkah and Purim are national feasts proclaimed by the people and are not God-ordained (1 Mac 4:36-61; 2 Mac 10:1-8; Est 9:20-32).

ISRAEL'S LITURGICAL AND CIVIL CALENDAR YEAR				
Month	Liturgical year order	Civil year order	Modern equivalent	Feast days & Agricultural Season (+ = God ordained annual and ++ pilgrim feasts * = national feasts)
Aviv/Abib (Nisan)	1	7	Mar/Apr	+Passover 14th ++Uneavened Bread; 15-21st (sacred assembly on 15th and 21st), +Firstfruits on Sunday of Unleavened Bread holy week. Spring equinox 15th. The "Latter rains" & flood season, beginning of barley and flax harvest
Ziv (Iyyar)	2	8	Apr/May	The dry season, apricots ripen

ISRAEL'S LITURGICAL AND CIVIL CALENDAR YEAR (cont)				
Month	Liturgical year order	Civil year order	Modern equivalent	Feast days & Agricultural Season (+ = God ordained annual and ++ pilgrim feasts * = national feasts)
Sivan	3	9	May/Jun	++Weeks (Pentecost) 50 days from Firstfruits as ancients counted; wheat harvest, dry winds, early fig harvest, grapes ripen
Tammuz	4	10	Jun/Jul	Hot, dry season: grape harvest
Ab	5	11	Jul/Aug	Hot, olive harvest
Elul	6	12	Aug/Sep	Dates and summer figs
Ethanim (Tishri)	7	1	Sep/Oct	+Trumpets = 1st , +Day of Atonement =10th, ++Tabernacles = 15-21st & 22nd sacred assembly; Fall equinox 15th; "Former (early) rains," plowing & seed time

ISRAEL'S LITURGICAL AND CIVIL CALENDAR YEAR (cont)				
Month	Liturgical year order	Civil year order	Modern equivalent	Feast days & Agricultural Season (+ = God ordained annual and ++ pilgrim feasts * = national feasts)
Bul (Heshvan)	8	2	Oct/Nov	Rains, winter figs, wheat, and barley sown
Chislev	9	3	Nov/Dec	*Hanukkah (feast of dedication); winter begins
Tebeth	10	4	Dec/Jan	Coldest month, rains and snow in mountains
Sebat	11	5	Jan/Feb	Growing warmer, almond trees in bloom
Adar	12	6	Feb/Mar	*Purim; spring: "Latter rains" begin, citrus & fruit harvest

GLOSSARY

Altar of Burnt Offerings: According to God's command, the altar of sacrifice was in the inner courtyard of the desert Sanctuary and the same location in the Jerusalem Temple. The altar fire entirely consumed anything placed on it and burned continually (Ex 27:1-8; 38:1-7; 1 Kng 8:64).

Altar of Incense: A chest-high golden altar located in the Holy Place in front of the curtain that shielded the entrance to the Holy of Holies. The High Priest or his priestly representative chosen by lot burned the holy incense twice a day, during the morning liturgical worship service and again in the afternoon, which was the evening for the Jews since their day ended at sunset (Ex 30:1-10; 1 Kng 6:20-21; 7:48).

Arnion Hestekos: These Greek words meant "Lamb Standing" and were used for Christ the Lamb in the heavenly Sanctuary in Revelation 5:6 and 14:1. If the inspired writer of the Book of Revelation was using Greek to express a Hebrew concept, then he was describing Jesus as the eternal Tamid, the "standing" Lamb that the Old Covenant daily sacrifice of the Tamid prefigured (the literal meaning of the word *tamid* is "standing" as in continual). The Tamid sacrifice was the premier sacrifice of the entire Old Covenant sacrificial system (see the listing for "Tamid" in the glossary).

Ark of the Covenant/Ark of the Testimony: The wooden box overlayed inside and out with gold that held the Ten Commandments, the two stone covenant documents of the Sinai Covenant. A solid gold lid called the Mercy-seat (Kapporeth) covered the top of the Ark. The Ark was the most sacred shrine of the Sinai Covenant. The presence of God rested upon the Mercy-seat of the Ark, and it was the only piece of furniture placed in the Holy of Holies. The Ark disappeared at the time the Babylonians destroyed Solomon's Temple in 587/6 BC (Ex 25:10-22; 37:1-9; 2 Macc 2:1-8).

Atonement: The expiation for an offense that occurs through a voluntary act that outweighs the injustice initially committed.

Bread of the Presence: In Hebrew, these consecrated loaves of bread were the "bread of the face" of God. The twelve loaves of bread, representing the twelve tribes of Israel, were placed on a golden table in the Holy Place of the Sanctuary and later the Jerusalem Temple. The priests ate the previous week's bread every Sabbath and replaced them with new loaves (Ex 25:30; Lev 24:5-9).

Catechesis: The form of ecclesial teaching and the application of that teaching that promotes the practice of right doctrine for individuals and faith communities. The purpose of catechesis is to lead both the individual and the congregation of the faithful to a deeper understanding of the rites and rituals of the Catholic faith, to a more committed level of faith in action, and therefore to a deeper level of spiritual maturity.

Censer: A device in which the holy incense was either carried or burned.

Chagigah: See Hagigah.

Charoset/haroset: The mixture of chopped fruit mixed with wine and cinnamon was one of the traditional foods served at a Passover meal. Jewish rabbis disagree as to whether it was a required dish at the feast of the Passover victim on the first night of Unleavened Bread.

Code: A standard of conduct.

Communion: This word is from the Latin meaning "sharing unity." In the liturgy of Christian worship, communion is the shared union with Christ in which the faithful consume the Body, Blood, Soul, and Divinity of Jesus Christ whole and entire under the form of bread alone or bread and wine. It can also refer to the spiritual unity between the saints in heaven, the souls in purgatory, and the faithful living on earth and defined as "the communion of saints."

Covenant: A covenant is an agreement based upon intangibles like justice, truth, and personal commitment, unlike a contract that is concerned with material goods like property. Biblical covenants formed by God in the Old Testament were agreements between God and a person and his family or a people as a unity (the Sinai Covenant and the New Covenant in Christ Jesus) in which God promised protection and blessings in return for exclusive loyalty. See the chart on Yahweh's Eight Covenants in the chart section.

Covenant ordeal: A test to determine covenant obedience in which the choice to obey God requires personal sacrifice, while the temptation to be disobedient is perceived as beneficial or of earthly reward.

Creed: A statement of belief.

Cult: Rituals of worship.

Curtain/veil: In the desert Sanctuary and Jerusalem Temple, one curtain covered the entryway to the Holy Place and a second covered the entrance to the Holy of Holies. According to the Jewish Mishnah, they were as thick as a man's hand.

Daily Sacrifice: See Tamid.

Doctrine: A doctrine is any formal instruction approved by the Magisterium and taught by the Church.

Dogma: A dogma is any teaching by the Church defined as theological truth and necessary for acceptance by the faithful.

Eucharist: From the Greek word *eucharistia,* meaning "thanksgiving." In the Catholic Mass, the Eucharist is the summit of worship when, after the words of consecration, the priest offers the Body and Blood of Jesus Christ, who is truly and substantially present under the appearance of bread and wine, to the faithful as their spiritual food in Holy Communion.

Expiation: Atonement for a wrong act and the attempt to undo the wrong by suffering a penalty, or by making reparation or redress.

Feasts (of the Sinai Covenant): The liturgical calendar of the Sinai Covenant consisted of festivals that included one monthly feast (Feast of the New Moon) to establish the beginning of each new month, two periodic feasts (the every seventh year Sabbath Year and the Jubilee Year every fiftieth year), seven annual remembrance feasts, and the weekly Sabbath feast. A lunar calendar determined the dates of all the God-ordained feasts (see Lev Chapters 23, 25, and Num Chapters 28-29). See the Liturgical Calendar in the charts section.

Feast of Atonement: Yom Kippur was the sixth annual remembrance feast in the liturgical calendar of the Sinai Covenant. It was a day of fasting and communal reconciliation with sacrifices offered in atonement for the collective sins of the covenant people. The feast fell on the 10th of Tishri in the fall (Lev 16; 23:26-32; Num 29:7-11).

Feast of Firstfruits: Yom HaBikkurim was the third annual remembrance feast in the liturgical calendar of the Sinai Covenant. This feast did not have a designated date like the other yearly feasts but fell on the day after the Sabbath of the week-long feast of Unleavened Bread (Lev 23:9-11). Therefore, it always fell on the first day of the week, our Sunday. Jesus' Resurrection was on the

Feast of Firstfruits, and because of this, the Jews changed the date of the feast to the 16th of Nisan to ensure that it and the Feast of Weeks/Pentecost (Hag HaShavuot) fifty days later as the ancients counted without a zero place-value no longer always fell on a Sunday.

Feast of Passover: Passover was the first annual remembrance feast in the liturgical calendar of the Sinai Covenant. The sacrifice of multiple lambs and goat kids took place in the spring on the 14th of Abib/Nisan in remembrance of the first Passover in Egypt (Ex 12:2, 6; 13:4; Lev 23:5; Num 28:16).

Feast of Pentecost/Weeks: Hag HaShavuot, later known in Greek as *he penetkoste* "the fiftieth day," was the fourth annual feast in the liturgical calendar of the Sinai Covenant and the second "pilgrim feast" (Dt 16:16). Like Firstfruits, this feast did not have a specific date but was to be celebrated 50 days after Firstfruits as the ancients counted, and therefore, like Firstfruits, it also always fell on a Sunday. It was the Jewish feast when God the Holy Spirit came to fill and indwell the New Covenant Church in Jerusalem 50 days after Jesus' Resurrection (Lev 23:15-22; Num 28:26-31).

Feast of Tabernacles/Booths/Shelters: Sukkot, also known as Chag HaAsif, the Festival of Ingathering, was the seventh and last annual feast in the liturgical calendar of the Sinai Covenant, and the third pilgrim feast (Dt 16:16). It was celebrated in the early fall from the 15th of Tishri to the 21st, with a Sacred Assembly on the 1st day and the 8th day of the 22nd (Lev 23:33-44; Num 29:12-38). The feast fell during the fall equinox and recalled the gift of God's Sanctuary and later the Jerusalem Temple. It also prefigured the future ingathering of the nations to worship God in the Messianic Era (Zec 14:16-18).

Feast of Trumpets: Rosh Hashanah was the fifth annual remembrance feast in the liturgical calendar of the Sinai Covenant, and the first day of the New Year in the civil calendar. The feast recalled the Exodus experience when God commanded the blowing of trumpets to announce the beginning of Israel's march from Mount Sinai to the Promised Land (Lev 23:23-25; Num 29:1-6).

Feast of Unleavened Bread: Hag Hamatzot was the second of the seven annual remembrance feasts in the liturgical calendar of the Sinai Covenant (Ex 34:18; Lev 23:4-8; Num 28:16-25). It was also the first of the three "pilgrim feasts" when the Law commanded every man of the Covenant to present himself before God's holy altar (Ex 23:15; Dt 16:16; 2 Chr 8:13)). The feast fell on the full moon and the spring equinox, beginning at sunset after the Passover sacrifice and lasting for seven days. The Last Supper took place on the first night of Unleavened Bread (Mt 26:17-20, 26-29; Mk 14:12-17, 22-25; Lk 22:7-20).

Fiat: The origin of this word is Latin and means "let it be done;" 3rd singular present subjunctive of *fierī*, "to become." 1. An authoritative decree, sanction, or order: *a royal fiat.* Synonyms: authorization, directive, ruling, mandate. 2. a fixed form of words containing the word *fiat* by which a person in authority gives sanction, or authorization. 3. An arbitrary decree or pronouncement, especially by a person or group of persons having absolute authority to enforce it; i.e., *The king ruled by fiat.*

First Temple Period: The period of the Jerusalem Temple built by King Solomon that extended from circa 970 to 587/6 BC when the Babylonians destroyed the Temple.

Firstborn: First life to issue from the womb whether animals or human males.

Gemarah: The commentary on the Mishnah. There is a Babylonian and a Palestinian version of the Gemarah. Together the Mishnah and the Gemarah form the Jewish Talmud.

Gethsemane: The garden on the Mount of Olives where Jesus went to pray with His disciples after the Last Supper and where the Temple guards arrested Him. The Aramaic name means "olive press."

Glory Cloud: The visible manifestation of God's glory. The Glory Cloud led the children of Israel on their exodus out of Egypt and continued to guide them until they entered the Promised Land.

Golgotha: The word represents in Greek letters the Aramaic word *Gulgaltha*, which is in Hebrew *Gulgoleth*, "place of [the] skull." It is the hill outside the gates of Jerusalem and the site of Jesus' crucifixion. The Greek for "place of [the] skull" is *Kraníou Tópos*, rendered in Latin as *Calvariœ Locus*, and in English expressed as *Calvary.*

Hagigah: The Hagigah/Chagigah was a festival communion offering of either a male or female animal from the flock or herd.

Herod's Temple: When King Herod the Great commissioned a renovation and expansion of the Second Temple complex, his name came to be associated with the monumental reconstructed. The Romans destroyed the Temple reconfigured and embellished by King Herod in AD 70.

Holocaust: 1. In the sacrificial system, a holocaust was an animal sacrifice consumed by fire, often called a "whole burnt offering," in which God accepted the sacrifice in its ascending smoke (Lev 1:3-7; 6:8-13). Such offerings were either compulsory communal sacrifices like the Tamid and festival offerings or an individual's voluntary offering expressing gratitude to God. 2. The Nazi German government's orchestrated murder of millions of Jews and others during World War II.

Holy of Holies: The Holy of Holies was a cube-shaped space that was the innermost sanctum of God's Sanctuary where the Ark of the Covenant rested in the desert Sanctuary and Solomon's Temple. It was an empty room in the Second Temple built after the return from the Babylonian exile.

Holy Place: The Temple proper was composed of the Holy Place and the Holy of Holies. The Menorah, Table of the Bread of the Presence and the Incense Altar were in the Holy Place.

Kapporeth: See Mercy-Seat.

Karaites: A sect of Jews who claim they are the descendants of the Sadducees. They continue to celebrate the Feast of Firstfruits on the day after the Sabbath of the holy week of the Feast of Unleavened Bread as commanded in Leviticus 23:9-14, as was the practice until after Jesus' Resurrection in the first century AD when the Jews changed the set time of the observance.

Kipper: A Hebrew word meaning "ransom." The animal offered in sacrifice (*kipper* in Hebrew) regarded as a ransom (*kopher* in Hebrew).

Korban: A Hebrew word derived from a root meaning "to draw near to" or "to establish fellowship with" and appears forty times in the liturgical instructions in the Book of Leviticus. The use of the word *korban* for the offering of sacrifice reveals that the Hebrew concept of sacrifice is much more than merely making a pleasing gift to appease a deity by offering something of material value. Any form of offering to God, whether animal sacrifice, grain offerings, first-fruit offerings, or Sanctuary gifts was *korban.*

Levant: An approximate historical and geographical term that refers to a large area in the eastern Mediterranean. In its widest historical sense, the Levant included all of the eastern Mediterranean with its islands, that is, it included all of the countries along the eastern Mediterranean shores, extending from Greece to Turkey, Syria, Israel and Cyrenaica in North Africa. The term "Levant" became an English word in the late 15th century AD from French. Both the French and English words derive from the Italian word *levante*, meaning "rising," implying the rising of the sun in the east. Today the term mostly refers to the land area along the Mediterranean coast from Syria to Israel and Gaza.

Levites: The lesser ministers of the Sinai Covenant. They were men from the three clans of the tribe of Levi. They served the chief priests of the tribe of Levi who were the descendants of Aaron. They were chosen as lesser ministers to replace the "firstborn sons" in the sin of the Golden Calf, and they could not perform any of the chief priests' duties to include offering the sacrifice at the Bronze Altar of Sacrifice (Num 3:6-13; 8:19; 18:1-7).

Liturgy: A public duty, service, or work; from Latin *liturgia;* from Greek *leitos,* "of the people" + *ergon,* "work" = *leitourgia*, "public duty/public worship." In the Old Testament, it refers to the religious duties performed by the chief priests, Levitical lesser ministers, and the faithful participating in Temple services, especially those works related to worship and sacrifice. For Christians, it refers to the official public worship of the Church as opposed to private prayer. For those who are Catholic and those in the Eastern Rites, it means the Eucharistic Sacrifice.

Liturgy of the Eucharist: The second part of the Catholic Mass following the Liturgy of the Word that is the most solemn part of the liturgical celebration from the Presentation of the Gifts to the Post Communion Rites.

Magisterium: The teaching authority of the Catholic Church vested in bishops, who are the successors of the Apostles, under the Roman Pontiff, who is the successor of Christ's Vicar, St. Peter. Latin = *magister,* "master."

Magrefah: A gong-like instrument was used in the Jerusalem Temple worship services to announce that the High Priest or his priestly representative was about to perform the ritual of burning the sacred incense in the Holy Place on the golden Altar of Incense (Ex 30:1-9; Lk 1:8-10).

Mass: The Mass is the Sacrifice of the Eucharist that is the central act of worship for the faithful of the Catholic Church. The word "Mass" is from the Latin word *missio*, which means "sending," and from the closing words of the worship service "to go forth," *ite missa est* in Latin. These are the words that send the faithful out into the world to use the graces they have received in the Eucharistic liturgy and to put into practice what they have learned in sharing the Gospel of salvation.

Menorah: The seven-branched lampstand with seven oil lamps that stood in the Holy Place of the Sanctuary/Temple (Ex 25:31-40; 37:17-24).

Mercy-Seat/Kapporeth: The solid gold lid of the Ark of the Covenant embellished with the images of two golden cherubim that faced each other. It was where God's Divine Presence dwelt among His people (Ex 25:21; 26:34).

Mikveh: A pool with flowing water used for ritual purification.

Minhah: It is a Hebrew word designating a tribute offering that signifies one's allegiance to God the Great King of the universe. The High Priest's wafer offering was both his *korban* that allowed him to draw near to God and his *minhah* tribute offering.

Mishnah: A document that contains the detailed record of ritual and worship in the Jerusalem Temple in the first century AD. It was written and compiled by Jewish scholars in the third century AD, about 130 years after the destruction of the Jerusalem Temple in 70 AD. The two commentaries on the Mishnah form the Palestinian and Babylonian Talmud. After the Hebrew Scriptures, the Mishnah is the first canonical document of Rabbinical Judaism and the major source and continuing expression of Jewish law and theology. The Mishnah united with the Gemarah (its commentary), forms the largest compendium of rabbinic Biblical exegesis ever compiled.

Mt. Moriah: Where Abraham was prepared to obediently offer up his son Isaac in sacrifice according to God's command (Gen 22:1). Later it was the location of the Jerusalem Temple built by King Solomon (2 Chr 3:1). Jesus' crucifixion was on a lower elevation of Mt. Moriah on a hill called Golgotha.

Mt. of Olives: Three hills were east of the city of Jerusalem across the Kidron Valley. The middle hill directly across from the Temple Mount was the Mt. of Olives. Jesus visited the village of Bethany on the Mt. of Olives frequently during His ministry. It was the home of several of His disciples including Martha, Mary, and Lazarus and Simon the Leper. He Ascended to Heaven from the Mt. of Olives and will return in His Second Advent to the same site (Acts 1:9-12; Zec 14:4-5).

Mt. Sinai/Horeb: Site of God's Theophany to the children of Israel after their Exodus out of Egypt. It was where God gave the first articles of divine Law beginning with the Ten Commandments, ratified His covenant with Israel, and established the liturgy of worship.

Mt. of Transfiguration: Jesus revealed Himself in His divine glory to the Apostles Peter, James, and John in the presence of the Old Testament prophets Moses and Elijah on this mountain (Mt 17:1-8; Mk 9:2-8; Lk 9:28-36).

Mt. Zion: It was the location of the City of David in ancient Jerusalem. Later the term "Zion" came to represent the faithful of the Old Covenant Church of Israel.

Novena: A novena is a nine-day prayer with one intention which, hopefully, receives an answer to the petition on the tenth day.

Olah: The rising smoke from the sacrificial altar that signified God's acceptance of the offering.

Ot: A symbolic act which represented something much more profound than the act itself.

Paraclete: A title for God the Holy Spirit that means "Advocate," from the Greek *para* = "besides" + *kalein*, "to call" = *parakletlios.* Jesus Christ is and remains our first Advocate, but He promised that when He left the earth in His visible form that He would send "another Advocate" so that His disciples would not be orphans (Jn 14:16; 1 Jn 2:1). God the Holy Spirit is the Advocate of the Mystical Body of Christ, pleading God's cause for the covenant family of the Church, keeping her from error and sanctifying souls.

Passover: A word from the Hebrew verb *pasha*, and the noun *pesah [pesach].* It is not the common Hebrew word for passing over something to avoid contact, which is the Hebrew verb *a-bhar* or *gabhar.* Biblical scholars have noted that the words *pasha and pesah* have no connection to other Hebrew words and suggest these words derive instead from a word of Egyptian origin. There are several other words and names in the Exodus story that are Egyptian and not Hebrew. Some scholars suggest the Hebrew words for "Passover" are from the Egyptian verb *pesah* meaning "to hold" or from the Egyptian noun *pesh*, meaning "wings of protection." Jewish and Christian commentators often express the protection of the Israelites eating the sacred meal of the Passover victim in their houses the night of the tenth plague as death "passing over." However, it was God's hovering protection over the "sign" of the blood on the doors of Israelite houses and the eating of the flesh of the Passover victim that brought redemption (Ex 12:23b). The Egyptian redemption and liberation are expressed in terms of God's "wings of protection" in Exodus 19:4, *You have seen what I did to the Egyptians, and how I bore you on eagles' wings and brought you to myself.*

Pilgrim feasts: The three God-ordained "pilgrim feasts" were Unleavened Bread, Pentecost/Weeks, and Tabernacles/Shelters (Ex 23:14-17; 34:18-23; Dt 16:16; 2 Chr 8:13). Every man of the covenant thirteen years old and older was required to present himself before Yahweh's altar in a sacred assembly three times a year at the celebration of these feasts.

Pharisees: In the first century AD, the Pharisees were the most influential political and religious group of the Jews. They considered themselves to be strict observers of the Law of Moses.

Praetorium: It was where the Roman governing authority presided and made judgments.

Priests: Unlike a prophet, whose mission was to communicate God's words to the people, the priest's mission was the reverse: mediating from the people to God. Jewish priests had to be the physical descendants of Aaron, the first high priest, who were ordained to offer sacrifice in God's Sanctuary. Jesus Christ, who is fully God and fully man, is the first, last, and greatest priest of New Covenant Law whose authority comes not from a hereditary link but God Himself. Jesus is our eternal High Priest who offered Himself once and for all on the altar of the Cross, a victim of infinite value and merit. He continually renews that sacrifice on the altar of every Catholic Church through the ministry of the Church. Within the Church, there are men ordained to the ministerial priesthood whose mission is, as Christ's representatives, to consecrate and offer the Body and Blood of Christ in the sacrifice of the Mass in the person of Christ, "Persona Christi." They are the spiritual descendants of the Apostles: those who were the first ordained priests by Jesus on Holy Thursday in the ceremonial washing of their feet at the sacred covenant meal of the Last Supper.

Purification: An outward ritual sign of an internal condition of purity.

Ritual: A ritual is a religious or solemn ceremony consisting of actions performed according to a prescribed order.

Sacrament: The Latin word *sacramentum* means "oath or sacred obligation"; from *sacrare*, "to set apart as sacred, consecrate." The Sacraments are visible signs instituted by Jesus Christ and entrusted to the Church through which the Holy Spirit communicates invisible grace, divine life, and inward sanctification to the soul. The formation of Biblical covenants takes place through oath swearing, sacrifice, and a sacred meal. The participation of the faithful in the Sacraments instituted by Christ is a continual oath swearing of covenant fidelity.

Sacrifice: The highest form of adoration of God under the old covenants was an offering of an animal victim, often accompanied by grain and wine. The community or an individual offered the material sacrifice that represented the offer's humbled heart in acknowledgment of God's supreme authority and sovereignty over all human beings and of humanity's total dependence upon God.

Sadducees: They were one of the most influential religious/political groups in the 1st century AD. Most of the priests and Herodian aristocracy were Sadducees. Both the Sadducees and Pharisees opposed Jesus' ministry.

Samaritans: The descendants of five pagan peoples brought in by the Assyrians to repopulate the territory of the Northern Kingdom of Israel after they exiled the Israelites of the northern tribes into Assyrian lands to the east (2 Kng 17:24). They adopted the illicit worship of Yahweh on their own terms and did not worship at the Jerusalem Temple (2 Kng 17:25-41). Jesus told the Samaritan woman that her people worshipped what they did not understand (Jn 4:22).

Second Temple: The Temple built by the returning citizen of Judah after the Babylonian captivity circa 517/6 BC. King Herod the Great refurbished and expanded the Second Temple later destroyed by the Romans in 70 AD.

Septuagint: Greek translation of the Old Testament identified by the abbreviation LXX, the number 70 in Roman numerals.

Scribes: Teachers of the Law of Moses. Most of the Levitical lesser ministers were also scribes.

Shekinah: The Hebrew word for the visible presence of God in the form of a cloud; also called the "Glory Cloud."

Shema Israel: The ancient profession of faith from Deuteronomy 6:4-9; 11:12-21; and Numbers 15:37-41.

Sheol: The grave or the netherworld to which all souls, the righteous and the wicked, were consigned before the coming of Christ (see Lk 16:19-31). He preached the Gospel to those souls imprisoned there after His death and entombment and before His Resurrection and led all the redeemed into Heaven. The Greek designation is Hades. Sheol/Hades, now called Purgatory, will continue as a destination for all souls deemed worthy of Heaven but in need of further purification until the Final Judgment (Rev 20:13-14).

Shewbread/Showbread: See Bread of the Presence.

Sin: A sin is a deliberate transgression of a law of God, defined by St. Augustine as, "A word, deed, or desire in opposition to the eternal law." Such transgressions disrupt the flow of divine grace and fellowship with God. The remedy is sincere repentance and an appeal to the mercy of God in forgiveness through the atoning work of Jesus Christ.

Soul: The soul is the immortal spiritual part of human beings that animates the body.

Spirit: Spirit is that which is immaterial and has no dependence on matter either for its existence or for any of its activities. God is uncreated pure Spirit, while the angels are created pure spirits. In Latin, *spiritus* means "breath, life, soul, mind, spirit, power." When God created the first man, He breathed His spirit into Adam that was the "breath of life" (Gen 2:7).

Synoptic Gospels: Gospels of Matthew, Mark, and Luke. The word "synoptic" means "at a glance." The first three Gospels are called "synoptic" because they follow the same general plan and reflect similar events in the life and teachings of Jesus.

Talit: Hebrew word meaning "tent," and used to refer to the Jewish cloak in ancient times and to the modern Jewish prayer shawl.

Talmud: An encyclopedic compendium of Jewish civil law, religious law and a description of worship in the Second Temple period. The Mishnah and the commentary on the Mishnah called the Gemarah, comprise the Jewish Talmud. The Mishnah united with the Gemarah forms the largest compendium of rabbinic biblical exegesis ever compiled. There are two versions of the Talmud: the Jerusalem and the Babylonian Talmud.

Tamid (olat-ha-tamid): The daily/perpetual, whole-burnt offering of the single sacrifice of two lambs in sacrifice during two liturgical worship services with one lamb offered in the morning and the other in the afternoon (evening to the Jews). Unleavened wheat flour mixed with oil, an unleavened wheat wafer (offering of the presiding priest), and a libation of red wine accompanied the burning of each lamb on the altar. Yahweh ordained the communal sacrifice of the Tamid (Ex 29:38-42; Num 28:1-8) as a perpetual offering for the atonement and sanctification of the covenant people and all peoples of the earth. Viewed as a single sacrifice, the Tamid was the center of liturgical worship; no other sacrifice was to take precedence over the Tamid (repeated 15 times in Num 28-29), and it was to be continually offered as a sacrifice on Yahweh's altar so long as the Sinai Covenant endured.

Temple of Solomon: The "house" for God's name in Jerusalem that was built by King Solomon in the 10th century BC. It was destroyed by the Babylonians in 587/6 BC and referred to as the First Temple.

Teni: The device in which a priest carried the live embers from the bronze Altar of Burnt Offerings in the Temple courtyard to the Altar of Incense in the Holy Place.

Titulus: Latin name for the plaque that hung on Jesus' Cross.

Theophany: In a Biblical context, the direct manifestation or communication by God to human beings. From the Greek, *theophaneia, Theo* = God + *phainein*, "to show."

Todah: The *Toda/Todah* was the communion, peace offering of the Sinai Covenant. Toda is a Hebrew word meaning "thanksgiving" and translated as *eucharistia* in the Greek translation of the Old Testament and is also the Latin word for "thanksgiving." It was a voluntary sacrifice that reestablished fellowship with God and was eaten in a sacred meal by the offeror, his family, and any other members of the covenant in the presence of God within the Sanctuary along with bread and wine on the day of the sacrifice. The sacred meal of the Eucharist is the New Covenant Todah.

Torah: In Hebrew, the word means "instruction," and refers to the five books of Moses: Genesis, Exodus, Leviticus, Numbers, and Deuteronomy.

Transubstantiation: The term which defines the miracle by which the Holy Spirit transforms the community's gifts of bread and wine into the Body and Blood of Jesus Christ in the sacrifice of the Mass.

INDEX

Made in the USA
Columbia, SC
12 December 2023

28453429R00271